The French language:
present and past

To my wife

The French language: present and past

Glanville Price

Professor of Romance Languages,
University College of Wales, Aberystwyth

Grant & Cutler

© Grant & Cutler Ltd 1984

First published 1971 by
Edward Arnold (Publishers) Ltd
and reprinted with corrections and
additional bibliographical notes 1975 and 1979

Reprinted and published by Grant & Cutler Ltd 1984

ISBN: 0 7293 0208 3

I.S.B.N. 84-599-0261-7
DEPÓSITO LEGAL: V. 34 - 1985

Printed in Spain by
Artes Gráficas Soler, S.A., Valencia

for

GRANT & CUTLER LTD
11 BUCKINGHAM STREET, LONDON WC2N 6DQ

Contents

Preface

The aim of the book. The aim of this book is to show how the French language as we know it today has emerged, after two thousand years of change and reconstruction, from the language once known as Latin in the area once known as Gaul. I have tried to avoid going into overmuch detail but rather to concentrate on the main features of pronunciation and grammar. Inevitably, some aspects of the subject have had to be presented in as simplified a way as is possible without undue distortion and others left out of account altogether. For a fuller treatment of particular points, the reader is referred to the works listed in the bibliography. My hope is that this book may in itself provide an adequate introduction to the subject for many students and that, for those who wish to take their study further, it will facilitate their understanding of other more ambitious and more specialized works.

Ⓞ zero

\> 'becomes', e.g. Latin *murum* > French *mur*

\< 'comes from', e.g. French *mur* < Latin *murum*

* indicates either (a) a form that is not attested in writing but whose existence is assumed on the basis of other evidence, e.g. the existence in the Romance languages of forms such as Old French *podeir* (> *pouvoir*), Italian *potere*, Rumanian *putere* ('power'), Spanish *poder*, leads us to assume that the verb 'to be able' in Vulgar Latin was *potere, whereas the Classical Latin form was *posse*;

or (b) a form that does not exist, as when we say that regular phonetic development of Old French *chastel* would have given Modern French *châtel, whereas the form that actually occurs is *château*

~ indicates forms that stand in opposition to one another, e.g. masc. *beau* ~ fem. *belle*

[ ] indicates phonetic transcription (see **2.1.5–2.1.9**)

/ / indicates phonemic transcription (see **2.2.3**)

ABBREVIATIONS

ClLat	Classical Latin (see **1.2**)
MidFr	Middle French (see **1.10**)
ModFr	Modern French
OFr	Old French (see **1.8** and **1.9**)
VL	Vulgar Latin (see **1.2**)

TECHNICAL TERMS

allophone: see **2.2**

apophonous verbs: see **14.4.3.6**.

aspect: a verbal category indicating the way in which the action of the verb is envisaged other than in relation to time (past, present, future); the action may, for example, be envisaged with reference to its beginning, end, duration or repetition; see **13.3–13.5** and **18.2**.

assimilation: see **2.4**.

blocked vowel: a vowel occurring in a closed syllable.

close and **open vowels**: these are relative terms referring to the degree of aperture of the mouth when various vowels are pronounced; e.g. the vowel [e] of *été* is more open than [i] of *lit* and more close than [ɛ] of *fête*; in particular, in the pairs [e] ~ [ɛ] and [o] ~ [ɔ] (see **2.1.6**), [e] and [o] are (relatively) close and [ɛ] and [ɔ] are (relatively) open.

xiv

closed syllable: a syllable ending in a consonant; see **2.3**.
combinative sound changes: see **2.5.2**.
complementary distribution: see **2.2.4**.
dissimilation: see **2.4**.
falling diphthong: a diphthong consisting of a vowel followed by a semi-consonant (semi-vowel), e.g. [aw], [ɔj].
free vowel: a vowel occurring in an open syllable.
glide consonant: see **3.7**.
isolative sound changes: see **2.5.2**.
open syllable: a syllable ending in a vowel; see **2.3**.
open vowels: see above, **close** and **open vowels**.
phoneme: see **2.2**.
reflex: the form taken in a later stage of a language by a given element occurring at an earlier stage, e.g. (i) French *rive* is a reflex of Latin *ripa*, (ii) the *-v-* of *rive* is a reflex of the *-p-* of *ripa*.
rising diphthong: a diphthong consisting of a semi-consonant (or semi-vowel) followed by a vowel, e.g. [jɛ], [wa].
semi-consonant, semi-vowel: see Ch. 5.
supporting vowel: see **4.3.3**.
syntagm: a succession of linguistic elements forming a syntactic unit, e.g. *to have* + PAST PARTICIPLE as in ' (I) have seen'.
yod: the semi-consonant *y* of *yes*, etc., represented in phonetic script by [j], e.g. French *fille* [fij]; see **2.1.7**.

Bibliography

This bibliography is not intended to list all important works on the history of the French language or on major aspects thereof. I include only those works that I have found particularly helpful in writing this book. It would have been uneconomical of space to indicate on nearly every page of the book my indebtedness to a particular source for examples or comment. I have therefore indicated such a debt only at those points where I have drawn particularly heavily on any of the works listed here. It would, however, be unfair and ungracious not to acknowledge freely that nearly every book listed has contributed something, and many of them a great deal, to the present work, not only in what I have consciously drawn from them for this specific purpose but also in what I have absorbed from them during the years that, as a student and as a teacher, I have been in the habit of consulting them.

Most of the works listed here are referred to in the body of the book by author's name only. Where two works by the same author are listed, reference is made by means of the abbreviation quoted at the end of the entry in the bibliography.

Works dealing with more specific features of the history or description of French are referred to at the appropriate place in the book.

For an extensive bibliography on all aspects of French linguistics, see R.-L. Wagner, *Introduction à la linguistique française*, Lille and Geneva, 1947, and the *Supplément bibliographique* thereto, Lille and Geneva, 1955. For more recent works, reference should be made to the relevant sections of such annual publications as the *Bibliographie linguistique*, published by the Permanent International Committee of Linguists, and *The Year's Work in Modern Language Studies*, published by the Modern Humanities Research Association.

Latin
C. H. Grandgent, *An Introduction to Vulgar Latin*, Boston, 1907
J. Herman, *Le Latin vulgaire*, Paris, 1967
L. R. Palmer, *The Latin Language*, London, 1954

V. Väänänen, *Introduction au latin vulgaire*, 2nd edn., Paris, 1967

The Romance Languages
E. Bourciez, *Éléments de linguistique romane*, 4th edn., Paris, 1946
W. D. Elcock, *The Romance Languages*, London, 1960

French
G. Alessio, *Grammatica storica francese*, Bari:
  I *Introduzione—Fonetica*, 1951
  II *Morfologia*, 1955
Lilias E. Armstrong, *The Phonetics of French*, London, 1932
H. Bauche, *Le langage populaire*, new edn., Paris, 1951
Ch. Beaulieux, *Histoire de l'orthographe française*, 2 vols., Paris, 1927
E. and J. Bourciez, *Phonétique française: étude historique*, Paris, 1967
  (This work is based on E. Bourciez's earlier *Précis historique de phonétique française*, 9th edn., Paris, 1958.)
Ch. Bruneau, *Petite histoire de la langue française*, 2 vols., Paris, 1955–1958
F. Brunot, *Histoire de la langue française des origines à nos jours*, 15 vols. (Vols. 14 and 15 in preparation), Paris, 1905–1953 (Reprinted 1966–1968) (Abbr: Brunot, *Histoire* . . .)
F. Brunot, *La pensée et la langue*, Paris, 1922 (Abbr: Brunot, *La pensée* . . .)
F. Brunot and Ch. Bruneau, *Précis de grammaire historique de la langue française*, 4th edn., Paris, 1956
J. Chaurand, *Histoire de la langue française*, Paris, 1969
M. Cohen, *Histoire d'une langue: le français*, 3rd edn., Paris, 1967
J. Damourette and E. Pichon, *Des mots à la pensée. Essai de grammaire de la langue française*, 7 vols., Paris, 1931–1950 (Reprinting) See also the authors' *Glossaire des termes spéciaux ou de sens spécial employés dans l'ouvrage*, Paris, 1949
A. Dauzat, *Histoire de la langue française*, Paris, 1930 (Abbr: Dauzat, *Histoire* . . .)
A. Dauzat, *Tableau de la langue française*, Paris, 1939 (reprinted 1967) (Abbr: Dauzat, *Tableau* . . .)
C. de Boer, *Syntaxe du français moderne*, 2nd edn. Leiden, 1954
J. Dubois, *Grammaire structurale du français*, Paris:
  I *Nom et pronom*, 1965
  II *Le verbe*, 1967
  III *La phrase et ses transformations*, 1969
A. Ewert, *The French Language*, 2nd edn., London, 1943 (reprinted with corrections and bibliographical additions, 1964)
P. Fouché, *Le verbe français: étude morphologique*, new edn., Paris, 1967 (Abbr: Fouché, *Le Verbe*)

P. Fouché, *Phonétique historique du français*, 3 vols., Paris, 1952–1961 (Abbr: Fouché, *Phonétique* . . .)

P. Fouché, *Traité de prononciation française*, 2nd edn., Paris, 1959 (Abbr: Fouché, *Traité* . . .)

L. Foulet, *Petite syntaxe de l'ancien français*, 3rd edn., Paris, 1930

J. Fox and R. Wood, *A Concise History of the French Language*, Oxford, 1968

A. François, *Histoire de la langue française cultivée*, 2 vols., Geneva, 1959

H. Frei, *La grammaire des fautes*, Paris, 1929

E. Gamillscheg, *Historische französische Syntax*, Tübigen, 1957

G. Gougenheim, *Grammaire de la langue française du seizième siècle*, Paris, 1951 (Abbr: Gougenheim, *Grammaire* . . .)

G. Gougenheim, *Système grammatical de la langue française*, Paris, 1938 (reprinted 1966) (Abbr: Gougenheim, *Système* . . .)

M. Grevisse, *Le bon usage*, 10th edn., Gembloux and Paris, 1975

P. Guiraud, *Le français populaire*, Paris, 1965

A. Haase, *Syntaxe française du XVIIe siècle* (translated from the German by M. Obert), 5th edn., Paris and Munich, 1965 (1st edn., 1898)

L. C. Harmer, *The French Language Today*, London, 1954

L. Kukenheim, *Grammaire historique de la langue française*, Leiden:
I *Les parties du discours*, 1967
II *Les syntagmes*, 1968

G. and R. Le Bidois, *Syntaxe du français moderne*, 2 vols., 2nd edn., Paris, 1968

Ph. Martinon, *Comment on parle en français*, Paris, 1927

P. Ménard, *Manuel d'ancien français: 3, Syntaxe*, Bordeaux, 1968

K. Nyrop, *Grammaire historique de la langue française*, Copenhagen:
I *Histoire générale de la langue française. Phonétique historique*, 4th edn., 1935
II *Morphologie*, 2nd edn., 1924
V *Syntaxe. Noms et pronoms*, 1925
VI *Syntaxe. Particules et verbes*, 1930

M. K. Pope, *From Latin to Modern French*, Manchester, 1934 (reprinted with corrections, 1952)

M. Regula, *Historische Grammatik des Französischen*, Heidelberg:
I *Lautlehre*, 1955
II *Formenlehre*, 1956
III *Syntax*, 1966

H. Rheinfelder, *Altfranzösische Grammatik*, Munich:
1. *Lautlehre*, 3rd edn., 1963
2. *Formenlehre*, 1967

K. Sandfeld, *Syntaxe du français contemporain*, 3 vols, 1928–1943 (reprinted 1965, Vol. I, Paris, Vols. II and III, Geneva)

S. A. Schane, *French Phonology and Morphology*, Cambridge (Mass.), 1968

K. Sneyders de Vogel, *Syntaxe historique du français*, 2nd edn., Groningen, 1927

R. L. Wagner and J. Pinchon, *Grammaire du français classique et moderne*, Paris, 1962

L. Warnant, *Dictionnaire de la prononciation française*, 3rd edn., Gembloux, 1968

W. von Wartburg, *Évolution et structure de la langue française*, 8th edn., Berne, 1967 (Abbr: Wartburg, *Évolution* . . .)

W. von Wartburg and P. Zumthor, *Précis de syntaxe du français contemporain*, 2nd edn., Berne, 1958

ADDITIONAL BIBLIOGRAPHY

J. Chaurand, *Introduction à la dialectologie française*, Paris, 1972

F. de la Chaussée, *Initiation à la phonétique historique de l'ancien français*, Paris, 1974

C. Désirat and T. Hordé, *La langue française au 20e siède*, Paris, 1976

P. MacCarthy, *The Pronunciation of French*, London, 1975

R. and E. Martin, *Guide bibliographique de linguistique française*, Paris, 1973

A. Martinet, *La prononciation du français contemporain*, Paris, 1945 (reprinted 1971)

P. Rickard, *A History of the French Language*, London, 1974

A. Rigaud (ed.), *La grammaire du français parlé*, Paris, 1971

A. Sauvageot, *Analyse du français parlé*, Paris, 1972

A. Viatte, *La Francophonie*, Paris, 1969

1 From Latin to Modern French

1.1. Latin is not dead in the sense in which, say, Cornish is. A language lives in the minds and on the lips of living people, and when, around 1800, the last few speakers of Cornish who had learned the language from their elders died without passing it on to the younger generation, then the language died with them. But the language—whatever it may be called—that the children of the 1970s are learning to speak in Rome, in Paris, in Madrid, in Bucharest, in Quebec, in Rio de Janeiro, is the same language that Caesar spoke, handed down and in the process undergoing gradual but constant and in the long run far-reaching changes, from one generation to another for more than two thousand years.[1] Though we do not refer to the language of, say, present-day Rome as 'Modern Latin' (or one form of Modern Latin) but as 'Italian', this is really just a question of terminology and custom: Italian stands in much the same relationship to Latin as Modern Greek does to Ancient Greek.

The variety of forms that Latin has taken in different areas in the course of two thousand years of change is incalculable, if one tries to imagine all the dialects and patois that exist in Europe, even more if one thinks of the French, Spanish, and Portuguese dialects of the Americas and elsewhere. There are, however, nine principal varieties of 'Modern Latin', known as the 'Romance languages'. These are: French, Occitan (often—but less accurately—known as Provençal, see footnote 11), Catalan, Spanish, Portuguese, Sardinian, Italian, Romansh[2] and Rumanian.[3]

[1] In the sense that the language as Caesar knew it is not now in use, Latin is of course dead. But in that sense, so is the English of Shakespeare—his English may be much closer to ours than Caesar's Latin is to modern Italian, or Spanish or French, but the difference is one of degree, not of kind.

[2] Romansh, or Raeto-Romance, consists of a group of dialects—numbering rather less than 50,000 speakers in all—in the Swiss canton of the Grisons (Graubünden). The term is often extended to cover related dialects spoken in some valleys in the Dolomites and the Friulan dialects of north-east Italy (spoken in a wide area around the town of Udine).

[3] A tenth Romance language, Dalmatian, spoken along the coast of what is now Yugoslavia, died out when the last speaker was killed in 1898. The group of dialects collectively known as 'Franco-Provençal' (see **1.9**) are generally regarded as being distinct from both French and Occitan, and so constitute an eleventh variety of Romance speech.

1

1.2. The Latin that is at the origin of the Romance languages is not Classical Latin (abbreviation: ClLat) as we find it in the works of such masters of Latin prose as Caesar, Cicero and Livy but everyday spoken Latin, which is usually referred to as Vulgar Latin (abbreviation: VL). ClLat was a highly polished literary language, differing to some extent from the language of conversation both in vocabulary and in grammar and maintaining an orthography that failed to keep pace with changes in pronunciation (just as, for example the -*gh*- of English *light*, *night* represents a sound that, except in Scots, has long since disappeared). The existence of different levels of language is sometimes expressly recognized by Latin writers, as when, for example, Quintilian (1st century after Christ) draws a distinction between the language of eloquence and the *sermo vulgaris* 'popular speech' or *sermo cotidianus* 'everyday speech' that one uses in speaking to one's friends, family, freedmen and slaves:[3a] Not that the spoken language itself, of course, was always and everywhere the same. It is a reasonable assumption not only that there were regional varieties and that the language changed in process of time but that there were also social differences: as Bourciez puts it,[4] the patricians chatting together at the Senate did not express themselves in the same way as the market-gardeners of the Appian Way or the gladiators in the taverns.

1.3. If VL is by definition a *spoken* language, how then can we know anything about it? There is first of all the evidence of those Latin writers who occasionally draw attention to features of the spoken language. Then there are the conclusions to be drawn from the mistakes committed by the semi-literate authors of inscriptions of one kind or another[5] or the deviations from ClLat usage that characterize the prose of various late Latin writers whose achievement frequently falls short of their ambition to write good Latin. These texts, some in better Latin than others,

[3a] The point that VL and ClLat co-existed and that VL does not derive from ClLat is worth emphasizing. It may however be assumed that the divergence between the two widened as the spoken language changed over the centuries and that some of the VL features revealed by later evidence (see **1.3**) were not necessarily present in the language in, say, the 1st century B.C.

[4] E. Bourciez, *Éléments de linguistique romane*, 31

[5] Particularly interesting in this respect are the inscriptions that decorated— or defaced—the walls of Pompeii and that came to light when the ruins of the city, which was buried in ash from Vesuvius in 79 A.D., were excavated. These inscriptions range from public proclamations and electoral slogans to the kind of writing-on-walls that one might expect to find in the street of the brothels.

2

include agricultural treatises, a veterinary treatise and a cookery book both dating from the 4th century, and an account by a nun of her journey to the Holy Land.

An indirect source of evidence about VL is provided by a comparison of the Romance languages. For example, the Latin word for 'fire', *ignis*, has disappeared in all the Romance languages and been replaced by reflexes of *focus* 'hearth' (Fr. *feu*, Spanish *fuego*, Italian *fuoco*, Rumanian *foc*, etc.), which entitles us to assume that *focus* had already come to mean 'fire' in VL. Or again, the Romance past participles of the verb 'to lose', Fr. *perdu*, Old Spanish *perdudo*, Catalan *perdut*, Italian *perduto*, Rumanian *pierdut*, etc., are an indication that the VL past participle of *perdĕre* was **perdutum*,[6] whereas the ClLat participle was *perditum*.

1.4. Our concern in this book is with the changes in pronunciation, forms and syntax in the Latin of northern Gaul that have produced the French language as we know it today.

The Romans moved into the territory now known as France but then known as Transalpine Gaul in the 2nd century B.C. and after a four-year campaign (125–121 B.C.) against the Ligurians and the Gauls founded the Provincia Narbonensis, extending from Toulouse to the Alps. The rest of Gaul, as far as Brittany and Flanders, was conquered by Caesar in the Gallic War of 58–51 B.C.

Before the Roman conquest, Gaul was mainly occupied— except for the Iberians in the south-west and the Ligurians in the Alpine region—by the Celtic-speaking Gauls. Though the Romans had no deliberate policy of linguistic assimilation, it is possible that by the 5th century after Christ the Gaulish tongue had disappeared,[7] except perhaps in a few remote areas, and that

[6] For the significance of the asterisk, see the list of symbols on p. xiv.

[7] The view generally held by Celticists is that the present-day Celtic language of Brittany is not a relic of Gaulish but a continuation of the Celtic speech reintroduced on to the mainland by emigrants from Devon and Cornwall in the 5th and 6th centuries. Professor F. Falc'hun, however, has recently argued that Breton *is* descended from Gaulish, and that, though some dialects have been affected by the language of the immigrants from Britain, the dialect of the Vannes area is 'une survivance gauloise peu influencée par l'apport breton', i.e. it is almost pure Gaulish (see his *Histoire de la langue bretonne*, 2 vols., Rennes, 1963, esp. Vol. I, 180 and 341; see also his articles 'La doctrine de Joseph Loth sur les origines de la langue bretonne' in *Revue de linguistique romane*, XXX [1966], 324–43, and 'Langue bretonne et langue gauloise' in his book *Les noms de lieux celtiques: deuxième série*, Rennes, 1970, 43–96). Falc'hun's view is rejected as quite untenable by Professor K. H. Jackson in his *Historical Phonology of Breton*, Dublin, 1967, 31–2.

Latin had become the normal speech of all sections of the population. Romanization probably started in the towns, where Latin was the language of the military garrisons, of administration and of trade, and then spread outwards into the country districts. The schools set up in the larger towns, to which the Gaulish nobles sent their sons to be educated, were an important contributory factor, and at a later stage the growing influence of the Christian church also worked in favour of Latin. Gaulish, however, contributed some elements to the vocabulary of the Latin of Gaul, particularly in the fields of agricultural and domestic terminology. It has been estimated[8] that some 180 such words are still to be found in the various French patois, though only about a third of these remain in the literary language, including *bouleau, bruyère, chêne, if, mouton, bouc, ruche, charrue, soc, suie, glaner.*

1.5. At the death of the emperor Trajan (117 A.D.), the Roman Empire extended from the Forth-Clyde valley to the Nile and the Euphrates. In the 3rd century, however, the decline began and one barbarian tribe after another invaded the imperial provinces. Gaul was lost to various Germanic-speaking tribes in the 5th century, when the south was occupied by the Visigoths, the eastern central area by the Burgundians and the north by the Franks. The Franks were the most powerful of these Germanic tribes and their king, Clovis (c. 465–511), succeeded in extending his rule over most of Gaul. However, whereas the Roman occupation had led eventually to a change of language on the part of the community as a whole when Gaulish faded out and was replaced by Latin, this time it was the invaders who, after a period of some centuries of bilingualism, abandoned their Germanic speech[9] and adopted the Romance speech of the area. The reasons for this are probably that the Franks did not settle *en masse* and remained a minority, albeit a ruling minority, and that the cultural prestige of Latin, even at a period when Roman rule had long ended and the Romance speech of the area had already undergone considerable changes, was still a powerful factor—the more so since Clovis's conversion to Christianity (496) had given considerable influence to the church. However, it seems likely that, when they adopted the Romance speech, the Franks carried over into it some of their Germanic speech-habits

---

[8] W. von Wartburg, *Evolution* . . . , 25.
[9] The Frankish language remained however in the extreme North, where one dialect of it survives as Dutch and another as the German dialects of the Rhineland.

4

(i.e. they spoke with a 'Germanic accent') and that their privileged position in the community led to the adoption of these speech-habits by the population in general. Frankish has also influenced the vocabulary of French which adopted over 200 Frankish words (some of which did not, however, outlast the Old French period). These include a number of words having to do with military and administrative matters (*heaume, fourbir, maréchal, éperon, baron,* etc.), with agriculture and the countryside (the Franks were not a nation of town-dwellers) (*gerbe, blé, jardin, haie, osier, houx, cresson, gazon,* etc.) with social customs (*banc, fauteuil, gant, épervier, rôtir,* etc.) or with the emotions (*haïr, honte, orgueil,* etc.).

1.6. Opinions differ widely as to the period at which the spoken language of the former Roman provinces had developed so far as no longer to be termed Latin. Some would have it that the written Latin of the 7th and 8th centuries corresponded fairly closely to the spoken language of the time. It is a more reasonable assumption, however, that those late Latin writers who, from the 6th century onwards, composed chronicles, legal documents, religious works and so on in what is still recognizably Latin, even though by classical standards often a very incorrect Latin, were trying within the limits of their education to manipulate the language in which such works had traditionally been composed and not the language that they used in everyday life.

Striking testimony to the fact that the Latin of the Vulgate (the 4th-century translation of the Bible by St. Jerome) was no longer easily intelligible by the 8th century is provided by the Glossary of Reichenau (so named after the monastery in which it once was), which consists of a list of some 1200 words from the Vulgate with equivalents, most of which are also Latin—if not always ClLat—though some are Germanic words dressed up in a Latin garb. The following are some examples, the Germanic words amongst them being indicated by (G):

semel 'once': *una vice* (> *une fois*)
liberos 'children': *infantes* (> *enfants*)
flare 'to blow': *suflare* (> *souffler*)
canere 'to sing': *cantare* (> *chanter*)
optimos 'best': *meliores*[10] (> (*les*) *meilleurs*)
pulcra 'beautiful': *bella* (> *belle*)

---

[10] In ClLat, *meliores* = 'better', *bucca* = 'cheek', *hibernus* = 'wintry', *coxa* = 'hip-bone'.

in ore 'in the mouth': *in bucca*[10] (> *bouche*)
hiems 'winter': *ibernus*[10] (> *hiver*)
vespertiliones 'bats': *calvas sorices* (> *chauves-souris*)
femur 'thigh': *coxa*[10] (> *cuisse*)
pignus 'pledge': *wadius* (G) (> *gage*)
galea 'helmet': *helmus* (G) (> *heaume*)
manipulos 'bundles': *garbas* (G) (> *gerbes*)
cementarii 'masons': *mationes* (G) (> *maçons*)

The gloss *Gallia: Frantia* (> *France*) is an indication that one part of the country at least had already taken its name from the Franks.

The Reichenau Glossary was almost certainly composed in the extreme north of France. At about the same period, the Emperor Charlemagne (742–814), conscious of the fact that the written Latin of his age was by classical standards intolerably corrupt, determined to restore the language of church and administration to an acceptable level of correctness. To this end he called on the help of scholars from countries where the monasteries had maintained a high standard of Latin culture, and foremost amongst them Alcuin of York. The effect of this successful reform was to emphasize the gulf that separated the Romance speech of the time from Latin, and in 813 the Council of Tours was obliged to instruct priests, whose Latin sermons were apparently unintelligible to the mass of the faithful, to translate them, according to the speech of the area, into the Germanic tongue or into the *rustica romana lingua*, 'the Romance speech of the countryside'.

By this time, and perhaps as early as the 6th century, there must have been sufficient difference between the Latin of Gaul, the Iberian peninsula, Italy and Dacia (Rumania) to justify us in speaking of Gallo-Romance, Hispano-Romance, Italo-Romance and Daco-Romance. Within Gallo-Romance itself, some at least of the distinctions that were to result in the creation of two main linguistic zones, a northern French-speaking one and a southern Occitan-speaking one (see **1.9**), were also already in existence or in process of development in the 8th century. To the extent that the speech of Northern Gaul was already marked out from the speech of other areas by characteristics of its own, we might in retrospect consider the *rustica romana lingua* referred to by the Council of Tours as being specifically 'French'. However, the term 'French' is better reserved for the language of the period

[10] See page 5.

from about the year 900 or shortly before, a stage that is known to us from the earliest surviving literary texts. When referring to characteristically French features that developed before this period, we shall use the term 'proto-French'.

One short text of 125 words has come down to us from the proto-French period. In the year 842, two of Charlemagne's grandsons, Louis the German, the leader of the Germanic-speaking Franks, and Charles the Bald, the leader of the Romance-speaking Franks, met at Strasbourg and joined in alliance against their brother Lothair. Oaths were sworn by the two leaders and their armies, each leader using the other's language and each army its own language. The text of the two Romance oaths (those sworn by Louis and by Charles's army) and the two Germanic oaths is recorded in a Latin chronicle of the times by Nithard. The following is an extract from the oath sworn by Louis:

> '. . . d'ist di in avant, in quant Deus savir et podir me dunat, si salvarai eo cist meon fradre Karlo, et in aiudha et in cadhuna cosa, si cum om per dreit son fradra salvar dift . . .'
> ('From this day forward, insofar as God gives me knowledge and power, I will support this my brother Charles, both in help and in everything, as a man must by right support his brother.')

The Strasbourg Oaths are the earliest known connected Romance text emanating from Gaul and one of the earliest in any Romance dialect. Unfortunately, their evidential value is limited: they do, it is true, cast a certain amount of light on the language of their time, but in many more respects they themselves require to be interpreted in the light of knowledge derived from other sources. Two fundamental difficulties are:

(a) that we do not know how faithfully Nithard managed—or even tried—to record this presumably hitherto unwritten language;
(b) that the sole surviving manuscript of Nithard's chronicle (which was written about 843) dates from about the year 1000, and there is no means of establishing how closely the text of the oaths as we have them corresponds to what Nithard actually wrote.

1.7. The earliest text in what is indisputably French (an extreme northern dialect thereof) is a short poem—29 lines—on the martyrdom of St. Eulalia, composed about 880 and handed down to us in a manuscript of about the same period. It begins:

> Buona pulcella fut Eulalia;
> Bel auret corps, bellezour anima.
> Voldrent la veintre li Deo inimi,
> Voldrent la faire diaule servir.
> Elle nont eskoltet les mals conseilliers,
> Qu'elle Deo raneiet chi maent sus en ciel,
> Ne por or ned argent ne paramenz.

('A good maid was Eulalia; she had a beautiful body and an even more beautiful soul. The enemies of God wanted to overcome her, they wanted to make her serve the devil. She does not listen to the evil counsellors, that she should deny God who dwells up in heaven, for gold or silver or fine adornments.')

From the 10th century we have some notes—partly in French, partly in Latin—for a sermon on Jonah and two more religious poems (756 lines in all) and then, in a number of 11th-century manuscripts, an important poem, the *Vie de St Alexis*, of which the following is a brief extract:

> An icest secle nen at parfit' amor;
> La vithe est fraisle, n'i ad durable honur;
> Cesta lethece revert a grant tristur.

('In this world there is no perfect love; life is fragile, there is no lasting honour; this joy turns to great sadness.')

1.8. It was in the 12th century that French literature first came into full flower and during the Old French (abbreviation: OFr) period, which lasts until 1300 or a little later, the language came to be used for an ever-increasing range and variety of ends. We can safely assume that the vernacular *Vie de St Alexis* and other early religious works (see **1.7**) owe their existence to an attempt to edify the faithful in a more immediate and more palatable way than by preaching at them. This didactic strain continues through later centuries and the use of the vernacular for the presentation of the teachings of the church in a way that might be accessible and acceptable even to the unlearned can be compared to the depiction of stories from the Scriptures or the lives of saints in the stained glass windows of medieval churches. Soon, however, other themes appear. The OFr epics or *chansons de geste*—many of them running to several thousand lines—deal with the exploits

8

(largely apocryphal) of Charlemagne and various feudal lords in their campaigns against the Moors in Spain and the south of France or against one another. The earliest and finest of these is the *Chanson de Roland* (abbreviation: *Roland*), a poem of 4002 lines, which in the earliest surviving manuscript, dating from the 12th century, begins:

> Carles li reis, nostre emperere magnes,
> Set anz tuz pleins ad estét en Espaigne.
> Tresqu'en la mer cunquist la tere altaigne.
> N'i ad castel ki devant lui remaigne,
> Mur ne citét n'i est remés a fraindre,
> Fors Sarraguce, ki est en une muntaigne:
> Li reis Marsilie la tient ki Deu nen aimet.

('Charles the king, our great emperor, seven full years has been in Spain. As far as the sea he conquered the proud land. There is no castle that holds out before him, no wall or city has remained to be broken, except Saragossa which is on a mountain: King Marsilie holds it who loves not God.')

There has been much debate as to whether the *Roland* is a profoundly Christian work, seeking to expound and illustrate Christian ideals and virtues, or whether the Christian element is merely part of the general cultural background to a tale of conflict between armies (Christian and Saracen) and between personalities. However this may be, it is certain that the inspiration of many other *chansons de geste* is primarily secular: the interest is in the personalities and exploits of the protagonists. With these *chansons de geste*—which were composed not to be read as books are read but to be recited or intoned by *jongleurs* or travelling minstrels who wandered about the country from castle to castle and from market-place to market-place—the French language has come to be used not merely, as in the case of the early saints' lives, for edification but also for entertainment. A little later in the 12th century, we find 'verse novels' based on themes drawn from antiquity (e.g. the *Roman d'Énéas*) or on the Arthurian legends and related material (the most outstanding of these are the *romans* of the late-12th-century poet, Chrétien de Troyes). Comedy, satire and ribaldry are well-represented, too, in the theatre—which, however, had its beginnings in religious drama—and such stories as those of Reynard the Fox. Apart from some translations of sermons, French prose—and the use of French for 'serious' purposes other than religious edification—begins with

9

the chronicles of the Fourth Crusade (1202–1204) by Villehardouin and Robert de Clari. Here is a short extract from Villehardouin:

> 'Seignor, fait li roys, je vois envoierai le frere ma fame, si le met en la Dieu main, qui le gart de mort, et en la vostre. Porce que vos alez por Dieu et por droit et por justise, si devez a ceus qui sont desherité a tort rendre lor heritages, se vos poez.'
> ('My lords, says the king, I shall send you my wife's brother; I put him in the hand of God, that he may keep him from death, and in yours. Because you go for God and for right and for justice, you must restore their inheritance to those who are wrongly deprived of their inheritance, if you can.')

Soon after this, French also came into use for purely utilitarian purposes: the earliest examples of legal documents—bills of sale, etc.—in French date from the early 13th century and by the end of the century such examples are comparatively common—though Latin still predominates.

1.9. At the beginning of the OFr period, the dialect of the Ile-de-France, i.e. the area around Paris, was merely one of a number of dialects: by the end of the period its dominant position was already recognized.

We have already referred (**1.6**) to the existence of a northern, French-speaking area and a southern, Occitan-speaking area. The division between the two runs approximately from the Gironde estuary to the north of the Massif Central and thence to the Alps. The Occitan[11] area includes amongst its main dialects Limousin, Auvergnat, Dauphinois, Provençal, Languedocien and Gascon. In the east, between the French- and Occitan-speaking areas, most Romance linguists recognize an intermediate zone of what are known as 'Franco-Provençal' dialects; this Franco-Provençal zone includes western Switzerland and a wedge-shaped area of France embracing Switzerland to north and south and extending further west than Lyons.

---

[11] In the Middle Ages, French and Occitan were sometimes known respectively as the *langue d'oïl* and the *langue d'oc*, from their characteristic words for 'yes', viz. *oïl* (= *oui*) and *oc*. The term 'Provençal' is frequently applied to the *langue d'oc* in general, but this term has the disadvantage that it also refers to one particular dialect, that of Provence, and the term 'Occitan' is consequently becoming more and more widely used. In medieval Latin the term *lingua occitana* is found as a translation of *langue d'oc*. It is not until the 19th century that the terms *occitanien, occitanique, occitan*, borrowed from this Latin form, are first used in French.

It has been plausibly suggested[12] that this division between the north and south of the Gallo-Romance area is to be explained as a result of the occupation of the north of Gaul by the Franks and the consequent carrying-over of Frankish speech-habits into the language of that area (see **1.5**). It is further suggested that the Franco-Provençal area corresponds to the territory occupied by another Germanic tribe, the Burgundians.

The principal OFr dialects are Francien (the dialect of the Ile-de-France),[13] Norman (including Anglo-Norman, i.e. French as used in England), Picard and Champenois, all of which were widely used for literary purposes;[14] others include Walloon, Lorrain, Burgundian and various western dialects.

As it happens, none of the earliest French texts in the form in which we have them is in Francien. This does not necessarily imply that none of them was written in the Ile-de-France: some of them could well have been, in which case the Norman or Picard colouring of the language of the existing manuscripts is due to their having been copied by Norman or Picard scribes. Indeed, it is more than likely that many texts which we have in manuscripts written in England—the *Roland,* for example—were originally composed in France. In the later 12th century and the 13th century, Champenois is represented by Chrétien de Troyes and Villehardouin, and Picard by many texts particularly in the more popular, less aristocratic genres (e.g. satirical and comic works). It is significant, however, that as early as 1182 or thereabouts, the northerner Conon de Béthune writes a poem expressing his resentment when the royal family pick him up for his northern speech:

> Encor ne soit ma parole françoise,
> Si la puet on bien entendre en françois

('Although my speech is not *français* [i.e. Francien], it can be perfectly well understood in *français*')

—and, he says, it is impolite to take such an attitude, *car je ne fui*

[12] W. von Wartburg, *Evolution . . .* , 64–65.

[13] In the Middle Ages, the term *françois* (= 'français') referred specifically to the dialect of the Ile-de-France; as this term now relates to the language in general, the term *francien* was coined in the 19th century to denote the medieval dialect of the Ile-de-France.

[14] When we speak of 'Norman' texts, 'Picard' texts, etc., this is not to be taken as implying that such texts are written in 'pure' dialect; more extreme dialectal features, which might cause undue difficulty for speakers of other dialects, tend to be avoided but a dialectal 'colouring' remains, more or less marked according to the text or manuscript.

pas noriz a Pontoise ('for I was not brought up at Pontoise [near Paris]').

It is clear that, by the end of the 12th century, the speech of the Paris area enjoyed a special prestige, and Garnier de Pont-Sainte-Maxence, the author of the first text of known Francien provenance, a verse life of St. Thomas à Beckett (c. 1174), brags:

Mis langages est boens, car en France fui nez

('My language is good, for I was born in France (i.e. the Ile-de-France)').

The reasons for the gradual rise of Francien to a position of dominance are many and varied. The fact that it was geographically a central dialect meant that it was less strange to speakers of other dialects than, say, northern and eastern dialects were to people from the west and south of the French-speaking area, and vice versa, and therefore a generally more acceptable basis for a common literary language. The principal reasons, however, were non-linguistic. Paris had been the chief residence of the kings since the 10th century and the prestige accruing to Paris from the presence there not only of the monarchy but also of the main law-courts and schools (including the University) conferred a special prestige also on the speech of the capital. We saw above that from the early 13th century French came into use in legal documents, and, whereas at first such documents reflect the dialect of their own particular area, by the end of the OFr period Francien is widely used in non-Francien areas and soon predominates over other dialects.

1.10. The Middle French (abbreviation: MidFr) period corresponds approximately to the 14th and 15th centuries. It is a period of unsettled social conditions (the Hundred Years' War lasted intermittently from 1335 to 1453) which may be one reason why there is something of a falling-off, as compared with the OFr period, in the production of imaginative literature. On the other hand, the frontier between the domain that was reserved for Latin and that in which French could operate was pushed back to the advantage of French. In 1314—i.e. right at the end of the OFr period—Henri de Mondeville produced a treatise on surgery in French, in the middle of the century Livy was translated and a little later Aristotle (from Latin, not from the original Greek), the number of French chronicles increased (most important among them being Froissart's lengthy chronicle of the

12

campaigns of the Hundred Years' War). Froissart (c. 1337–1410), whose language, particularly in the early part of his chronicle, has a marked Picard colouring, is the last important writer to deviate from Francien French in his work.

The new uses to which French was put in the MidFr period inevitably brought changes. Latin had for so long been the language of virtually all 'serious' writing that the vernacular had not developed the necessary vocabulary for coping with the new needs. It was natural that the gaps should be filled by drawing on Latin. There was indeed nothing new in this. As early as the 11th century, there are in the *Vie de St Alexis* some 30 words whose form indicates that they were not part of the traditional word-stock handed down through the centuries but borrowings from the Latin of the church; they include *affliction, celeste, habiter, miracle* and *paradis*. Throughout the OFr period, other Latinisms continue to enter the language, but they were not taken in in such quantities as to alter significantly the character of the language. All this changes in the MidFr period. 'The borrowing of learned loan-words, which had been an *infiltration* in Old French, became a stream in the fourteenth and almost a deluge in the fifteenth and sixteenth centuries.'[15] Amongst the hundreds of 14th-century borrowings from Latin quoted by Brunot[16] are *acte, classe, commerce, examen, médecin, poème, évidence, dictateur, comédie, tragédie, atrocité, supplément, agitation, collection, position, agricole, énorme, détestable, fatal, final, immortel, absent, différent, agile, habile, circulaire, adapter, assister, communiquer, habituer, procéder.*

Whereas very many of these borrowings from Latin served a useful purpose, some 15th-century writers went to grotesque lengths in larding their works by way of ornamentation with unnecessary Latinisms, most of which were never integrated into the language and had only an ephemeral existence.

As an example of MidFr, we quote a passage from Alain Chartier's *Quadrilogue invectif* (1422):

'De ce temps la peus tu avoir remembrance, car Dieu sceit le bruit, la rumeur et l'esclandre obprobrieux, que tu donnoyes a ceulx qui en plantureuse union et transquilité te gouvernoient. Icellui temps detestoies et tenoies a mauvais, en tresgrant ingratitude a Dieu et vers ton prince.'

('You may well remember that time, for God knows the noise, uproar and shameful scandal that you caused to those who governed you in plentiful unity and tranquillity. You hated

[15] M. K. Pope, 30   [16] F. Brunot, *Histoire* . . . , I, 571–6

13

that time and held it to be evil, in great ingratitude to God and your prince.')

1.11. Between 1494 and 1525, the French embarked on a series of military campaigns in Italy. This contact with the flourishing civilization of the Italian Renaissance had a three-fold influence on the French language:

(a) The arrival in France of Italian architects, painters, musicians and writers, particularly under the encouragement of Henri II's Italian queen, Catherine de Médici. The influence of Italian fashions affected not only the arts but also the language, so much so as to provoke a reaction against the excessive use of Italianisms by some courtiers: the attack was led by Henri Estienne in such works as his *Deux dialogues du nouveau langage françois italianizé* (1578). Many words borrowed from Italian in the 16th century have, however, remained, particularly in the fields of military and artistic terminology (e.g. *alerte, attaquer, bataillon, escale, escorte, infanterie, manquer, réussir, risque, arcade, balcon, façade, grotesque, modèle*).

(b) The Renaissance stimulated the study of vernacular tongues. The first grammar of French is Palsgrave's *Esclarcissement de la langue françoyse* (London, 1530), meant for English learners of French; in 1531, the first French grammar to be published in France was brought out by Dubois; this was written in Latin but was followed later in the century by other grammars written in French. The first French-Latin dictionary was published in 1540 by Robert Estienne who had earlier also produced a Latin-French dictionary.

(c) Side by side with this interest in the study of the language went a concern to encourage the use of French for all purposes, including those that had hitherto been the exclusive domain of Latin. The Latin that had served for centuries as the medium for nearly all scholarly writing, whilst far superior to the Latin in use before the Carolingian reform in the 8th century, was nevertheless not pure Classical Latin. Classical Latin lacked the vocabulary to serve adequately all the purposes it was called on to fulfil in the Middle Ages, and so medieval Latin—'Low Latin'—was characterized by many non-Classical neologisms; furthermore, the syntax of Low Latin is often influenced by that of the writer's mother tongue. One immediate effect of the efforts made by Erasmus (1466–1536) and others to restore the written language to an acceptable classical standard, particularly by abolishing all non-classical elements from its vocabulary, was to unfit it for many functions that it had hitherto fulfilled. This redounded to the advantage of the vernaculars, and the example of the literary achievements of Italian was a further stimulus to the use of French. In 1549 Du Bellay's *Deffence et illustration de la langue françoyse*, which can be regarded as the manifesto of the school of poets (chief among them being Ronsard) known as the Pléiade, urged the claims of the French language as a medium for all purposes, whilst recognizing that it might be necessary in some respects to supplement its vocabulary by borrowing from the classical languages. The Pléiade also saw the possibilities of enriching the language by drawing on other sources—provincial words, archaisms and new derivatives based on French roots (e.g. *survivance, délicatesse, aboutir*, based on *survivre, délicat, à bout*, are all first attested in the 16th century). 'Plus nous aurons de mots en notre langue, plus elle sera parfaite,' says Ronsard, and though some writers went too far and indulged in the mass importation and creation of new words, many of which were only ephemeral, nevertheless the word-stock of the language was substantially enriched in the course of the 16th century. Even before Du Bellay's *Deffence et illustration*, French had been put to a number of new uses—the first complete translations of the Bible date from 1523–1530 (Lefèvre d'Etaples—Catholic) and 1535 (Olivetan—Protestant), the first serious theological work in French is Calvin's *Institution de la religion chrestienne* (1541—the Latin version had appeared in 1536), and an important surgical treatise by Ambroise Paré appeared in 1545. These were followed later in the century by numerous works in French on theology, mathematics, astronomy, medicine, geography, history, etc.

1.12. Early in the 17th century came a reaction, the most influential figure in which was Malherbe, who took upon himself the task of 'purifying' the language and pruning drastically the luxuriant growth of the 16th century. Taking the line that the literary language should not admit any words that would not be intelligible to all, he proscribed archaisms, neologisms, learned borrowings, provincialisms, technical terms, and also sought to regulate the syntax of the language. Malherbe's activity, says Brunot, 'ouvre le règne de la grammaire, règne qui a été, en France, plus tyrannique et plus long qu'en aucun pays'.[17] He took his doctrine to excess, but nevertheless his activity had a positive side too: as a result of the work of Malherbe and his

[17] F. Brunot, *Histoire . . .*, III, Part I, 4

successors, and particularly as a result of their achievements in defining words more closely than had ever been done before,[18] the French language, if it lost in richness and colour, gained in clarity and precision. Malherbe had his opponents, but much of the linguistic activity of the 17th century continues in his tradition. Discussion of points of language and style was a favourite activity at the literary *salons* of the time, and from these *salons* and this activity emerged, to quote only two outstanding examples, the *Académie Française* (founded 1635) and Vaugelas. 'La principale fonction de l'Académie', says its Constitution, 'sera de travailler avec tout le soin et toute la diligence possible à donner des règles certaines à notre langue, et à la rendre pure, éloquente et capable de traiter les arts et les sciences.'[19] Vaugelas, a distinguished frequenter of the *salons* and a founder member of the Academy, published in 1647 his *Remarques sur la langue françoise*. He considered himself not as a legislator but as an observer and arbiter of 'good usage', which he defined as 'la façon de parler de la plus saine partie de la Cour, conformément à la façon d'écrire de la plus saine partie des auteurs du temps'. Generally, if not invariably, he avoids the excesses of artificiality and doctrinaire purism of some other grammarians of the period and his decisions on matters of vocabulary and syntax are often a positive contribution to the fixing of literary usage.

1.13. By the mid-17th century, the activity of the literary *salons* and academies, in concurrence with that of outstanding individuals such as Vaugelas and eminent writers such as Corneille, Racine and others who sought to conform to current standards of clarity and taste, had forged a highly polished literary language unrivalled at its time by any other European vernacular in terms of lexical precision and grammatical rigour. The price at which this was achieved was, however, a high one: though it is a commonplace in all literate communities that the written language diverges in some measure from everyday spoken usage, the gap that separated the language of literature (and the cultivated conversation of the *salons*) from the speech of the mass of the

[18] It was Malherbe who, for example, established a clear distinction in meaning between such near-synonyms as *sommeiller* and *dormir*, *contraire* and *différent*, *faible* and *débile*.

[19] The Academy was also charged to produce a dictionary, a grammar, a *poétique* and a *rhétorique*. The first edition of the dictionary appeared in 1694, the eighth in 1932–35. The grammar did not appear until 1932, and at once attracted a deal of scornful and well-founded hostility. The other works were not proceeded with.

people was accentuated—and deliberately so—by those who, in 17th-century France, codified what they considered to be 'good usage' and succeeded in imposing this as the only acceptable form of French for literary purposes.

In its grammatical structure, modern literary French is still in most respects the language as codified in the 17th century. On the other hand, the restrictions imposed on vocabulary have gradually been lifted. It is true that the aim of many in the 18th century was to maintain the purity of language achieved in the 17th century; some indeed wished to carry the refining process further and even objected to some elements in the vocabulary of classical writers like Corneille and Racine. However, with the scientific developments of the century, new approaches to religion and politics, an interest in foreign countries and their institutions, it was inevitable that new words should come into the language. For the technical terms they required, scientists had recourse to Latin and especially Greek, creating with elements drawn from these languages new words that had never themselves existed in the classical languages (*oxygène* and *hydrogène*, for example, are 18th-century creations). The great interest in England and English political institutions brought in words such as *budget, club, congrès, jury, session, vote, pudding, punch, grog, redingote* (< *riding-coat*), *sandwich*. The broadening of cultural and scientific horizons led also to borrowings from many other languages, e.g. German (*cobalt, gneiss, quartz*) and Spanish (e.g. *cigare, embarcadère, sieste, tomate* < Sp. *tomate*, itself borrowed from Nahuatl *tomatl*), and particularly Italian which provided many terms in the fields of music and the plastic arts (e.g. *contralto, cantate, mandoline, sonate, solo, aquarelle, pittoresque*).

1.14. The upheavals of the revolutionary period (1789 onwards) led to the introduction of a number of new words (e.g. the words *révolutionnaire* and *plébiscite* and the completely new terminology required for the metric system, *gramme, litre, mètre, kilogramme,* etc.) and the attribution of new senses to other words (e.g. *arrondissement, département, préfet*).[20] The linguistic consequences of the Revolution, however, were less far-reaching than those of the Romantic movement, which swept away most of the last remaining

---

[20] The triumph of the popular Parisian pronunciation [wa] over the aristocratic pronunciation [wè] in words having the spelling -*oi*- is also due to the Revolution. Before the overthrow of the monarchy, words such as *roi, soir,* etc. were pronounced [rwè], [swèr], etc., in Court circles (see **4.10**); this pronunciation still occurs in, for example, rural Normandy.

restrictions on the vocabulary of the literary language: with their interest in affectivity, expressiveness, picturesqueness, the Romantics admitted freely archaisms, neologisms, provincialisms, foreign words, the 'mots bas' that previous ages had spurned— almost all the categories of words that had been excluded for two centuries from the literary language came flooding in. Whereas the 17th-century classicists had sought to 'fix' the language, Victor Hugo, one of the foremost spokesmen of the Romantics, proclaimed that 'la langue française n'est point fixée et ne se fixera point' and, referring to the red cap of Liberty, the emblem of the Revolution, he wrote: 'Je mis le bonnet rouge au vieux dictionnaire', and declared all words free and equal.

During the last century and a half, the continued needs of literary expressivity and scientific and technological precision have so swollen the word-stock of the language with neologisms based on Greek and Latin roots[21] and borrowings from foreign tongues, and in particular from English, as to constitute in the eyes of some purists a real threat to the French language.[22]

1.15. The shackles imposed on the vocabulary of literary French by Malherbe and his successors have long since been shattered. Yet the 'official' grammar of the language, the grammar taught in schools and adopted for nearly all 'serious' purposes in writing, has changed comparatively little: if the language of 17th-century writers now has a certain period flavour about it, this is for stylistic rather than grammatical reasons. Meanwhile, however, the spoken language has been developing. The theoreticians of the 17th century were, as we have seen, well aware that their linguistic norms were based on the usage of a select section of society and there was already at that time a considerable gap between 'accepted' usage and popular usage. Popular speech, however, has of course continued in use and developed along its own lines and in recent decades has been put to literary use, particularly in the transcription of dialogue, but also on occasion as a narrative medium itself, for such varying ends as comedy (e.g. Queneau, *Zazie dans le métro*) and vituperative aggressiveness (Céline, *Voyage au bout de la nuit*), realism (Aragon, *Les communistes*) and lyrical beauty (Giono, *Présentation de Pan*). The following passage will illustrate Queneau's use of popular French:

[21] Some such words have even—to the horror of pedants—been formed by combining roots from both languages, e.g. *pluviomètre* 'rain-gauge', in which *pluvio-* is Latin and *-mètre* Greek.

[22] For a witty if exaggerated onslaught on the current mania for using English (including American) words, see Étiemble, *Parlez-vous franglais?*, Paris, 1964.

18

'Dans le journal, on dit qu'il y a pas onze pour cent des apparte-
ments à Paris qui ont des salles de bain, ça m'étonne pas, mais
on peut se laver sans. Tous ceux là qui m'entourent, ils doivent
pas faire de grands efforts. D'un autre côté, c'est tout de même
pas un choix parmi les plus crasseux de Paris. . . . On peut pas
supposer que les gens qu'attendent à la gare d'Austerlitz
sentent plus mauvais que ceux qu'attendent à la gare de Lyon.'

It is always dangerous to predict the future development of a
language. It is perhaps not going beyond the bounds of legitimate
speculation, however, to suggest that, gradually, various features
that are already well-established in popular speech, and in some
cases in spoken usage at all but the most formal levels, may well
come to be adopted in literary usage not merely for particular
expressive effects but as generally accepted practice.

1.16. The principal countries outside France in which French
is the first language of a sizeable community are Belgium,
Switzerland and Canada (where it has been well established since
the 17th century). It is noteworthy that in both Belgium, where
French is in competition with Dutch (Flemish), and Canada,
where it is in competition with English, the linguistic situation
has led to notorious social and political crises.[23] Even Switzerland
has its linguistic problem, the *problème jurassien*, arising out of the
fact that a section of the French-speaking community in the
predominantly German-speaking canton of Bern felt itself at a
disadvantage; this led to the setting up in 1978 of a separate
French-speaking canton of the Jura.

French is also the official language of the few remaining territories of the French colonial empire, including the *Territoire
français des Afars et des Issas* (formerly French Somaliland), French
Guiana and the islands of St. Pierre et Miquelon off Newfound-
land (all that remains to France of French Canada), Guadeloupe
and Martinique in the West Indies, Réunion and the Comores
archipelago in the Indian Ocean, and various Pacific islands. It
is also the official language of Luxembourg (where the everyday
spoken language is a Germanic dialect), of Haiti (where the
everyday spoken language is a form of French-based creole) and
of numerous African republics that were, until comparatively
recently, French or Belgian colonies or mandated territories.

---

[23] For a discussion of the Belgian situation, seen from the point of view of the
Walloon (French-speaking) section of the population, see Lucien Outers, *Le
divorce belge*, Paris, 1968.

2 Pronunciation: Preliminaries

2.1. *Classification of sounds and phonetic transcription.*[1]

2.1.1. Voice is the sound produced when the air expelled from the lungs passes between the so-called 'vocal cords'[2] and causes them to vibrate—just as the vibration of the reed of a clarinet or the strings of a violin produces a musical note. Voice can be heard when we utter any vowel or such consonants as *l*, *m*, *n*, *v*; such sounds are known as *voiced* sounds. If, however, the gap between the vocal cords is wide enough to allow the air to pass through without causing them to vibrate, any sounds produced in the mouth are *voiceless*. The principal difference between *b* and *p*, *d* and *t*, *v* and *f*,[3] is that in each of these pairs of consonants the first is voiced and the second voiceless.

2.1.2. Consonants are classified according to (i) whether they are voiced or voiceless (**2.1.1**), (ii) their point of articulation (**2.1.3**), and (iii) their manner of articulation (**2.1.4**).

2.1.3. 'Point of articulation' refers to the place in the mouth at which the consonant is produced. We shall here consider only the following:

(a) *lips*: consonants pronounced with both lips are known as *bilabials* (e.g. *p*, *b*);

[1] This chapter does not purport to be more than a brief introductory survey. For a fuller, though elementary, discussion, see B. Malmberg, *La phonétique*, Paris, 1962 (in the *Que sais-je?* series) translated under the title *Phonetics*, New York, 1963. More advanced text-books are of course available, one of the most recent being D. Abercrombie's *Elements of General Phonetics*, Edinburgh, 1967, which contains an extensive bibliography.
[2] In reality, the 'vocal cords' are not cords at all, but two movable membranes attached to either side of the larynx.
[3] In both English and French, voiceless consonants are also pronounced with greater muscular effort than voiced consonants; see B. Malmberg, *op. cit.*, 59–60 and A. C. Gimson, *An Introduction to the Pronunciation of English*, 2nd ed., London, 1970, 149. Voiceless consonants may therefore be referred to as strong or *fortis* and voiced consonants as weak or *lenis*. For a full discussion of the pronunciation of consonants in French and English respectively, see Armstrong, Ch. XI and Gimson, Ch. 8.

20

(b) *lips and teeth:* consonants pronounced with the top teeth and the bottom lip are *labio-dentals* (*f*, *v*);

(c) *teeth:* (i) consonants produced by placing the tongue between the teeth are *interdentals* (English **thin** and **then**); (ii) consonants produced by raising the tip of the tongue to the top teeth are *dentals* (French *t, d, n*);

(d) *alveolae* (i.e. the hard ridge behind the top teeth): English *t, d, n* are pronounced by raising the tongue to the alveolae not to the teeth (as in French) and so are *alveolars; s* and *z* are also alveolar consonants;

(e) *palate* (i.e. the hard front part of the roof of the mouth): consonants produced by raising the tongue towards the palate are known as *palatals:* apart from the semi-consonant *y* as in *yes,* English has no palatals; French has a similar semi-consonant to English *y*, viz. the sound transcribed as *i* in *pied* and as *ll* in *fille* (see Ch. 5), and in addition the *gn* sound of *signe,* etc; as we shall see (**3.9**), other palatal sounds were important at the proto-French stage;

(f) *velum* (i.e. the soft back part of the roof of the mouth): sounds produced by raising the tongue towards the velum are *velars* (English *c, g* as in *cool, good,* and *ng* as in *sing*);

(g) *uvula:* the only *uvular* sound that need concern us is the modern Parisian *r.*

2.1.4. 'Manner of articulation': the consonants we shall be concerned with are produced in one or other of the following ways:

(a) The flow of air is stopped by a complete closure of the passage at some point or other, and then released; closure may be made at such points as the following:

   (i) both lips (*p, b*)
   (ii) at the teeth (Fr. *t, d*) or alveolae (Eng. *t, d*)
   (iii) at the palate (see **3.9**)
   (iv) at the velum (*k, g*).

These sounds are known as *stops* (or *plosives*): so, *p* and *b* are respectively a *voiceless bilabial stop* and a *voiced bilabial stop,* French *t* is a *voiceless dental stop,* etc.

(b) The flow of air is not completely stopped but is restricted so that audible friction occurs when the air is forced through the narrow remaining gap; such sounds we know as *fricatives;* the friction may occur:

(i) between both lips: the *b* of Spanish *saber* is a voiced bilabial fricative;

(ii) between top teeth and bottom lip (*f, v*);

(iii) interdentally (English voiced and voiceless *th*);

(iv) at the alveolae (*s, z*);

(v) just behind the alveolae—French *ch* and *j,* corresponding more or less though not exactly to English *sh* and '*zh*' (=*s* in *measure*) are post-alveolar;

(vi) at the palate—the German *ch* in *ich* is a voiceless palatal fricative;

(vii) at the velum—*ch* in German *ach* (or Scottish *loch*) and Spanish *g* in *haga* are respectively voiceless and voiced velar fricatives.

(c) Sounds having a stop as first element and a fricative second element—e.g. English *ch* (=*t*+*sh*), German *z* (=*t*+*s*)—are known as *affricates.*

(d) The flow of air is stopped at some point in the mouth, but is allowed to escape through the nose; consonants so produced are known as *nasals*; the point of articulation may be:

(i) the lips (*m*)

(ii) the teeth (French *n*)

(iii) the alveolae (English *n*)

(iv) the palate (French *gn*)

(v) the velum (English *ng*)

(e) The centre of the passage is closed at the teeth (or alveolae) but the air is allowed to escape at the sides: this produces the *lateral* consonant *l*; in French, the tip of the tongue touches the teeth, in English the alveolae; if, in addition, the back of the tongue is raised, the sound produced is a 'velar *l*', the so-called 'dark *l*', found in most varieties of English at the end of a word or before a consonant (*cool, field*) (the initial *l* of English—*like, leave*—is, in most areas, a 'clear *l*', i.e. it has no velar colouring).

(f) There are numerous varieties of *r* sound; we shall here mention, in addition to the uvular fricative of modern Parisian French, the rolled or trilled *r* produced by vibrating either the tip of the tongue or the uvula.

2.1.5. The Latin alphabet is not fully adequate for coping with the numerous sounds we shall need to refer to. We must therefore

22

adopt some kind of phonetic transcription. The following table shows most of the symbols we shall use for consonants; these are drawn from those of the International Phonetic Alphabet; where two symbols are given in the same box, the first stands for a voiceless sound, the second for a voiced sound:

	Bilabial	Labio-dental	Dental or Inter-dental	Alveolar	Post-alveolar	Palatal	Velar
Stop	p b		t d				k g
Frica-tive	β	f v	θ ð	s z	ʃ ʒ		χ ɣ
Nasal	m		n			ɲ	ŋ
Lateral			l			λ	ɫ

The following may require some explanation:

β = Spanish *b* as in *saber* [saβer]
θ ð = Eng. *th* of *thin* [θin] and *then* [ðen] respectively
ʃ ʒ = Fr. *ch* (Eng. *sh*) and *j* (Eng. *s* of *measure*) respectively: *chou* [ʃu], *joue* [ʒu]
χ ɣ = German *ch* of *ach* [aχ] (Scottish *loch* [lɔχ]) and its voiced equivalent (Spanish *agua* [aɣwa])
ɲ = Fr. *gn* (*signe* [siɲ])
ŋ = Eng. *ng* (*sing* [siŋ])
ɫ = Eng. 'dark *l*' (*full* [fuɫ])
λ = palatal *l*, the sound represented in Spanish by *ll* and in Italian by *gl*

In addition:

(a) [h] represents English *h* as in *house*.
(b) To represent palatal sounds (other than [ɲ] and [λ]) we shall use the symbol for the corresponding non-palatal sound followed by ['], e.g. palatal [s] = [s'].
(c) We shall use [r] for all varieties of *r* sound.

2.1.6. The vowels of French are classified on the basis of the following criteria:

(a) the extent to which the tongue is raised: at one extreme we

23

have vowels such as *a* in which the tongue is comparatively flat and which are therefore known as 'low' vowels, and at the other *i*, *ou* (as in French *loup*) and *u* (as in French *tu*) in which the tongue is raised almost to the roof of the mouth and which are therefore known as 'high' vowels; in between are the various *e*, *o* and *eu* vowels of French;

(b) the part of the tongue—front, centre, back—that is raised during the production of the vowel: on this basis, we have 'front', 'central' and 'back' vowels;

(c) whether the lips are rounded (for *o*, *ou*, *u* etc.) or not (as for *i*, *é* etc.);

(d) whether or not the air escapes only through the mouth or through the nose as well: on this basis, we have 'oral' and 'nasal' vowels.

The oral vowels of modern French can be tabulated thus, using the International Phonetic Alphabet symbols:

	Front unrounded	Front rounded	Back rounded
High	[i] lit	[y] du	[u] bout
High-mid	[e] été	[ø] peu	[o] dos
Low-mid	[ɛ] bête	[œ] peur	[ɔ] porte
Low	[a] patte		[ɑ] pâte

There is also the vowel [ə] of *le* [lə], *cheval* [ʃəval], etc.; in ModFr. it is a central vowel pronounced with rounded lips.

Nasal vowels are represented by the symbol for the corresponding oral vowel[4] surmounted by a tilde [~]. The ModFr nasal vowels are [ɛ̃] *vin*, [œ̃] *un*, [ɔ̃] *bon*, [ã] *dans*.

2.1.7. The symbols [j], [w] and [ɥ] represent the three semi-consonants of French, as in *paille* [paːj] (cf. English *yap* [jæp]), *poire* [pwaːr] and *huit* [ɥit]. These are discussed more fully in Chapter 5.

2.1.8. A colon indicates that a sound is long, e.g. *pâte* [paːt]

2.1.9. Phonetic transcriptions are given in square brackets, e.g. *chanter* [ʃãte].

2.2. *Sounds and phonemes.*

2.2.1. Human speech consists not of a succession of sounds with

---

[4] 'Corresponding' does not necessarily mean 'having identical tongue- and lip-positions'. Though the tongue- and lip-positions for [œ̃] and [ã] are much the same as those for [œ] and [ɑ] respectively, [ɛ̃] is a more open vowel than [ɛ] and [ɔ̃] a less open vowel than [ɔ]. See Armstrong, Ch. IX.

clear lines of demarcation between them, not, that is, of a succession of discrete units like the succession of letters on a printed
page, but of a continuum of sound: all the time we are speaking,
the quality of any sound we utter is likely to be affected *both* by
the fact that our speech organs are in the process of moving away
from the position they were in for a preceding sound *and* by the
fact that we are already preparing to utter a following sound. In
the English word *can* [kæn], for example, the quality of the [k]
is determined by the fact that it is followed by [æ], not by [i] or
[u], and the quality of the [æ] is affected, if only slightly and in
general imperceptibly, by the fact that the speaker has just
uttered a [k] and not, say, a [p] or a [z] or an [l], and also by
the fact that he is preparing to say [n] and not [t] or [b] or [m].

Variations in the pronunciation of what is basically the same
'sound' (to use for the moment a term that is not strictly appropriate) when it occurs in different phonetic circumstances occur
in all languages. Two examples from English will enable us to
make the point clear:

(a) the point of articulation of [k] in *cool* [kuːl], in which it is
followed by a back vowel [u], is towards the back of the velum;
before a front vowel, as in *keen* [kiːn], it is towards the front of the
velum; the point of articulation varies slightly for each vowel
that follows the [k];
(b) in English as spoken in most areas, *l* is pronounced differently
according to whether it precedes a vowel (e.g. *leave*) (in which
case we have the so-called 'clear *l*') or whether it precedes a
consonant (*salt*) or comes at the end of a word (*cool*) (in which
case we have the so-called 'dark *l*'—see **2.1.4.** (e)).

2.2.2. The man-in-the-street is not generally aware of these
shades of pronunciation which serve no functional purpose in
the language. In other words, whereas the difference between,
say, [t] and [d], or [t] and [θ], or [θ] and [ð], is distinctive, in
that it enables us to distinguish between such pairs as *toe/doe*
tick/thick, *thigh/thy*, the difference between, say, 'clear *l*' and
'dark *l*' serves no such purpose. We can therefore distinguish,
within any given language, between what we might call *functional*
or *distinctive* 'sounds' (such as [t], [d], [θ], [ð] in English) and
non-functional or *non-distinctive* sounds (such as 'clear' and 'dark' *l*
or the varieties of [k] mentioned above, in English). The technical
term for what we have called a functional or distinctive 'sound'
is a *phoneme*, and the varieties of one phoneme within a given

25

language are its *allophones*—so, in English, clear *l* and dark *l* are allophones of the same *l* phoneme.

2.2.3. Whereas the number of allophones in a given language is very great even within the speech of one person, the number of phonemes is comparatively small: Professor Barbara Strang, for example, lists 37 consonant and vowel phonemes for one variety of English,[5] and André Martinet says[6] that Parisian French as spoken by him has 34 phonemes; some languages have far fewer.

We may wish to represent the pronunciation of a language taking account only of the phonemes and not of the allophones. In this case, we place the symbols between oblique strokes: so, if we use /l/ for the English *l* phoneme, we can transcribe *lip* and *full* phonetically as [lip], [fuł], and phonemically as /lip/, /ful/.

Different sounds that are phonemic—i.e. constitute separate phonemes—in one language may be merely allophones in another. Two examples will illustrate this:

(a) in some varieties of Polish, 'clear' and 'dark' *l* are separate phonemes, e.g. *laska*[laska] 'walking-stick' ~ *łaska*[łaska] 'favour';
(b) in Spanish, [d] and [ð] are allophones of one phoneme: [d] is used initially and after [l] or [n], and [ð] is used between vowels, so *han dado* 'they have given' is [an daðo], but *ha dado* 'he has given' is [a ðaðo]; if we decide to represent this phoneme as /d/, we shall transcribe these as /an dado/ and /a dado/ respectively.

2.2.4. Allophones are said to be in *complementary distribution* when —like, for example, Spanish [d] and [ð]—each occurs in phonetic circumstances in which the other does not.

2.3. *Syllables.* We shall see that in discussing sound change (e.g. **4.5**), or the distribution of certain sounds at a given period (e.g. **4.13**), it is sometimes necessary to take into account the nature of the relevant syllable. We must therefore discuss briefly the principles governing syllabification.

In both Latin and French (but *not* in English) the following principles apply:

(a) a single consonant[7] between vowels forms part of the following syllable:

[5] *Modern English Structure*, 2nd edn., London, 1968, 47–50
[6] *Éléments de linguistique générale*, Paris, 1960, 25
[7] i.e. a single *pronounced* consonant

26

ma-ri-tum, va-ti-ci-na-ri, re-ti-rer, a-van-ta-geux [a- vɑ̃-ta-ʒø]

(b) clusters composed of a stop + *l* (*bl, gl, pl,* etc.) or of a stop + *r* (*br, pr, tr,* etc.) are not divided and so form part of the following syllable:

de-cli-na-re, pa-trem, ca-pra, bi-bli-o-gra-phie, beu-gler, sou-plesse, a-bré-ger, â-pre-té, é-cri-vain

(c) other pairs of consonants are split, the first going with the preceding syllable, the second with the following syllable:

ar-gen-tum, por-ta, fac-tum, mit-tere, ar-gent, por-teur, fes-ti-val

Syllables ending in a vowel are known as *open* syllables (e.g. all three syllables in *o-pe-ra*, both syllables in *tomber* [tɔ̃-be]).

Syllables ending in a consonant are known as *closed* syllables (e.g. the first syllable in *por-ta*, both syllables in *porteur* [pɔr-tœːr]).

2.4. *Assimilation and dissimilation. Assimilation* is the process whereby one sound takes on some or all of the characteristics of another sound that precedes or follows it. In English, for example, *have* [hæv] often becomes [hæf] in *I have to go* [. . . . hæf tə . . .], i.e. the voiced [v] becomes the voiceless [f] in contact with the voiceless [t] ([v] is partially assimilated to [t]); or again, in the pronunciation [ðækkɔːnə] for [ðæt kɔːnə], *that corner*, the [t] has changed its point of articulation and become fully assimilated to the following [k].

Dissimilation is the process whereby a sound becomes more markedly differentiated from another, as when Latin *peregrinum* becomes *pelegrinum* (> *pèlerin*) (the first of two [r]s is dissimilated to [l]) or when *chimney* is pronounced *chimley* (one nasal consonant, [n], is dissimilated to [l] after another nasal consonant, [m]). Dissimilation of consonants in contact (as in *chim**n**ey*) and dissimilation of consonants not in contact (as in *peregrinum*) are usually considered as different processes arising from different causes.[7a]

[7a] 'Consonantal dissimilation itself is usually sub-divided into two categories: dissimilation of consonants in contact, or *differentiation*; and dissimilation of consonants not in contact—*Ferndissimilation, dissimilation harmonique.* Some linguists believe these two types of dissimilation to spring from quite different psychic causes: *differentiation* results from an instinctive effort on the part of the speaker to avoid assimilation; *dissimilation* proper is a mechanical product of lack of attention.' (Rebecca R. Posner, *Consonantal Dissimilation in the Romance Languages,* 1961, 4) Without necessarily accepting the distinction, Dr. Posner confines herself in her book to what she calls dissimilation proper.

27

2.5. *Sound laws.*

2.5.1. Let us imagine a language that has in its vocabulary such words as *datum, pratum* and *natum* and let us imagine that, after being rolled on the tongues of successive generations for some 2000 years, these words became, in one particular district, [dat], [praðo] and [ne]——*atum* has given something different in each word. Suppose too that, in the same district,

(a) *cervum, centum* and *centrum* (*c* = [k]) became [tʃɛrb], [θjɛnto] and [sãːtr] (with three different developments of *c* before *e*),
(b) *plicare, plangere, plus, plorat* and *plenum* became [plie], [pjandʒere], [prus], [ʎora] and [ʃeju] (with five different developments of initial *pl*), and
(c) a similar apparent chaos emerged whenever the modern forms of a number of words having some feature in common are compared.

Clearly, in such circumstances, it would be hopeless to try and discuss systematically the evolution of the pronunciation of the language.

Fortunately, we are not faced with this situation. Our 'imaginary' language is of course Latin, but though the modern forms of Latin words quoted are all authentic, they are drawn from different languages: [praðo] *prado*, [θjɛrto] *cierto* and [ʎora] *llora* are Spanish, [dat] *dat* and [tʃɛrb] *cerb* are Rumanian, [pjandʒere] *piangere* is Italian, [ʃeju] *cheio* is Portuguese, [prus] *prus* is Sardinian and the rest are French. If we now look at the French forms of these words, we shall see that the words within each group have undergone a parallel development:

(a) datum > dé, pratum > pré, natum > né: -atum > [e]
(b) cervum > cerf [sɛrf], centum > cent [sã], centrum > centre [sãːtr]: [k] before *e* > [s]
(c) plicare > plier, plangere > plaindre, plŭs > plus, plorat > pleure, plenum > plein: initial [pl] remains.

We can now come to two tentative conclusions: first, that there is a degree of regularity in the way a given sound develops and that certain general conclusions can be drawn; but secondly, that any such general conclusions relate only to one particular area, as the development of the same sound may be very different in different languages.

Let us now compare the following groups of Latin words with the corresponding ModFr forms:

(a) contra > contre [kɔ̃ːtr]   placent > plaisent [plɛːz]
    centum > cent [sɑ̃]   pacare > payer [pɛje]
    campum > champ [ʃɑ̃]   jocare > jouer [ʒwe]

(b) partem > part [paːr]   manum > main [mɛ̃]
    passum > pas [pɑ]   annum > an [ɑ̃]
    pratum > pré [pre]   capïllos > cheveux [ʃəvø]
    patrem > père [pɛːr]   porta > porte [pɔrt]

These words show six different developments in the same language of Latin [k]—viz. [k], [s], [ʃ], [z], [j] and total disappearance—and eight different developments of Latin [a]—viz. [a], [ɑ], [e], [ɛ], [ɛ̃], [ɑ̃], [ə] and complete disappearance: and the lists are not exhaustive. Our tentative conclusion that there is a degree of regularity in the way a given sound develops in a given language is not however invalidated, but it must be stated with greater precision. By way of example, we can take some of the words listed above and place them in sets of comparable words:

contra > contre [kɔ̃ːtr]   costa > côte [koːt]
corpus > corps [kɔːr]   cumulare > combler [kɔ̃ble]
collum > col [kɔl]   cura > cure [kyːr]

centum > cent [sɑ̃]   cera > cire [siːr]
cervum > cerf [sɛrf]   circulum > cercle [sɛrkl]
cessare > cesser [sɛse]   cinerem > cendre [sɑ̃ːdr]

campum > champ [ʃɑ̃]   carbonem > charbon [ʃarbɔ̃]
cantare > chanter [ʃɑ̃te]   carum > cher [ʃɛːr]
calidum > chaud [ʃo]   capra > chèvre [ʃɛːvr]

Each of these lists could be added to. On the basis of this new evidence we could conclude (i) that when it was followed by *o* or *u*, Latin [k] at the beginning of a word remained as [k] in French; (ii) that before *e* or *i* it has become [s]; and (iii) that before *a* it has become [ʃ]. Additional examples of the same types as *placent, pacare, jocare* would show that, between vowels, the development of [k] depended on which particular vowels preceded and followed it. Similarly, the development of *a* depends upon the degree of stress it bore, upon the nature of the syllable

29

(open or closed) and upon the influence of neighbouring sounds (e.g. palatals or nasals). In other words, the development of a sound depends upon its 'phonetic circumstances'.

We have now established that, provided they are properly framed, we can make general statements about the way sounds have changed (i) in a given language or dialect (i.e. in a certain geographical area) and (ii) in certain specified phonetic circumstances.

We have just seen that Latin initial *c* [k] before *a* becomes *ch* [ʃ] in French. But anyone with even an elementary knowledge of French can point to apparent exceptions to this. These can usually be explained in one of the following ways:

(1) *casser*, for example, comes from Latin *quassare*, not from a word having initial *c* in Latin: in French, Latin *qu* [kw] becomes [k], cf. *quadrare* > *carrer* [kare], *quattuor* > *quatre* [katr], *quando* > *quand* [kɑ̃];

(2) the word in question may have been borrowed either (i) from a different dialect of the same language which did not undergo the sound change in question, or (ii) from another language: for example, (i) *câble* is borrowed from one of the northern dialects of French in which [k] + *a* remained unchanged (cf. the place name *Le Câteau'* = 'château'); (ii) *cadavre* and *calcul* are 16th-century borrowings from written Latin, *cap* and *cadeau* are borrowed from Occitan, *cascade*, *casino*, *cavalier* from Italian, *camping* from English.

These considerations enable us to emphasize that our general statements or 'sound laws' refer to what happened *at a given period* in the past. The change by which [k] + *a* > [tʃ] (and later [ʃ]) took place before the 10th century; so by the time [kwa] had changed to [ka]—perhaps not till the 11th or 12th century—it was too late for the development of [k] + *a* > [tʃ] to take place; likewise, nouns that entered the language later from other sources—*cadeau*, etc.—were not affected.

As a final working definition of a sound law, therefore, we can say that it is a *descriptive statement* of a sound change that took place (i) in a *particular language* or dialect, (ii) at a *particular time*, (iii) in *specified phonetic circumstances*.

2.5.2. *Combinative and isolative changes.* Sound changes that take place only in certain phonetic circumstances, e.g. under the influence of particular neighbouring sounds or in certain types of syllables (for numerous examples, see Chs. 2 and 3), are known as 'combinative' changes. Some sound changes, however, come about independently of phonetic circumstances and are known as 'isolative' changes (for some examples, see **3.2**).

2.5.3. Even a moderately full treatment of all the sound laws relating to the development of French is far beyond the scope of this book. Our aim is to show the main features and trends of phonetic development, without going into the mass of detail that a comprehensive survey would require. Those who wish to look into problems not covered here are referred to the books listed in the bibliography.

2.5.4. Though most—if not all—sound changes begin at the phonetic level, their effects may also be felt at the phonemic level. At this level, there are various possibilities:

(a) a new phoneme may arise—e.g. when [n] in contact with a palatal became [ɲ] (**3.9.4** (b)), with the result that French has pairs such as /pɛn/ *peine* and /pɛɲ/ *peigne*, a new phoneme /ɲ/ entered the system;

(b) a phoneme may disappear—e.g. when [ʎ] became [j] (as in [fiʎ] *fille* > [fij], **3.9.4** (b)), the fact that French already had a phoneme /j/, as in /pɛje/ *payer*, meant that henceforth, instead of the two phonemes /ʎ/ and /j/, the language had only the phoneme /j/;

(c) the original phoneme may remain in some circumstances, but in other circumstances may disappear completely or merge with another phoneme—e.g. Latin /p/ remains in *portare* > *porter*, but has disappeared in *campum* > *champ* [ʃɑ̃], *rupta* > *route*, has merged with /v/ in *ripa* > *rive*, and has merged with /f/ in *caput* > *chef*.

Ideally, we ought to state at what stage a given sound change became phonemicized, i.e. at what stage a sound B resulting from sound A in certain circumstances is to be considered as a different phoneme from sound A (or a different reflex of sound A) in other circumstances. In practice, this is often difficult or even, in the present state of our knowledge, impossible. A great deal of work remains to be done on this aspect of the history of French.

One example will suffice to illustrate the nature of the problem. We shall see (**3.9.2** (b)) that the phoneme /k/ before *a* had in proto-French an allophone [t'] that later became [tʃ] and then [ʃ]: e.g. *campum* [kampo] > [t'ampo] > [tʃɑ̃mp] > [ʃɑ̃] *champ*. It is certain on the one hand that [t'] was merely an allophone of /k/, and on the other hand that [ʃ] has long been an independent phoneme (witness pairs such as *champ* /ʃɑ̃/ and *camp*[8] /kɑ̃/). But at what stage did the reflex of /k/ + /a/ become phonemic? The answer is probably that it became phonemic at the time (11th century?) when [kwa] became [ka], as in *quattuor* > *catre* (now written *quatre*), *quadrare* > *carrer*, etc.

Whilst recognizing that changes at the phonemic level are of prime importance, in practice we shall find ourselves obliged to discuss changes at the phonetic level. However, there will frequently be a clear implication that by a certain period given changes have become phonemicized.

2.6. *Sounds and spellings.* The gulf that exists between pronunciation and spelling in ModFr, as in English, is notorious. Space does not allow of an extended discussion of French orthography. The reader is referred to the chapter on orthography in Ewert, *The French Language*, to P. Burney, *L'orthographe*, Paris, 1955 (in the *Que sais-je?* series) or, for a much fuller treatment, to Ch. Beaulieux, *Histoire de l'orthographe française*, 2 vols., Paris, 1927. However, a few points should be made briefly here.

The discrepancy between the written and the spoken language arises from various causes, the following being the most important:

(a) The letters of the Latin alphabet were inadequate for representing all the sounds of French and so recourse was had to various combinations of letters, e.g. *ch* for [tʃ] (> [ʃ]) as in *chanter*, *ign/gn* for [ɲ] as in *peigne* [pɛɲ], *il/ill/ll* for [ʎ] (> [j]) as in *travail* [travaʎ] > [travaj], *fille* [fiʎə] > [fij].

(b) Orthography has not kept pace with changes in pronunciation, with the result that it now reflects many features of pronunciation that have not been current since the Middle Ages. In particular, (i) consonants (especially final consonants) that disappeared in pronunciation in the MidFr period (see **3.8.4**) are still retained in spelling (e.g. *champ*, *lit*, *porter*, *les murs*), and (ii) spellings that originally represented fairly accurately various diphthongs or triphthongs (see in particular **4.5.4**, **4.7** and **4.8**) remain, though they now represent quite different sounds and in many cases simple vowels (see **4.9** and **4.10**) (e.g. *foi*—pronounced [fɔj] in the 12th century—*aube* [awbə] > [oːb], *eux*, *eau*, *fait*, etc.).

(c) Words from the Classical languages and living foreign languages have been adopted with only a minimum, if any, of

---

[8] It is uncertain whether *camp* was borrowed from a northern dialect of French, from Occitan or from Italian.

32

orthographical adaptation,[9] e.g. *nation, ascension, théâtre, photo-graphe, tramway, football, building, gneiss, pronunciamiento, spaghetti.*
(d) The spelling of many words was altered—in most cases in MidFr or the 16th century—under the influence of Latin spelling, e.g. OFr *grant > grand* (Latin *grandem*), though in liaison there is still a final [t] (*un grand homme* [œ̃ grɑ̃t ɔm]), *pie > pied* (Latin *pedem*), *cors > corps* (Latin *corpus*), *vint > vingt* (Latin *viginti*), *sis > six* (Latin *sex*), *set > sept* (Latin *septem*), *erbe > herbe* (Latin *herba*), *catre > quatre* (Latin *quattuor*), *conter > compter* (Latin *computare*), *povre > pauvre* (Latin *pauper*).[10]

On the credit side, it must be recognized that the unphonetic nature of French orthography makes it possible to distinguish in the written language between homonyms, e.g. *sain, saint, sein,* (*je*) *ceins,* (*il*) *ceint, seing,* all pronounced [sɛ̃], or *comte, conte, compte,* all pronounced [kɔ̃ːt].

In some words, spelling has influenced pronunciation, e.g. *advenir* for *avenir* [adv-], *extraire* for *estraire* [ɛks-], and numerous words having a final consonant (*bec, chef, sens,* etc., see **3.8.4**).

[9] One may contrast this with the practice of other languages that adapt the spelling of loan-words in conformity with their own orthographical conventions, e.g. German *Büro < bureau,* Spanish *chofer < chauffeur,* Rumanian *creion < crayon,* Welsh *sgôr < score.*
[10] Many of these 'etymological' spellings have not survived, e.g. *debte, aultre, poinct, advocat* for *dette, autre, point, avocat.* In some cases the etymologizing was erroneous, as when *pois* (*< pensum*) was changed to *poids* by faulty association with *pondus.*

33

3 Consonants

3.1. *French and Latin consonant phonemes.* The consonant phonemes of ModFr are:

Stops: p   b   t   d   k   g
Fricatives: f   v   s   z   ʃ   ʒ   r
Nasals: m   n   ɲ
Lateral: l

(For our purposes, the sounds [j], [ɥ] and [w] are treated as semi-consonants—see Ch. 5, where their phonemic status is also discussed.)

A comparison with ClLat shows, briefly, that:

(a) one phoneme, /h/, has been lost;
(b) four fricative phonemes, /v/, /z/, /ʃ/ and /ʒ/, and the palatal nasal phoneme /ɲ/ have been gained;
(c) one phoneme, /r/, has changed its point of articulation (see **3.2** (b)).

A further comparison with Latin shows that, depending on the phonetic context:

(i) some phonemes have remained, e.g.

bene > bien	natum > né	talpa > taupe
dentem > dent	gula > gueule	clavem > clef
factum > fait	sola > seule	plena > pleine

(ii) some phonemes have been replaced by others, e.g.

ripa > rive /p/ > /v/	cantare > chanter /k/ > /ʃ/
rosa > rose /s/ > /z/	centum > cent /k/ > /s/

(iii) Some phonemes have disappeared altogether, e.g.

vita > vie [vi]	talpa > taupe [toːp]
bonum > bon [bɔ̃]	factum > fait [fɛ]
partem > part [paːr]	testa > tête [tɛt]

(iv) some phonemes have been introduced, e.g.

camera > chambre	tenerum > tendre

In the rest of this chapter we shall consider some of the more important changes affecting consonants. We shall not however attempt to cover everything. For a fuller treatment, the reader is referred to the relevant works listed in the bibliography, and in particular to E. and J. Bourciez, Ewert, Fouché (*Phonétique . . .*, Vol. III), Nyrop (Vol. I) and Pope.

3.2. *Isolative changes.* In most cases, the development of consonants depends on their position in the word or phrase (i.e. they are combinative changes). Three isolative changes, however (see **2.5.2**), call for particular comment:

(a) /h/ disappeared in Late Latin in all positions, and so has left no trace in the Romance languages—e.g. *herba* > OFr *erbe*, Spanish *yerba*, Italian *erba*, Rumanian *iarbǎ*. Though in many words an initial *h* has been reintroduced in French *in spelling*, under the influence of Latin spelling, they still function as if they began (as indeed they do in pronunciation) with a vowel (e.g. *l'herbe*):

hominem > OFr ome > homme   hibernum > OFr iver > hiver
heri > OFr ier > hier   hospitalem > OFr ostel > hôtel

The *h* has not been introduced in such words as *orge* < *hordeum* and *avoir* < *habere*.

/h/ re-entered the French phonemic system with words borrowed from the languages of the Germanic invaders (5th to 8th centuries). By the 16th century we find grammarians criticizing those who dropped their *h*s, which is an indication that the sound was then on its way out. The dropping of *h* became generally accepted in the 18th century, but these words are still treated as if they began with a consonant (the so-called '*h* aspirée'—a misnomer, as a non-existent sound is certainly not an aspirate!):

la hache   le houx   la haine   le hibou
la haie   la hâte   je hais   la honte

(b) The point of articulation of /r/ has changed. In Latin, as in modern Italian or Spanish, /r/ was probably a trill produced by the vibration of the tip of the tongue; this was the pronunciation of the French /r/ as late as the 17th century and is still general in many French provinces. The 'back' /r/, i.e. the rolled or fricative uvular /r/, may date from no further back than the 18th century.

35

This is a case of change at the phonetic but not at the phonemic level: French has one /r/ phoneme which has been pronounced in different ways at different periods and is still pronounced in different ways in different areas.

(c) There was no [v] in Latin. The V or U represented either a vowel [u], as in *murum*, or a semi-consonant [w], as in *villa, vivere*. If, when intending to say [w], we draw the lips close enough together for the passage of the air between them to produce friction, we utter the sound [β], the bi-labial fricative found in, for example, Spanish *saber* [saβer]. In late Latin, [w] seems to have become [β] and in proto-French [v], so we have *vivere* [wiwere] > *vivre* [viːvr], *servire* [sɛrwire] > *servir* [sɛrviːr], *lavare* [laware] > *laver* [lave], etc.

3.3. *Initial consonants and clusters.* This section relates both to the initial consonants and clusters of a word (*patrem, clavem*, etc.) and to the initial consonants and clusters of a syllable when the preceding syllable ends in a consonant (e.g. *tal-pa, mus-ca, in-trare*, etc.).

Most initial consonants, and clusters having [r] or [l] as their second element, remain (with the usual change in the point of articulation in the case of /r/, see **3.2** (b)), e.g.:

bonum > bon	tela > toile	man-dare > mander
cura > cure	flamma > flamme	in-fantem > enfant
dentem > dent	clavem > clef	sub-mittere > soumettre
factum > fait	pluma > plume	or-nare > orner
gula > gueule	brachium > bras	tal-pa > taupe
lana > laine	credere > croire	scrip-ta > écrite
manum > main	grandem > grand	por-tare > porter
natum > né	fratrem > frère	in-flare > enfler
panem > pain	pratum > pré	um-bra > ombre
ripa > rive	tres > trois	in-trare > entrer
solum > seul	al-ba > aube	fenes-tra > fenêtre

The following initial consonants and clusters, however, call for comment:

(a) [k] *c* and [g], which remain when followed by *o*, *u* or a consonant:

collum > col clavem > clef gustum > goût grandem > grand

became [s] and [ʒ] respectively when followed by *e* or *i*:

centum [kɛnto] > cent [sɑ̃]   gelare [gelare] > geler [ʒəle]

and [ʃ] and [ʒ] respectively when followed by *a*:

cantare > chanter [ʃɑ̃te]   gamba > jambe [ʒɑ̃:b]

An initial yod also became [ʒ], e.g. *iocum > jeu.*

These developments are discussed more fully in **3.9.**
(b) Initial *qu-* [kw] was reduced to [k] in proto-French, except
before *a*, where it probably became [k] only at the beginning of
the OFr period:

qui [kwi] > qui [ki]   quindecim > quinze [kɛ̃:z]
quando > quand [kɑ̃]   quassare > casser
quattuor > quatre   quadratum > carré

gu [gw] occurred in Latin only internally—*lingua* > *langue* [lɑ̃:g]
—but was introduced at the beginning of words when Germanic
words beginning with [w] were borrowed; it became [g] during
the OFr period:

Germanic *wardon > *[gwardare] > garder   *warnjan > garnir
Germanic *werra > guerre   *wisa > guise

A few Latin words that had *v-* [w] underwent this development, perhaps because they were influenced by Germanic words
of similar form and meaning:

vastare (Germanic *wost-) > guaster > gâter
vadum (Germanic *wad) > gué
vespa (Germanic *wespa) > guêpe

(c) Initial clusters consisting of [s] + [p], [t] or *c* [k] developed
an initial vowel in VL. This perhaps began as a fleeting 'on-
glide', a very light [ə] or [i]—e.g. spina [ᵊspina] or [ⁱspina]—at
which stage [ᵊs] or [ⁱs] was no more than the allophone of initial
/s/ when followed by a consonant. Later it became a fully syllabic
vowel, a stage occasionally represented in late Latin spelling (e.g.
iscripta for *scripta*) and clearly reflected in modern Spanish, e.g.
escudo < *scutum, estado* < *statum.* As we shall see (**3.5.2**), [s] followed
by a consonant later disappeared:

scutum > OFr escu > écu   scriptum > escrit > écrit
spatha > espethe > espee > épée   spina > espine > épine
sparsum > espars > épars   strictum > estreit > étroit

37

After a word ending in a vowel, no 'on-glide' appeared as the preceding vowel itself served the same purpose. Consequently, we find in early OFr such forms as *ta spose* 'ton épouse', *une spede*, *la spée* 'épée'.[1] Later, the forms in *es-* were generalized and we find *l'espose*, *une espée*, etc.

3.4. *Intervocalic consonants.*

3.4.1. In this section we take no account of:

(a) intervocalic consonants affected by palatalization (see **3.9.3** and **3.9.4**),
(b) intervocalic consonants that became final in OFr (see **3.8.3** (b)).

3.4.2. Intervocalic [l], [m], [n] and [r] remain:

tela > toile   fumat > fume   farina > farine

3.4.3. The development of intervocalic [p], [t], [k] and [b], [d], [g] is one of partial or total assimilation to the preceding and following vowels. For example, the pronunciation of [p] in *ripa* requires the vibration of the vocal cords to be stopped after the [i] and started again for the [a]; if however the cords are allowed to continue to vibrate, what is produced is the corresponding *voiced* stop, [b], and we have [riba]. Likewise, *vita* > [vida] and *securum* > [seguro]. This stage is represented by modern Occitan *riba* [ribo], *vida* [vido] and *segur* [segyr]. A further stage in the assimilation of these stops—and likewise of original voiced stops, as in *faba, nuda, plaga*—to the vowels occurs when the tongue is no longer raised high enough to block the flow of air completely, but only high enough to leave a narrow passage and so produce audible friction; the result is that, instead of [b], [d], [g], we have the corresponding fricatives [β], [ð], [ɣ]. This is the stage reached by modern Spanish, e.g. *riba* [riβa], *vida* [βiða], *seguro* [seɣuro]. At some proto-French stage, the pronunciation of these words must have been similar to that of modern Spanish, probably [riβa], [viða] and [seɣur] or [seɣyr]. The pronunciation has since evolved further:

(a) [ð], which existed in early OFr, disappeared when speakers

---

[1] In Italian a similar alternation is still possible: though forms in *s-* have been generalized—e.g. *scuola*, 'school', *strada* 'street', *scritto* 'written'—forms in *is-* can occur, in literary style, after consonants, e.g. *in iscuola, in istrada, per iscritto* ('in writing').

failed to raise the tongue high enough even to produce audible friction, i.e. assimilation to the vowels was now total:[1a]

vita > vide [viðə] > vie   maturum > [maðyr] > mēur > mûr
nuda > nude [nyðə] > nue   videre > vedeir > vēeir > vēoir > voir
mutare > muer   nativum > naïf   laudare > louer

An identical development took place between a vowel and [r]:

patrem > pedre [peðrə] > père   nutrire > nodrir > nourrir
credere > VL[kredre] > creidre [krejðrə] > creire > croire

(b) The bi-labial fricative [β] was completely assimilated—i.e. it disappeared—only when it preceded (or, in certain cases, followed) a labial vowel, i.e. one pronounced with rounded lips:

*nuba > [nuβa] > nue   tabonem > [taβone] > taon
*habutum > ēut [əyθ] > ëu [əy] > eu [y]
*bibutum > bēu [bəy] > bu

Elsewhere, [β] became [v]:

ripa > [riba] > [riβa] > rive   nepotem > neveu
capillos > cheveux   papilionem > pavillon
debere > OFr deveir > devoir   habere > avoir
hibernum > hiver   caballos > chevaux

Here too an identical development took place between a vowel and [r]:

capra > chèvre   labra > lèvre   febrem > fièvre

(c) Just as [β] was fully assimilated only to a labial vowel, so the velar fricative [ɣ] was fully assimilated only when preceded or followed by a velar vowel, i.e. one produced by raising the back of the tongue towards the velum, e.g.:

securum > [seɣuro] > sēur [səyr] > sûr
augustum > août [u]   locare > [loɣare] > louer   jocare > jouer
advocatum > avoué   verruca > verrue   ruga > rue

[1a] Cf. modern Spanish in which the ending -ado [-aðo] (as in *cantado* 'chanté') is often pronounced [ao].

39

Elsewhere, [ɣ] moved forward to become [j] (which disappeared after [i]):

pacare > [paɣare] > payer [peje]   baca > baie
necare > OFr neiier > noyer   plaga > plaie   paganum > païen
amica > amie

As we shall see (**3.9.3**), intervocalic [k] and [g] when followed by *e* or *i* underwent a quite different development, never reaching the stage [ɣ], and so are left out of account here.

This weakening of the intervocalic stops has therefore resulted in:

  (i) the complete disappearance of many of them;
  (ii) a number of additional examples of the new, non-Latin phoneme /v/;
  (iii) a number of words having a [j], with consequential effects on the development of vowels (see **4.8**).

3.4.4. When intervocalic, the voiceless fricative [s] also voiced, namely to [z], a sound that was not characteristic of Latin:

rosa [rosa] > rose [roːz]   resolvere > résoudre
causa [kausa] > chose   pausare > poser

As intervocalic [s] also occurred, in words that had -*ss*- in Latin (e.g. *bassa > basse, missa > messe*), the possibility of an opposition [s] ~ [z] henceforward existed and so the new sound [z] must be considered as already having phonemic status (see also **3.9.4. (c)**).

3.5. *The first consonant of non-initial clusters.*

3.5.1. The only consonant that regularly remains in this position in modern French is [r]:

perdere > perdre   argentum > argent   servire > servir

3.5.2. [s] + consonant disappeared in late OldFr[1b]; (but is still to be heard in English words borrowed from French shortly after the Norman conquest):

[1b] Before disappearing, pre-consonantal [s] probably first became a breathed sound, e.g. [h] (or perhaps [χ], see Pope, § 378); this is indicated by spellings such as *tschahtel* for *chastel* in German texts. A similar development may be seen in southern dialects of modern Spanish in which, for example, *España* 'Spain' may be pronounced [ehpaɲa] or even [epaɲa].

festa > feste > fête (feast)	magistrum > maïstre > maître (master)
costa > coste > côte (coast)	*sponsare > espouser > épouser (espouse)
nostrum > nostre > notre	asperum > aspre > âpre
testa > teste > tête	musca > mosche > mouche

Most words having *s* + consonant in ModFr are borrowed from written Latin (e.g. *espace, estomac, hostile, respirer, rester, question* and many others) or from another Romance language such as Italian (e.g. *escorte, masque, risque*), Spanish (e.g. *casque, sieste*) or Occitan (e.g. *escalier, escargot*). Some however are taken from English (e.g. *festival, test*) or other languages.

3.5.3. We have seen (**3.4.3** (a)) that, when follo·ved by [r], the dental stops [t] and [d] were treated as though they were intervocalic and eventually disappeared (*patrem > pedre > père*, etc.).

3.5.4. We have seen (**3.4.3** (b)) that, when followed by [r], the labial stops [p] and [b] were treated as though they were intervocalic (*capra > chèvre*, etc.). Before [l] they remain as [b] (*duplum > double, tab(u)la > table*) and before other consonants they disappear:

rupta > route   scriptum > écrit   subvenire > souvenir

3.5.5. It is clear from the evidence of inscriptions, and from the remark made by Quintilian (1st century after Christ) that 'we read the word *consules* without the *n*', that [n] before [s] disappeared very early in pronunciation:

mensem > [mese] > Fr. mois, Ital. mese, Sp. mes
insula > [isola] > OFr isle > île   mansionem > [masjone] > maison

Before other consonants, [n] and [m] remained in OFr but later disappeared after first nasalizing the preceding vowels (**4.14.4**), e.g. *vendere > vendre* [vã:dr], *campum > champ* [ʃã].

3.5.6. [l] + consonant remained in OFr as a velar or 'dark' *l* [ɫ] (see **2.1.4** (e)). The acoustic impression of a 'dark' *l*, i.e. the way a hearer interprets it, is not unlike that of [u] or [w] and the two are indeed similar in articulation, insofar as the back of the tongue is raised in both cases. It is therefore not surprising that the

41

THE FRENCH LANGUAGE: PRESENT AND PAST

development [ɫ] > [u] or [w] has occurred in many languages: in English as spoken in south-east England, for example, *milk* and *cold* are frequently pronounced [miwk] and [kowd].

In OFr, *l* vocalized—i.e. became a vowel—before a consonant, but not elsewhere: *caballos > chevals* [tʃəvaɫs] *> chevaus* [tʃəvaws] > [ʃəvo], but *caballum > cheval* [tʃəval] > [ʃəval]. The [w] combined with the preceding vowel to form a diphthong, which later became a simple vowel:

alterum > altre > autre [awtrə] > [oːtr]
poll(i)cem > polce [pɔɫtsə] > pouce [pus]
illos > els > eus [ews] > eux [ø]   capillos > chevels > cheveux
alba > aube   bellos > beaux   pŭlmonem > poumon

The consequences of this vocalization of *l* are discussed more fully in **4.7**.

After the two high front vowels [i] and [y], the *l* disappeared without leaving any trace:

filius > fis (> fils [fis])[2]   pūl(i)cem > pulce > puce

3.5.7. Before the OFr period, [k] before a consonant seems to have become first the corresponding fricative [χ] and then [j], which combined with the preceding vowel to form a diphthong (**3.9.5**), e.g. *factum > fait* [fajt], *tructa > truite*.

3.6. *Consonants in the middle of a cluster.* Some Latin words contained clusters of three consonants; the disappearance in VL or proto-French of vowels in unstressed penultimate and final syllables created further such clusters. In general,
(a) if the cluster ends in [l] or [r], we have the syllabification [n/fl], [r/br] etc. (see **2.3**), and [fl], [br] etc. remain, being in effect in initial position (see **3.3**):

inflare > enfler   circ(u)lum > cercle   ostrea > uistre > huître
rump(e)re > rompre   arb(o)rem > arbre   perd(e)re > perdre

(though [skl] became [sl], e.g. *masc(u)lum* > OFr *masle > mâle*),

[2] This word illustrates the fact that [λ] < [lj] also vocalized, probably after first becoming [ɫ]: *filius > filz* [fiλts] > [fits] (cf. *Fitz* in *Fitzgerald*='son of Gerald') > [fis]; cf. **tripalios > travailz* [travaλts] > *travaux*. The [t] in *filz, travailz*—N.B. *z*=[ts]—is a glide consonant (see **3.7**) that developed between [λ] and [s].

42

(b) in other types of cluster, the middle consonant disappeared, e.g.:

test(i)monium > témoin   forf(i)ces > forces 'shears'
dorm(i)torium > dortoir   serv(i)s > (tu) sers
galb(i)num > jalne > jaune
hosp(i)tem > oste > hôte
(though [t] remained before [s], e.g. *fortes* > OFr *forz* [fɔrts], *dentes* > OFr *denz* [dẽnts]).

3.7. *Glide consonants.* When the loss of the unstressed penultimate vowel (**4.3.2** (c)) brought about the creation of clusters such as [mr], [ml], [nr], [lr], [sr] or [zr], a 'glide consonant' developed. This process is illustrated in English by the surname *Hendry* < *Henry*: in anticipation of the [r], the nasal passage has been closed before the speaker has finished uttering the [n], with the result that the latter part of the [n] is denasalized and a [d], which has the same point of articulation, is heard. Likewise, if an [m] is similarly denasalized, we hear the corresponding labial consonant [b], as in the popular pronunciation *fambly* < *fam(i)ly*. A similar process results in the appearance of [t] or [d] between [s] or [z] and a following [r] in *Strath* (as in *Strathclyde*) < Gaelic *srath* and the pronunciation *Ezdra* for *Ezra*. Examples from French:

cam(e)ra > chambre   num(e)rum > nombre
*trem(u)lare > trembler   sim(u)lare > sembler
cum(u)lare > combler   in simul > ensemble
ten(e)rum > tendre   cin(e)rem > cendre
gen(e)rum > gendre   pon(e)re > pondre
*ess(e)re (ClLat esse) > estre > être
consuere > [kosere] > [kozre] > cosdre > coudre
mol(e)re > moldre > moudre
pulverem > [polre] > poldre > poudre

3.8. *Final Consonants.*

3.8.1. *Introduction.* The notorious discrepancy between the written and spoken forms of ModFr is nowhere more apparent than in the case of final consonants. If the two correspond in such words as *sec* [sɛk], *vif* [vif], *bal* [bal], *ours* [urs], *dur* [dyːr], *finir* [finiːr] and many others, there are nevertheless vast numbers of words in

43

which there is no such correspondence. The discrepancy may be one of two kinds:
(a) a written final consonant has no corresponding spoken consonant (except in certain cases in liaison forms), e.g.

lit [li]	part [paːr]	champ [ʃã]	fusil [fyzi]
tout [tu]	gros [gro]	murs [myːr]	chanter [ʃãte]

(but *tout à fait* [tut a fɛ], *un gros effort* [œ̃ groz efɔːr], *les murs épais* [le myrz epɛ], etc.).
(b) a consonant that is followed by -*e* in the written language is final in pronunciation, e.g.

vive [viːv]	demande [dəmãːd]	robe [rɔb]
plage [plaːʒ]	porte [pɔrt]	course [kurs]

Chronologically, final consonants fall into three categories, (i) those that were final in Latin (**3.8.2.**), (ii) those that became final at the proto-French stage (**3.8.3** and **3.8.4**), (iii) those that have become final since the OFr period (**3.8.5**).

3.8.2. *Latin final consonants.*
(a) Final -*m*. As early as the first century after Christ, if not before, final -*m* was probably silent and, apart from one or two monosyllables (*meum* > *mien*, *rem* > *rien*), it has left no trace in any Romance language—e.g. *florem* > Fr. *fleur*, Spanish and Occitan *flor*, Italian *fiore*, Romansh *flur*, Rumanian *floare*.
(b) Final -*t*. Latin final -*t* when preceded by a vowel remained in early OFr as -*t* (pronounced [θ]), but this disappeared probably before the end of the 11th century:

cantat > chantet [tʃãntəθ] > chante

After a consonant, -*t* remained in OFr but disappeared when final consonants in general disappeared (see **3.8.4**):

cantant > chantent [tʃãntət] > [ʃãːt]   dormit > dort[dɔrt] > [dɔːr]

It remains, however in liaison forms:

chantent-ils [ʃãtətil]   dort-il [dɔrtil]

(c) Final -*s* disappeared early in some parts of the Romance-speaking area, but still remains in Spanish (*muros* > *muros*, *mensas > mesas*) and some other western Romance languages. It was still pronounced in OFr, but began to disappear in late OFr before a word beginning with a consonant; before a vowel, it remains in liaison as [z] (*les murs épais* [le myrz epɛ]); before a pause, it probably remained as [s] till the 16th century (*les murs* [le myrs]), but disappeared when final consonants in general disappeared (**3.8.4.**). So, *muros > murs* [myrs] > [myːr], *cantas > (tu) chantes* [tʃãntəs] > [ʃãːt], etc.

3.8.3. *Old French final consonants.* Final consonants in OFr include some that were final in Latin (see **3.8.2.** (b) and (c)) and many that became final after the loss of the final unstressed vowel, e.g. *partem > part* [part], *campum > champ* [tʃãmp], *porcum > porc* [pɔrk], *cursum > cors* [kors] (*> cours*).

Those who know German will know that in words such as *Grab* 'grave', *Hand* 'hand' and *Tag* 'day', the final consonant, though written as *b*, *d*, *g*—and pronounced [b] [d] [g] in inflected forms such as the plural (*Gräber* [grɛːbər], *Hände* [hɛndə], *Tage* [taːgə])—is pronounced [p] [t] or [k]: [graːp], [hant], [taːk]: that is, the opposition between such pairs of phonemes as /p/ ~ /b/, /t/ ~ /d/, /k/ ~ /g/ is neutralized in final position where only the voiceless stop is possible. The reason for this is that, in anticipation of a pause when the vibration of the vowel cords would inevitably cease, the vibration is stopped before the final consonant is uttered, with the result that it becomes voiceless.

Old French resembled German in this respect. All final stops, fricatives and affricates were voiceless.[2a] We can divide the examples into three categories (in addition to words such as *part*, *champ*, *porc* in which the final consonant had always been voiceless):

(a) the originally voiced consonant of a cluster:

sanguem (ClLat sanguinem) > sanc		*longum > lonc*
tarde > tart		*viridem > [verde] > vert*
quando > quant	*grandem > grant*	*de unde > dont*
servum > serf	*nervum > nerf*	*salvum > salf > sauf*

After the disappearance in pronunciation of final consonants (**3.8.4**), the spelling of many of these words was remodelled under the influence of Latin spelling (*sang, long, tard, quand, grand*); the

[2a] Not, however, the lateral consonant [l] or the trilled consonant [r], as *cheval*, *finir*, etc.

voiceless consonant of OFr is still heard, however, in liaison forms: *un long hiver* [œ̃ lɔ̃k ivɛːr], *quand il viendra* [kɑ̃t il vjɛ̃dra], *un grand homme* [œ̃ grɑ̃t ɔm].

(b) We have seen (**3.4.3**) that intervocalic *v* [w], [p], [d], [t] and [s] became [v], [v], [ð], [ð] and [z] respectively; when these sounds became final, they unvoiced to [f], [θ] and [s] ([θ] disappeared in early OFr—there is a relic of it in English *faith < feit* [fejθ]):

vivum > vif clavem > clef novem, novum > neuf
*capum (for caput) > chief > chef bovem > bœuf
pedem > piet [pjeθ] > pie (now pied) [pje]
mercedem > mercit [mɛrtsiθ] > merci nudum > nu
fidem > feit [fejθ] > fei > foi nodum > nœud [nø]
scutum > escut [ɛskyθ] > écu nepotem > nevot >
nasum > nes [nes] > nez [ne] neveu

(c) Final consonants arising from the palatalization of [k] + *e*, *i*, or from [tj] (see **3.9.3.** (b) and **3.9.4** (d)).

3.8.4. *Final Consonants from Old French to Modern French.* The further development of final consonants from late OFr onwards depended mainly upon whether the word was (i) followed without pause by a word beginning with a consonant, (ii) followed without pause by a word beginning with a vowel, (iii) followed by a pause.

Before a word beginning with a consonant, final consonants began to disappear as early as the end of the 12th century, and by the end of the OFr period they had probably gone. Before a pause, however, and before a vowel they remained: consequently, words ending in a consonant had two different pronunciations, as is still the case with some of the numerals: *J'en ai cinq* [ʒɑ̃n e sɛ̃ːk], *cinq enfants* [sɛ̃k ɑ̃fɑ̃], but *cinq francs* [sɛ̃ frɑ̃]; *comptez jusqu'à huit* [kɔ̃te ʒyska ɥit], *huit heures* [ɥit œːr], but *huit jours* [ɥi ʒuːr]. In MidFr, therefore, words like *drap, lit, bec, vert, porc* had the dual forms [dra] ~ [drap], [li] ~ [lit], [be] ~ [bɛk], [vɛr] ~ [vɛrt], [pɔr] ~ [pɔrk], the first being used before a consonant, the second before a vowel or a pause.

The situation was even more complicated with words ending in [s] or [f], which not only disappeared before a consonant and remained before a pause, but voiced to [z] and [v] respectively before vowels. This state of affairs is still illustrated by the triple pronunciation of *six* and *dix* (earlier written *sis* and *dis*) and, if we take an old-fashioned pronunciation before consonants, of *neuf:* J'*en ai six* [sis] ~ *six heures* [siz œːr] ~ *six francs* [si frɑ̃]; j'*en ai dix* [dis] ~ *dix enfants* [diz ɑ̃fɑ̃] ~ *dix pages* [di paːʒ]; j'*en ai neuf* [nœf] ~ *neuf ans* [nœv ɑ̃]³ ~ *neuf livres* [nø liːvr].⁴

This dual or triple pronunciation was still current in the 16th century. We know, for example, that *les femmes sont bonnes* was pronounced [le famə sɔ̃ bɔnəs] and (*un homme) inventif et résolu* was pronounced [ɛ̃vɑ̃tiv e resoly]. There was, however, a tendency to generalize the pre-consonantal pronunciation: Ronsard, for example, uses or recommends such rhymes as *blond* and *tronc*, *or* and *fort*. Although grammarians strove until well into the 17th century to maintain the pronunciation of final consonants before a pause, in most cases it is the other form that has survived: e.g. *trop* [tro], *lit* [li], *part* [paːr], *pont* [pɔ̃], *long* [lɔ̃], *mis* [mi], *hommes* [ɔm], *chanter* [ʃɑ̃te].

In many such words, the form with pronounced final consonant survives in liaison, e.g. *trop aimable* [trɔp ɛmabl], *tout à fait* [tut a fɛ], *heureux homme* [œrøz ɔm], *pas encore* [pɑz ɑ̃kɔːr], *le premier enfant* [lə prəmjer ɑ̃fɑ̃]. In general, however, liaison is on the decrease even in careful speech and much more so in familiar speech, in which forms such as *pas encore* [pɑ ɑ̃kɔːr] are to be heard.⁵

On the other hand, in many words the form with a pronounced final consonant has been generalized: e.g. *un œuf dur* [ɛ̃n œf dyːr], *un coq blanc* [ɛ̃ kɔk blɑ̃], such words as *bec, duc, sec, arc, bœuf, chef, vif, neuf, os, ours*, and very many words in -*r*, including *or, cher, clair, fer, mer, hier, amer* and infinitives in -*ir* and -*oir* (*finir, vouloir,* etc.) (but not those in -*er: chanter*, etc.).⁶ Indeed, the combined influence of:

(a) spelling,
(b) liaison forms in which the final consonant is pronounced,
(c) the attempt to distinguish between homonyms (e.g. between *sens, sans, sang, cent* all pronounced as [sɑ̃], or between *cinq, saint, sein, sain* all pronounced as [sɛ̃]), and

---

³ Also *neuf heures* [nœv œːr]. Elsewhere, *neuf*+vowel is pronounced [nœf]: *neuf années* [nœf ane], *neuf arbres* [nœf arbr].
⁴ Nowadays the usual pronunciation before a consonant is [nœf]: *neuf livres* [nœf liːvr]. The pronunciation [sɛ̃k] for [sɛ̃] *cinq*+consonant is also gaining ground, e.g. *cinq francs* [sɛ̃k frɑ̃]
⁵ For a discussion of liaison in careful Parisian conversational usage, see Fouché, *Traité* ..., 434–77.
⁶ In 1625, Maupas condemned the dropping of final -*r* both in -*ir* and in -*er* endings, quoting as an example of what not to say *vous plaist il veni disné avec moy, vous me ferez plaisi.*

47

(d) an attempt to give more 'body' to words that had been reduced to two phonemes or even one (e.g. [u] *août*),

has led to a restoration of some final consonants that had previously ceased to be pronounced. The pronunciation [fis] *fils* (for earlier [fi]), for example, dates from the 18th century and [nɛt] *net* from the 19th. At the present time [sɛ̃k] *cinq* and [ut] *août* are well on the way to being generalized; [kɑ̃t] *quand* is to be heard even before consonants ([kɑ̃t vu vjɛ̃dre] *Quand vous viendrez*) and, although the plural of [œf] *œuf* is still usually [ø] *œufs*, forms like [yn duzɛn dœf] *une douzaine d'œufs* are often heard.

Various relics of an older pronunciation remain: for example, though *bœuf, cerf, chef,* and *sens* are now regularly pronounced [bœf], [sɛrf], [ʃɛf] and [sɑ̃:s], we still have the pronunciations [bøgrɑ] *bœuf gras*, [sɛrvɔlɑ̃] *cerf-volant*, [ʃɛdœːvr] *chef-d'œuvre* and [sɑ̃dsydsu] *sens dessus dessous*.

3.8.5. *Consonants that have become final since the OFr period.* With the loss of final [ə] -*e*—which probably dates in Parisian French from about the 16th century—many consonants have become final, e.g.[6a]

nette [nɛtə] > nɛt]	*vide* [vidə] > [vid]
rive [rivə] > [riːv]	*plage* [plaʒə] > [plaːʒ]
parle [parlə] > [parl]	*porte* [pɔrtə] > [pɔrt]

The fact that there has been no general tendency either for these to become voiceless[7] or for them to disappear illustrates the point made earlier (**2.5.1**) that a sound change that is characteristic of one stage in the evolution of a language is not necessarily characteristic of later stages.

[6a] After two consonants, [ə] remains in certain circumstances (see **4.12.4** (*d*)) e.g. *il parle bien* [il parlə bjɛ̃].

[7] Note that the final [l] and [r] have a voiceless allophone in words in which they are preceded by a voiceless stop, such as *peuple, siècle, âpre, mettre, fiacre,* i.e. they are partially assimilated to the preceding consonant. So, if we indicate voicelessness by [₀], we can transcribe the words quoted above as [pœpl̥], [sjɛkl̥], [ɑːpr̥], [mɛtr̥], [fjakr̥]. There is also a partial unvoicing of final [l] and [r] after voiced stops, i.e. in words such as *table, aigle, sabre, vendre, aigre.* In circumstances in which the final [ə] is pronounced (see note 6a above) or before another vowel, the voiced allophone however is used, as in for example *quatre jours* [katrə ʒuːr], *une table ronde* [yn tablə rɔ̃ːd], *mettre à part* [mɛtr a paːr]. In familiar speech, however, there is a tendency to reduce final clusters composed of stop + [l] or [r] to their first element, i.e. to eliminate the [l] or [r], when a consonant follows, e.g. *il me semble que* . . . [i m sɑ̃b kə], *articles de Paris* [artik də pari], *notre maison* [nɔt mɛzɔ̃], *Où est-ce qu'il faut mettre ça?* [. . . mɛt sa], *pour vous rendre service* [pur vu rɑ̃d sɛrvis]; similarly, [vr] may be reduced to [v], e.g. *pauvre type* [pov tip]. On features referred to above, see Armstrong §§ 284 and 306.

3.9. *Palatalization of consonants.*

3.9.1. Palatal consonants are those whose point of articulation is the palate (**2.1.3**). Those who know Russian will be aware of the importance of palatal consonants in the phonemic structure of that language: to give one simple illustration, the difference between брат [brat] 'brother' and брать [brat′] 'to take' is that in the former we have a dental [t] and in the latter a palatal [t′]. Although in ModFr there is only one palatal consonant, viz. [ɲ] *gn*, and a palatal semi-consonant [j] (as in *paille* [pɑːj]), it is clear that, in proto-French, there was a whole range of palatal consonants.

Palatalization—i.e. the process by which the point of articulation shifts from, say, the teeth or the velum to the palate—and the later developments of palatalized consonants have had far-reaching effects on the pronunciation of French.

Palatalization has been brought about in French by two main factors:

(a) the influence of a yod [j],
(b) the tendency of the velar stops [k] and [g] to shift their point of articulation to the palate in certain circumstances.

3.9.2. *Palatalization of initial consonants.* When they were followed by *e, i* or *a*, the consonants [k] *c* and [g] gave rise eventually to two new phonemes, /ʃ/ and /ʒ/, and to a much extended use of the phoneme /s/ in the initial position.

(a) In many languages including English and modern French, the allophone of /k/ before front vowels such as [i] is pronounced further forward in the mouth than the corresponding allophone before a back vowel such as [u], i.e. the point of articulation of the consonant is partially assimilated to that of the vowel. It is clear from the evidence of the Romance languages that in VL the allophones of /k/ and /g/ before *e* and *i* came to be pronounced so far forward in the mouth as to become palatal stops, [t′] and [d′],[7a] e.g. *centum* > [t′ɛnto], *gentem* > [d′ɛnte], i.e. these sounds became palatalized. In Italian and Rumanian these in turn became the affricates [tʃ] and [dʒ]—Italian *cento* [tʃɛnto], *gente* [dʒɛnte]—but in French, though [d′] also became [dʒ], [t′] became [ts]; in OFr, the affricates lost their first element and so

[7a] These sounds could equally be represented as [k′] and [g′].

were reduced to fricatives, [ts] and [dʒ] becoming [s] and [ʒ] respectively:

centum > cent [tsẽnt] > [sã]   civitatem > cité [tsite] > [site]
cinerem > cendre   cera > cire   mercedem > merci
gentem > gent [dʒẽnt] > [ʒã]   gelare > geler
generum > gendre   argentum > argent

(b) In French and some Occitan and Romansh dialects there was a later palatalization of [k] and [g] before *a*. As in the case of the earlier palatalization, [g] became [d'] and then [dʒ] and finally [ʒ]; [k] however passed from the stage [t'] not to [ts] but to [tʃ] and then to [ʃ]:

campum > [t'ampo] > champ [tʃãmp] > [ʃã]   calidum > chaud
cantare > chanter   mercatum > marché   calcem > chaux
caballum > cheval   sicca > sèche   canem > chien   vacca > vache
bucca > bouche   gamba > jamba [dʒãmbə] > [ʒãːb]
gaudia > joie   galbinum > jaune   larga > large

(c) Another source of the phoneme /ʒ/ was an initial yod. If, when a [j] is to be pronounced, the tongue is raised a little too far and touches the palate, the resulting sound is [d']; in proto-French, initial [j] went through this stage and then became [dʒ] and finally [ʒ]:[7b]

iam > ja [dʒa] > ja [ʒa] (remaining in *jamais* and *déjà*)
iocum > jeu   iungere > joindre   iurare > jurer   iugum > joug
iuvenem > jeune   iudicare > juger

3.9.3. *Palatalization of intervocalic* [k] *and* [g] *before* e, i. We have seen (i) that initial [k] *c* and [g] before *e*, *i* were palatalized to [t'], [d'] (**3.9.2** (a)), and (ii) that intervocalic voiceless stops became voiced and all intervocalic stops became fricatives (**3.4.3**). Both of these processes have to be taken into account in discussing the development of intervocalic [k], [g] +*e*, *i*.

(a) Intervocalic [k] *c* +*e*, *i* palatalized, as in the initial position, to [t'] and then apparently became the corresponding affricate [t's'] which, like certain other intervocalic sounds, voiced and so became [d'z']. This was an unstable sound in proto-French and an allophonic variant [jdz] developed—i.e. instead of correctly

[7b] Similarly, in modern Spanish, [j] sometimes becomes [d'], particularly in emphatic pronunciation, e.g. [d'o] for [jo] *yo* 'I', [d'a] for [ja] *ya* 'already'.

positioning the tongue so as to produce the palatalized dental-alveolar affricate [d'z'], the speakers of the language tended to raise the tongue first to the palate, producing a yod [j], before moving it forward to produce a non-palatal affricate [dz]; [jdz] was later simplified to [jz], the [j] meanwhile combining with the preceding vowel to form a diphthong:

placere [plakere] > [plat'ere] > [-t's'-] > [-d'z'-] > [plajdzir] >
[plajzir] plaisir
lĭcere [lekere] > leisir > loisir   racemum > raisin
vicinum [wekino] > veisin > voisin

(b) In words such as *pĭcem, crŭcem,* etc., the final vowel disappeared, probably at the period when the reflex of *-c-* was at the stage [jdz]. When this became final, it unvoiced like other final consonants (**3.8.3**) and so became [jts]. The [ts], written *z*, remained until the 13th century when it was simplified to [s] (cf. the reduction of initial [ts] to [s] in *cent,* etc., **3.9.2.** (a)). This later disappeared like other final consonants (**3.8.4**):

crŭcem [kroke] > croiz [kroɨts] > croix   vocem > voiz > voix
pĭcem [peke] > peiz [pejts] > poiz > poix
pacem [pake] > paiz > paix

(c) Intervocalic [g] + *e, i* palatalized, as in the initial position, to [d'], which, instead of becoming [dʒ], followed a similar development to other intervocalic stops (**3.4.3**) and became the corresponding voiced fricative [j], which in most cases was absorbed into a following [i]:

magis > maïs [mais] > mais [mɛ]   pagensem > pays [pei] or [peji]
magistrum > maïstre [maistrə] > maître   *fugire > fuir

3.9.4. *Palatalization before yod.*
(a) ClLat postconsonantal unstressed *i* and *e* became [j] in VL when followed by a vowel: e.g. *rationem* > [ratjone], *vinea* > [vinja]. The usual effect of a yod on the consonant immediately preceding it was to cause it to be palatalized: in other words, there was a tendency to anticipate the following [j], i.e. to prepare to utter it by raising the tongue towards the palate *whilst the preceding consonant was being uttered.* The consequence was that the point of

51

articulation of the consonant was assimilated to that of the yod and the consonant became palatalized.

(b) The effect of palatalization brought about by a following [j] is most easily appreciated if we consider the fate of the Latin groups [nj] and [lj]. In such words as *filia* [filja] and *vinea* [vinja], the anticipation of the following [j] caused the point of articulation of the consonant to shift from the teeth to the palate, with the result that dental [n] and [l] became palatal [ɲ] and [λ], and the yod was absorbed into these palatal consonants. The [ɲ] still remains in French (written *gn*); [λ]—the sound represented in Italian by *gl* and in Spanish by *ll*—also remained in early ModFr but during the course of the 18th and early 19th centuries became [j]:

seniorem > seigneur [sɛɲœːr]
vinea > [vinja] > vigne [viɲ] montanea > montagne
filia > fille [fiλə] > [fij] consilium > conseil [kɔ̃sɛλ] > [kɔ̃sɛj]
meliorem > meilleur [mɛλœːr] > [mɛjœːr] palea > paille

(c) The development of other consonants can best be explained by taking one or two of the simplest examples and following them through. We shall use the sign ['] to indicate a palatalized consonant (e.g. [r'], [z'] = palatalized [r] and [z] respectively).

In a word like *paria*, the fact of raising the tongue in anticipation of the yod caused the [r] to become palatalized to [r'], so that the word became [par'a] (the yod being absorbed in the [r']). [r'] however, like [d'z'] (**3.9.3** (a)), proved to be an unstable consonant—not surprisingly, since its pronunciation required the tongue to be simultaneously raised towards the palate and trilled. If these actions are not properly synchronized, so that the tongue is first raised towards the palate and *then* trilled, we get of course not *one* sound but a succession of two sounds, viz. [j] and a non-palatalized trilled [r], i.e. [jr]. So, from [par'a] we get [pajra] > [pajrə] *paire*. It must not be imagined that the stages [parja], [par'a], [pajra] succeeded one another at clearly defined intervals: in all likelihood, all three coexisted for a period before [parja] disappeared and [pajra] became the established pronunciation.

When [n] disappeared before [s] (**3.5.5**), *mansionem* became [masjone] and later, when intervocalic voiceless consonants became voiced, [mazjone]. With palatalization brought about by anticipation of the [j], it may be assumed that, perhaps via a

52

stage [maz'jone], a pronunciation [maz'one] arose: just as [r']
became [jr], so [z'] became [jz]—the [z'] depalatalized to [z]
but a trace of the palatal stage remained in the semi-consonant
[j]. The principal stages were therefore the following, or something not much different:

[masjone] > [mazjone] > [maz'on(e)] > [majzon] *or* [majzun] maison. Similarly, *tonsionem > toison.*

All of this may seem highly speculative, and it is true that there
is no objective evidence for most of the stages that have been
postulated. However, there is phonetically nothing implausible
about the suggested development and the hypothesis does explain
satisfactorily how, for example, [masjone] could have become
[majzon].
  One important result of the processes discussed above was
to create further instances of a phonemic opposition [s] ~ [z]
(see **3.4.4**), e.g. **bassiare > baissier* (*> baisser*) [8] ~ *basiare > baisier*
(*> baiser*).
  The development of words such as *rationem* is rather more complicated, but the principle is the same. The main stages were
something like this:

rationem [ratjone] > [ratsjone] > [rat's'one] > [rad'z'on(e)] >
                                        [rajdzon] > [rajzon/-un] *raison*

Similarly, *potionem* 'drink' *> poison* and *sationem* 'sowing' ('seed-
time'?) *> saison.*

(d) When intervocalic [jz] < *-ti-* became final after the disappearance of the final unstressed vowel, it unvoiced in the usual
way (**3.8.3**) to [js]:

palatium > palais[palajs] > [palɛ]   prĕtium > pris > prix [9]

(e) Intervocalic [dj] and [gj] both became [d'] which then
became [j] (cf. **4.8.5**):

gaudia > joie   hodie > ui (remaining in *aujourd'hui*)
medium > mi   corrĭgia > correie > courroie

[8] Latin long or 'double' consonants did not voice when intervocalic, cf.
bassa > basse, messionem > [messjone] *> moisson, gutta > goutte.*
[9] For the development of the tonic vowel in *prĕtium*, see **4.8.5**.

(f) When yod was preceded by a labial consonant (p, b, m, v), this did not palatalize; instead, [j] developed as an initial consonant, becoming [dʒ] and then [ʒ] (or [tʃ] and then [ʃ] after the voiceless p), and the preceding consonant (except m) disappeared, e.g. *tibia* > *[tibdʒə] > *tige*, *sapiam* > *[saptʃə] > *sache*. The development of [mj] can be illustrated by *simium* > [sindʒə] > *singe*.

3.9.5. [k] *and* [g] *before consonants*. Before the OFr period, [k] before most consonants seems to have become first the corresponding fricative [χ] and then [j], which combined with the preceding vowel to form a diphthong; during the OFr and MidFr periods these diphthongs developed further, in some cases becoming simple vowels (**4.8**):

factum > fait [fajt] > [fɛ]   tectum > teit > toit > [tojt] > [twa]
sacramentum > sairement > serment
tractare > OFr traitier > traiter   strĭctum > estreit > étroit
coxa [kɔksa] > cuisse   lactem > lait   directum > droit
vectura > voiture   noctem > nuit   octo > huit   fructum > fruit

Similarly, *nigru* > VL [negro] > *neir* > *noir*.
[kl] and [gl] became [ʎ] and, in early ModFr, [j]:

paric(u)lum > pareil [parɛʎ] > [parɛj]   *solic(u)lum > soleil
oc(u)lum > ueil [wɛʎ] > œil [œj]   auric(u)la > oreille
vig(i)lare > veiller [vɛje]   coag(u)lare > cailler

4 Vowels

4.1. *French and Latin vowel phonemes.*

4.1.1. *The different systems of ModFr and Latin.* The vowel systems of ModFr and ClLat differ even more widely from one another than do the consonant systems (see **3.1**).

As we have seen (**2.1.6**), ModFr has sixteen phonemic vowels:

Oral vowels:

	Front unrounded	Front rounded	Back
High	i	y	u
High-mid	e	ø	o
Low-mid	ɛ	œ	ɔ
Low	a		ɑ

and the central vowel [ə].

Nasal vowels: ɛ̃, œ̃, ɔ̃, ɑ̃

ClLat, however, had only five phonemic vowels, each of which could be phonemically either short or long, and three diphthongs, making a total of thirteen phonemes. In traditional orthography, and with the conventional symbols (˘) for short vowels and (¯) for long vowels, these are:

Simple vowels:

Front					*Back*	
High	ĭ	ī			ŭ	ū
Mid	ĕ	ē			ŏ	ō
Low			ă	ā		

Diphthongs: ae, au, oe

The differences between the two systems can be stated as follows:

(a) French has four degrees of aperture (high, high-mid, etc.) as opposed to Latin's three;
(b) French has a series of front rounded vowels unknown to Latin;
(c) French has a series of nasal vowels unknown to Latin;

55

(d) French has the central vowel [ə] unknown to Latin;
(e) Vowel length is phonemically significant in Latin but not in French (but see **4.15.3** for a possible exception);
(f) Latin has falling diphthongs whereas French has not.
The purpose of this chapter is to show how the French system has evolved from the Latin one.

4.1.2. *Classical Latin and Vulgar Latin vowels.* The precise quality of the ClLat vowels is unknown, but short vowels may have been more open than the corresponding long vowels: ĕ, ŏ for example may have been pronounced as [ɛ], [ɔ], and ē, ō as [eː], [oː]. However this may be, it is clear that vowel length ceased to be a distinctive feature (i.e. ceased to be phonemic) in VL and that a distinction between open and close vowels became important. The tendency in Gaul and most other western areas (elsewhere, e.g. in Sardinia and Dacia, there were different developments) was for long vowels to become (or remain) close and for short vowels to become (or remain) open. So, ē became [e], ĕ became [ɛ] and so on. One result of this was that certain vowels fell together, i.e. one opened and one closed to give the same result. So, ĭ and ŭ opened to [e] and [o], which were also the results of ē and ō respectively. The distinction between ă and ā was lost.

The correspondences between ClLat and VL vowels can be tabulated thus:

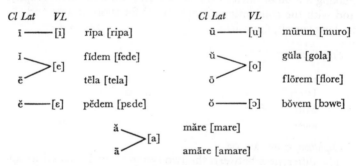

Cl Lat	VL		Cl Lat	VL	
ī —— [i]		rīpa [ripa]	ū —— [u]		mūrum [muro]
ĭ ⟩[e]		fĭdem [fede]	ŭ ⟩[o]		gŭla [gola]
ē		tēla [tela]	ō		flōrem [flore]
ĕ —— [ɛ]		pĕdem [pɛde]	ŏ —— [ɔ]		bŏvem [bɔwe]
ă ⟩[a]		măre [mare]			
ā		amāre [amare]			

Of the three ClLat diphthongs only *au* remained (as [au]), e.g. *aurum* > [auro], *causa* > [kausa]; *œ* and *æ* became [e] and [ɛ] respectively, e.g. *poena* > [pena], *caelum* > [kɛlo].

The later history of the VL vowels depends on such factors as:

(a) the degree of stress borne by the vowel,
(b) the nature of the syllable, i.e. whether it was open (as in

56

ma-re, de-be-re, ri-pa) or closed (as in the first syllable of *par-te, tes-ta, vil-la*),
(c) the influence of other sounds (see especially **4.7, 4.8** and **4.14**).

4.2. *Stress.* In many languages the syllables of a given word are pronounced with varying degrees of stress. For example, in English *dependent*, German *verkaufen*, Russian картина, there is greater stress on the second syllable than on the first or third, whilst in *competent, arbeiten*, комната the main stress falls on the first syllable. In some words, a given syllable bears a secondary stress, i.e. it is less strongly stressed than the syllable bearing the main stress but more so than the remaining syllables. If we indicate the main stress by (´) and the secondary stress by (`), we have in English such words as *còntradíction, ínterlòper*.

For our purposes, Latin vowels can be classified as follows:

(a) Tonic—the vowel that carries the main stress of the word;[1] we indicate this by (´): *pórta, cantáre, crédere, imperátor*;
(b) Initial—the vowel of the first syllable when this is not tonic; in these circumstances, the vowel seems to have borne a secondary stress, which we indicate by (`): *càntáre, òrnaméntum*;
(c) Atonic or unstressed—we may retain these widely-used terms, though they are not fully accurate: 'unstressed' syllables are only *relatively* unstressed, i.e. in comparison with those that bear the main or the secondary stress. So, in the English word *dependability*, the fourth syllable bears the main stress, the second the secondary stress, and the others are relatively unstressed: *depèndabílity*.

We shall not here go into the principles determining the position of the main stress in ClLat, nor shall we discuss the few categories of words in which the main stress in VL was on a different syllable from in ClLat.[2]

4.3. *Unstressed vowels.*

4.3.1. Unstressed vowels occur:

(a) between the initial and tonic syllables: òrnaméntum, cèrebéllum, hòspitálem, dòrmitórium, sìmuláre;

---

[1] It is possible that in ClLat the significant feature of the tonic syllable was not that it was pronounced *with greater force* (as in English, German, Russian, Italian, etc.) but that, as in Classical Greek, it was pronounced *on a higher note*, i.e. it was a *musical* not an *expiratory* accent. It is certain, however, that sooner or later it became an expiratory accent in VL.
[2] For details, see for example Ewert, §§ 21–22, Pope §§ 211–17; Nyrop, I, §§ 135–39.

(b) between the tonic and final syllables: cámera, númerum, hóminem, vívere;

(c) in final syllables: pórta, pánem, bónos, héri, múrum;

(d) in certain monosyllables, some of which were always unstressed (e.g. *et, ad, in,* etc.), while others were stressed or unstressed according to context (*non, me, te, se, quid,* etc.).

4.3.2. The fate of unstressed vowels can be briefly stated as follows (see **4.3.3** for an important exception):

(a) *a* remained in OFr as [ə],[3] written *e*:

òrnaméntum > ornement   pórtat > (il) porte

pórta > (la) porte   cántas > (tu) chantes

For a discussion of the circumstances in which [ə] remains or disappears in ModFr, see **4.12**.

(b) *e* and *i* in hiatus with a following vowel became yod:

vinea > [vinja]   filia > [filja]   basiare > [basjare]

(c) All other vowels disappear:

lìberáre > livrer   sìmuláre > sembler   hòspitálem > OFr ostel > hôtel

cámera > chambre   pérdita > perte   víridem > vert

pérdere > perdre   vívere > vivre   ásinum > OFr asne > âne

hóminem > homme   léporem > lièvre   másculum > OFr masle > mâle

(The reason for the preservation of the final vowel in the last six words in the above list is discussed in **4.3.3**.)

pártem > part   héri > hier   bónos > bons   múrum > mur

4.3.3. The principal exception to the sound laws discussed in **4.3.2** is illustrated by such words as:

léporem > lièvre   pérdere > perdre   nóstrum > notre

vívere > vivre   dúplum > double   ásinum > OFr asne > âne

---

[3] In ModFr the phoneme /ə/ is pronounced with rounding of the lips; it is uncertain whether this was so in OFr and MidFr or whether it was pronounced more like the *-e* of *Knabe* etc. in modern German.

in which a final vowel other than *a* remained in OFr as [ə] *e*
(though it has since disappeared, e.g. *vivre* [vivrə] > [viːvr]—but
see **4.12.4**). The reason is that final clusters [tr], [dr], [pl], [bl],
[pr], [br], [vr], [zn] etc. did not enter into the phonological
structure of OFr and so the final vowel remained as a 'supporting
vowel', namely [ə] *e*, wherever its disappearance would have left
such a group. In addition to such examples as those we have
already quoted, there are those in which a glide consonant (**3.7**)
developed between two consonants that had originally been
separated by a vowel:

núm(e)rum > nombre	*éss(e)re > OFr estre > être
tén(e)rum > tendre	cúm(u)lum > comble

In such words in which there was no final vowel in Latin, a
supporting vowel [ə] developed where one of the 'impossible'
consonant groups would otherwise have ended a word:

in simul > ensemble   minor > OFr mendre > moindre

In such groups as [ðr], [mn], [ln], [zn], the first of the two
consonants later disappeared, but the supporting vowel remained
for centuries afterwards:

patrem > OFr pedre [peðrə] > pere [perə] > père [pɛːr]
hóminem > *om'ne > homme[ɔmə] > [ɔm]   alnum > alne > aune
ásinum > OFr asne [aznə] > âne

A supporting vowel also remained in the third person plural of
verbs, where otherwise a group CONSONANT + [nt] would have
resulted:

vendunt > vendent   debent > doivent

This final [ə] has generally speaking disappeared (*tendre*
[tãːdr], *vendent* [vãːd] etc.); for fuller discussion, see **4.12**.

4.4. *Vowels in initial syllables*

4.4.1. We now look at what happened to vowels in initial syllables
other than tonic syllables.

4.4.2. The two high vowels, [i] and [u], and the low vowel, [a], cause no difficulty: [i] and [a] remain, and [u] becomes [y]:

àrgéntum > argent	làváre > laver	màrítum > mari
vìllánum > vilain	hìbérnum > hiver	lìberáre > livrer
*ùsáre > user [yze]	fùrórem > fureur	fùmáre > fumer
dùráre > durer	jùdicáre > juger	jùráre > jurer

4.4.3. The distinction between open and close vowels in the pairs [e, ɛ] and [o, ɔ] disappeared, i.e. the opposition between open and close vowels is neutralized. As the phonetic value of these two phonemes in this position is unknown, we shall here avoid the symbols that conventionally represent close vowels [e, o] or open vowels [ɛ, ɔ], and adopt the symbols /E/ and /O/, which are to be interpreted as follows:

/E/ = a phoneme of uncertain phonetic value deriving from VL [e] and [ɛ];
/O/ = a phoneme of uncertain phonetic value deriving from VL [o] and [ɔ].

4.4.4. The development of /E/ depends upon whether the initial syllable was *closed* or *open*. In closed syllables /E/ > [ɛ], in open syllables /E/ > [ə]:

fĭr-máre > fermer [fɛrme]	ves-tíre > vestir > vêtir	
pĕr-sóna > personne	ser-víre > servir	ĕr-ráre > errer

dē-bére > devoir [dəvwaːr]		fĕ-néstra > fenêtre
nĕ-pótem > neveu	lĕ-váre > lever	vĕ-níre > venir

For the circumstances in which /ə/ remains or disappears in ModFr, see **4.12.**

The development of these vowels from ClLat to ModFr in initial syllables can be tabulated as follows:

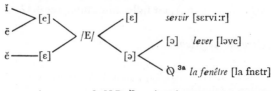

3a N.B. Ǫ = 'zero'.

4.4.5. The development of /O/ is a much debated problem. It seems that the 'regular' development was *probably* [u] in both closed and open syllables:

Closed syllables:

sŭb-veníre > souvenir   tŏr-méntum > tourment
pŏr-céllum > pourceau

Open syllables:

nŭ-tríre > nourrir   sŭ-bínde > souvent   cŏ-róna > couronne
prŏ-báre > prouver   mŏ-vére > mouvoir   nŏvéllum > nouveau

There are, however, very many words that have [ɔ] not [u] in French. These fall into two categories:

(a) Words for which there is no evidence that they ever had an [u] in French, e.g.

dormir < dormíre   mortel < mortálem
porter < portáre   sortir < *sortíre

Although some scholars consider [ɔ] as the 'regular' development in these words, it seems more likely that in fact the vowel of the initial syllable has been influenced by related forms in which the corresponding syllable bears the tonic stress, in which case the regular development is [ɔ] (**4.5.3**),[4] e.g.

dórmit > (il) dort   mórtem > mort
pórtat > (il) porte   *sórtit > (il) sort

(b) Words which had an [u] at one stage, e.g.

colonne < coulonne < colúmna   soleil < souleil < *solículum
colombe < coulombe < colúmba   oraison < ouraison < oratiónem
ortie < ourtie < urtíca   promettre < proumettre <
                                            promíttere

If the form in [u] is the 'regular' one, we are left with the problem of the replacement of [u] by [ɔ]. The reasons for this are uncertain. The influence of Latin spelling may have been decisive

---

[4] In Provençal, a variation in vowel between tonic and initial forms of the same stem does in fact occur: e.g. *pourtá* 'porter', *pórto* 'il porte', *dourmí* 'dormir', *dór* 'il dort', *mourí* 'mourir', *mórt* 'mort', *sourtí* 'sortir', *sórt* 'il sort'.

in many cases in the 16th century, with the result that *coulonne*, *coulombe, ouraison,* etc. were remodelled under the influence of *columna, columba, oratio,* etc. The pronunciation of such words as these was the subject of much debate in the 16th and early 17th centuries between the *ou-istes,* who advocated the pronunciation [u] *ou,* and the *non-ou-istes* who were partisans of [ɔ]. Neither side was wholly successful in its advocacy, sometimes [u] being finally adopted, sometimes [ɔ]. In most cases the issue was settled one way or the other in the early part of the 17th century.

4.4.6. When, as a result of the loss of certain intervocalic consonants (**3.4.3**), initial vowels came to be in hiatus with a following vowel, the development was as follows:

(a) reflexes of *ū, ī* and *ŏ, ō, au* became [y], [i] and [u] respectively, and then (in most circumstances) the semi-consonants [ɥ], [j] and [w], e.g.

mūtare > muer [mɥe]	*lūcorem > lueur [lɥœːr]
*fīdare > fier [fje]	lŏcare > louer [lwe]
nōdare > nouer [nwe]	laudare > louer [lwe]

(for circumstances in which [y], [u] and [i] occur in hiatus, see **5.2**);

(b) reflexes of *ĕ, ē* and *ĭ* became [ə] (as elsewhere in open syllables, see **4.4.4**); *a* > [a] (as in *lavare > laver,* **4.4.2**) and then [ə]; the [ə] from either of these sources later disappeared (see **4.12.2**), e.g.

*aetaticum [ɛt-] > ěage [əaʒə] > âge
sēcurum > sěur [səyr] > sûr   vĭdere > vedeir [vəðejr] > věoir > voir
maturum > [maðyr] > měur [məyr] > mûr

4.5. *Tonic vowels.*

4.5.1. As in initial syllables, [i] remains unchanged and [u] becomes [y],[5] whether they are blocked or free:

vīlla > ville	mīlle > mil	scrīptum > écrit
vīta > vie	venīre > venir	fīlum > fil
rīpa > rive	amīcum > ami	nīdum > nid
nūdum > nu	mūrum > mur	dūrum > dur
	nūllum > nul	fūstem > OFr fust > fût

[5] In most phonetic circumstances, *ū* becomes [y] in French, as also in Occitan and some Romansh and northern Italian dialects. In the other Romance languages it remains as [u]. Arguing that the area where *ū* > [y] was once a

4.5.2. The development of the other vowels depends on whether they are blocked (i.e. in a closed syllable) or free (i.e. in an open syllable). We shall consider the history of these vowels in two stages. In most cases but not all, Stage 1 is complete by the end of the OFr period. Stage 2 is discussed in **4.9** to **4.13**.

4.5.3. *Tonic blocked vowels*: *Stage 1*.

4.5.3.1. [a], [ɛ] < ĕ and [ɔ] < ŏ remained in OFr and generally speaking still remain (for some changes in Stage 2, see **4.11** and **4.13**):

árborem > arbre	arma > arme	partem > part

testa > OFr teste > tête	septem > OFr set > sept [sɛt]	
ferrum > fer	infernum > enfer	terra > terre
bella > belle	herba > herbe	pérdere > perdre

mortem > mort	porcum > porc	dormit > (il) dort
porta > porte	portum > port	corpus > OFr cors > corps

4.5.3.2. [e] < ĭ, ē and [o] < ŭ, ō probably remained in early OFr, but by the end of the OFr period, [e] had become [ɛ][6] and [o] had become [u]:

mĭttere > OFr metre [metrə] > mettre [mɛtr]

mĭssa > messe	ĭlla > elle	crĭsta > crête
lĭttera > lettre	sĭccum > sec	spĭssum > OFr espes > épais

gŭtta > OFr gote [gotə] > goutte [gut]

rŭpta > route	cŭppa > coupe	gŭstum > goût
tŭrrem > tour	sŭrdum > sourd	ŭrsum > ours
cŭrsum > cours	constat > VL [kostat] > coûte	

Celtic-speaking area and that similar phonetic developments are found in the Celtic languages, some scholars attribute this sound-change to the speech habits of the Celts who, it is argued, carried over into Latin a tendency to pronounce [u] further forward in the mouth than was so in Latin, with the result that it eventually became [y]. The theory is, however, disputed by other scholars.

[6] This is an early illustration of the tendency for French to have open vowels in closed syllables and close vowels in open syllables (see **4.13**). We know that [e] became [ɛ] in these words as early as the 12th century because they then rhyme with words having an original [ɛ]—e.g. *ele* (ModFr *elle*) < ĭlla rhyming with *bele* < bĕlla.

4.5.4. *Tonic free vowels: Stage 1.*

4.5.4.1. With the exception of [i] and [u] which, as in other positions, remained as [i] or became [y] respectively (**4.4.2** and **4.5.1**), tonic free vowels have undergone considerable changes.

Before we look more closely at the history of each vowel, some preliminary remarks must be made. The stage the various vowels, other than *i* and *u*, had reached in early OFr was as follows:

[e] > [ej]   [o] > [ow]
[ɛ] > [jE]   [ɔ] > [wɛ]
          [a] > *e*[7]

(The reflex of [ɛ] is transcribed as [jE] as authorities differ as to whether this was [je] or [jɛ] in OFr.)

When tonic and free, [e], [ɛ], [o] and [ɔ] all diphthongized; [a] perhaps also diphthongized, passing through a stage [aj] before becoming *e*.

The diphthongization of [ɛ] and [ɔ] occurs widely in other Romance languages whereas the diphthongization of [e] and [o] is a characteristically *French* phenomenon (though it also occurs in Romansh and some other dialects). There is therefore a *prima facie* case for considering that there were two phases in the diphthongization of tonic free vowels, one—that of [ɛ] and [ɔ]—beginning in VL and another taking place much later and affecting almost exclusively the north of France.

4.5.4.2. Various theories have been put forward to account for the diphthongization of tonic free [ɛ] and [ɔ], but none of them is universally accepted. Whatever the reason for this development, and whatever its early stages (which are by no means clear), these vowels had, by OFr, reached the stage they are still at in Spanish, namely, [jE][8] and [wɛ][9] respectively: *pĕdem* > OFr *piet* [pjEθ], cf. Spanish *pie*; *nŏvum* > OFr *nuef* [nwɛf], cf. Spanish *nuevo*. At the stage [wɛ], the lips are rounded for [w], and then unrounded for the [ɛ]; if the rounding of the lips is prolonged throughout the diphthong, [ɛ] will come to be pronounced [œ]—i.e. it is partially assimilated to the [w]—and so the diphthong

[7] For a discussion of the sound this represented, see **4.5.4.4.**
[8] For the reasons why this has sometimes given [je] in ModFr (e.g. *pĕdem* > *pied* [pje]) and sometimes [jɛ] (e.g. *hĕri* > *hier* [jɛːr]), see **4.13.**
[9] Before becoming [wɛ], [ɔ] probably went through the stage [wɔ], as in Italian (e.g. *nŏvum* > Ital. *nuovo*).

becomes [wœ]; it is likely that this happened in OFr and that the [w] was then absorbed into [i.e. completely assimilated to] the following sound so that we are left with a simple vowel [Ö] (we use this transcription as it is uncertain whether this was [ø] or [œ]). The reasons why [jE] and [Ö] sometimes become [je] and [ø] (*pied, bœufs*) and sometimes [jɛ] and [œ] (*hier, bœuf*) are discussed in **4.13**:

lĕporem > lièvre	pĕtra > pierre
hĕri > hier	pĕdem > pied

nŏvum > nuef > neuf	nŏvem > nuef > neuf
bŏvem > buef > bœuf	mŏvet > muet > meut
prŏba > prueve > preuve	ŏpera > uevre > œuvre

4.5.4.3. The diphthongization of tonic free [e] and [o], a characteristically *French* phenomenon, is perhaps to be attributed to the influence of the speech-habits of the Frankish invaders who occupied northern Gaul in the 5th century and gradually adopted the Romance speech of the area. It is suggested that they gave the tonic syllable of Romance the far stronger tonic stress that characterized their Germanic speech with the consequence that, in open syllables, the vowel tended to lengthen and diphthongize, so that [e] > [ej] and [o] > [ow].[10] The pronunciation [ej] remains in some early English borrowings from French, e.g. *vela* > OFr *veile* (ModFr *voile*) > English *veil* [vejl]. During the 12th century, these sounds underwent further changes:

(a) [ej] > [ɔj] (perhaps via such stages as [ɛj] [ɑj]): *tela* > *teile* [tejlə] > *toile* [tɔjlə]; by the 13th century, though the spelling *oi* remained, the pronunciation had evolved via a stage [ɔɛ] to [wɛ]; for later developments, see **4.10**:

fĭdem > [fede] > feit [fejθ] > foi	credere > creidre > croire	
me > mei > moi	vela > veile > voile	tela > teile > toile
vĭa > [vea] > veie > voie	seta > seie > soie	habere > aveir > avoir

(b) Words having [ow] from tonic free ō, which were written with *o* or *ou* in early OFr (e.g. *flōrem* > *flor, flour*; *plōrat* > *plore, ploure*), are soon found with the spelling *eu* (*fleur, pleure*, etc.). This probably

---

[10] The tendency of long vowels to diphthongize when given a strong tonic stress is to be seen in many Germanic languages, including English, e.g. Old English *is* [iːs], *hus* [huːs], *stan* [staːn] > modern English *ice, house, stone*.

65

represents the front rounded vowel [Ö][10a] (we use this transcription as it is uncertain whether the pronunciation was [ø] or [œ]); for the reason why this sometimes becomes [ø] in ModFr and sometimes [œ], see **4.13**;

[ø]	[œ]	
nepōtem > neveu [nəvø]	flōrem > fleur [flœːr]	sōlum > seul
nōdum > nœud	dolōrem > douleur	hōra > heure
vōtum > vœu	illōrum > leur	plōrat > pleure

4.5.4.4. Tonic free *a* gave in OFr a sound that is written *e*. The pronunciation of this *e* in early OFr is uncertain, but the fact that it rhymes or assonates[11] neither with [e] nor with [ɛ] indicates that it was not identical with either. It may have been a more open sound than [ɛ], rather like the [æ] of Southern English *hat* [hæt].[11a] This *e* < *a* has become [e] or [ɛ] in ModFr, according to whether it is in an open or a closed syllable (see **4.13** for further examples):

[e]	[ɛ]
datum > dé 'dice'	matrem > mère
nasum > nez	faba > fève
portatis > portez	clarum > OFr cler > clair

4.5.4.5. The development of *au* is the same whether it is initial or tonic; in OFr it became [ɔ] which either:

(a) remains: *auricula* > *oreille* [ɔrɛj], *claudere* > *clore* [klɔːr], *aurum* > *or*; or

(b) becomes [o] before [z] or [v]: *ausare > *oser* [oze], *pausat* > *pose* [poːz], *causa* > *chose*, *pauperem* > OFr *povre* > *pauvre* [poːvr]; or

(c) before a vowel becomes [u] and later, when in hiatus with a following stressed vowel, [w]: *laudat* > *loue* [lu], *laudare* > *louer* [lwe], *audire* > *ouïr* [wiːr].

[10a] [ow] probably became [Ö] via the stage [øw] or [œw]. The spelling *eu* was presumably adopted as it already existed for [ø] in the case of words in which *el* [el] had become *eu* [ew] and then [ø], e.g. *illos* > *els* [els] > *eus* [ews] > [øs] (> *eux*) (see **4.7** (b)).

[11] Assonance, a typical feature of OFr versification, differs from rhyme in that, whereas rhyming words have the same stressed vowel (*true—blue—shoe*, etc.) and the same following consonant if any (*deep—sheep—sleep*; *honey—money—funny*), for assonance only the stressed vowel need correspond; so, for example, *road—sole—soap—zone—coach* or *honey—dummy—fuzzy—sundry* assonate in English.

[11a] Pope however argues, § 233, that it was perhaps a high, close vowel.

4.6. *Summary.* The role of different degrees of stress in the development of vowels from VL to OFr can be summarized as follows:

(a) There is a tendency in many languages—including for example English[12] and Russian—to slur over unstressed vowels, which consequently weaken or even disappear; the result of this process was that, by the OFr period, Latin unstressed *a* had become [ə] (which has since disappeared in most circumstances, see below **4.12**) and other unstressed vowels had disappeared.

(b) Vowels having a secondary or a tonic stress were more clearly articulated and so not subject, in general, to the same process of reduction as affected unstressed vowels;[12a] initial and tonic blocked vowels (for tonic free vowels, see (c) below) are consequently fairly well maintained, with however a change of timbre in some cases, as when [u] becomes [y], [e] becomes [ε], and [o] and [ɔ] become [u].

(c) Whereas unstressed vowels tended to be weakened and initial and tonic blocked vowels to be maintained, tonic free vowels tended to diphthongize, i.e. to be strengthened; as we have seen (**4.5.4.2**), the reasons for the diphthongization of tonic free [ε] and [ɔ] are by no means clear, but the diphthongization of other tonic free vowels in French may be a consequence of lengthening brought about by a particularly strong Germanic stress (**4.5.4.3**).

The principal developments of vowels from VL to OFr in the circumstances we have so far dealt with can be tabulated as on page 68:

The tables call for the following comments:

(1) for the uncertainty regarding the pronunciation of *e* < tonic free *a*, see **4.5.4.4**;

(2) the transcriptions [jE] and [Ö] are used as it is uncertain whether these represent [je] or [jε], [ø] or [œ], respectively;

(3) for words that have [ɔ] instead of [u] in initial syllables, see **4.4.5**;

(4) one widespread source of [ə], namely its development as a supporting vowel, is not shown on the tables.

---

[12] On the reduction of unstressed vowels in English, see for example A. C. Gimson, *An Introduction to the Pronunciation of English*, 2nd edn., London, 1970, 82 and 125. Examples include *palate* [palət], *father* [faːðə], *bishop* [biʃəp], *upon* [əpɔn], *famous* [feiməs], *figure* [figə].

[12a] In some words, the initial vowel was lost between a stop and [r], e.g. *directum* > *droit, quiritare* > *crier,* *corrotulare* > *crouler.*

Vulgar Latin Vowels	Old French Vowels			
	Unstressed	*Initial Blocked Free*	*Tonic Blocked*	*Tonic Free*
a	ə	a		e (?)
ε		ε ə	ε	jE
e			e > ε	wε
i		i		
ɔ		u	ɔ	Ö
o				
u		y		

These developments are illustrated in the following table:

Vulgar Latin Vowels	Old French Vowels			
	Unstressed	*Initial Blocked Free*	*Tonic blocked*	*Tonic Free*
a	porte	argent	part	pré
ε	panem > pain	fermer neveu	belle	hier
e		devoir	sec	toile
i	herī > hier	hiver	ville	rive
ɔ	muros > murs	tourment	porte	neuf
o		souvent	route	fleur
u	manūs > mains	durer	nul	mur

VOWELS

4.7. *Consequences of the vocalization of* [l]. We have seen (**3.5.6**) that during the OFr period [l] vocalized to [w] before a consonant. This created a number of diphthongs, some of which coincided with diphthongs arising from other sources, some of which did not.

(a) [ol] and [ɔl] both became [u] by the end of the OFr period, probably via the stages:

[ol] > [ow] > [u]   [ɔl] > [ɔw] > [u]
pŭlsum > pols > pouls   fŏlles > fols > fous
pŭlverem > poldre > poudre   mŏlere > moldre > moudre

(b) [el] > [ew] which in late OFr became first [øw]—i.e. the lip position of the [e] was assimilated to that of the following [w]—and then a simple vowel [ø]:

ĭllos > els > eus > eux [ø]   capĭllos > chevels > cheveux
fĭltrum > feltre > feutre 'felt'

(c) In a few cases OFr had triphthongs, [jew] and [wew]; by dissimilation of the first element, [wew] also became [jew];[12b] in late OFr [jew] was reduced to [jÖ] (we use the symbol [Ö] as it is uncertain whether the pronunciation was [ø] or [œ]):

mĕlius > mielz [mieʎts] > mieuz [mjewts] > mieux [mjø]
ŏc(u)los > ueilz [weʎts] > [wewts] > ieus [jews] > yeux [jø]

(d) [al] > [aw], which remained as a diphthong until the 15th or 16th century, when it became [o]:

talpa > taupe [tawpə] > [toːp]   alba > aube
valet > valt > vaut   calidum > chalt > chaud
saltum > saut   alterum > autre

(e) In the case of [ɛl], the tongue when being drawn back from the [ɛ] position to the [w] position passed through the [a] position, thus giving rise to a triphthong [ɛaw] which by the end of the 12th century had become [əaw] (with the stress on the [a]). Just as [aw] < [al] became [o], this first became [əo], in the 15th or 16th century, and later the [ə] of [əo], like every other [ə] in

[12b] In some words there was no dissimilation, e.g. *vŏlet* > *vuelt* > [vwewt] > *veut* [vø]. Opinions differ as to the explanation for this; see Fouché, *Phonétique . . .* , II, 323–24, Pope §§ 555–56, Rheinfelder, I, § 330.

69

hiatus with a following vowel (see **4.12**), disappeared, leaving only the vowel [o]:

bĕllos > bels > beaus [bɛaws] > [bɔos] > [bo] beaux
*castĕllos > chastels > châteaux   pĕlles > pels > peaux

By late OFr, therefore, the diphthongs and triphthongs that had arisen as a result of the vocalization of [l] had nearly all been reduced to simple vowels that already had phonemic status in the language: the only remaining diphthong was [aw] (< [al] and in [əaw] < [ɛl]), which was not reduced to [o] until the 15th or 16th century.

4.8. *Diphthongs arising as a result of palatalization.*

4.8.1. We have seen that, in various circumstances, the effect of palatalization was to give rise to a yod: the principal phonetic circumstances in which this [j] developed were:

(a) intervocalic [k], [g] preceded by *a, e, i* and followed by *a* (*necare > neiier > noyer, plaga > plaie*, see **3.4.3** (c)),

(b) intervocalic [k], [g] + *e, i* (*placere > plaisir, crucem > croix*, etc., see **3.9.3**),

(c) consonant + yod (*feria > feire > foire, potionem > poison, palatium > palais*, see **3.9.4**),

(d) [k], [g] + consonant (*factum > fait, nĭgrum > neir > noir*, see **3.9.5**).

The resulting [j] combined with the preceding vowel to form a series of diphthongs, some of which coincided with diphthongs arising from other sources, some of which did not.

4.8.2. [e] + yod fell together with [ej] from tonic free [e] (**4.5.4.**_3_) and became [ɔj]; [o] + yod also became [ɔj] (via a stage [oj]):

lĭcēre > [lekere] > leisir > loisir
pĭcem > peiz > poix   messionem > meisson > moisson
vectura > veiture > voiture   feria > feire > foire
dirēctum > dreit > droit   tēctum > teit > toit
strĭctum > estreit > étroit   nĭgrum > neir > noir

crŭcem > [kroke] > croix   vōcem > voix
potionem > poison dormitorium > dortoir gaudia > joie

70

As we have seen (**4.5.4.**3(a)), by the end of the OFr period [ɔj] had become [wɛ], the later history of which is traced in **4.10** below.

4.8.3. [a] + [j] gave the diphthong [aj], which was reduced to [ɛ] during the 12th century[12c] (this conclusion can be drawn from such spellings as *fet* for *fait*):

placere > plaisir [plajzir] > [plɛzir]   paria > paire
mansionem > maison   rationem > raison   palatium > palais
fac(e)re > faire   factum > fait
sacramentum > sairement > serment

4.8.4. [y] + [j] gave a diphthong [yj], but during the OFr period the stress moved from the first element, [y], to the second, creating a diphthong [ɥi], with the stress on the [i]:

conduc(e)re > conduire   fructum > fruit

4.8.5. When followed by a palatal, tonic *ĕ* and *ŏ* (which elsewhere diphthongized to [jE] and [wɛ] only when free) diphthongized even when blocked (as in *pĕctus* and *nŏctem*). In either case, the resulting diphthongs combined with a following [j] to form the triphthongs [jEj] and [wɛj] which, by the beginning of the OFr period, had become [i] and [yj]; [yj] later became [ɥi] during the OFr period (cf. **4.8.4**):

(a) Tonic free *ĕ*, *ŏ* + palatal:

mĕdium > *[mjEj] > mi[13]   pĕjor > pire   prĕtium > prix
dĕcem > diz (now dix)   nĕgat > (il) nie   prĕcat > (il) prie
        hŏdie > *[wɛj] > ui (remaining in aujourd'**hui**)

(b) Tonic blocked *ĕ*, *ŏ* + palatal:

lĕctum > *[ljEjt] > lit[13]   lĕg(e)re > *[ljEjre] > lire
pĕctus > piz > pis 'udder'   sĕx > sis (now six)
nŏctem > *[nwɛjt] > nuit   ŏcto > uit (now huit)
            cŏxa [kɔksa] > cuisse

[12c] In intervocalic position the yod still remains, as in *pacare > paiier* [pajjɛr] > *payer* [pɛje].
[13] The evidence for supposing that forms such as *[mjEj] < *mĕdium* and *[ljEjt] < *lĕctum* existed includes (i) the existence of *miei* < *mĕdium* in some modern Occitan dialects and (ii) the fact that various French dialects have *leit* or *liet* respectively, both of which, together with *lit*, can be explained by postulating a stage [ljEjt].

4.8.6. Tonic free *a* and *e* normally became *e*[14] and [ej] respectively (*pratum* > *pré*, *tela* > *toile*, **4.5.4.**4 and 3). After a palatal, however, they became [jE] and [i]:

carum > chier	capra > chievre	*capum > chief
tractare > traitier	vigilare > veillier	dignare > deignier
vindicare > vengier	laxare [laksare] > laissier	
pietatem *[pijtate] > pitié		
medietatem *[mejtate] > meitié > moitié		

cēra > cire	mercēdem > merci	placēre > plaisir

The explanation of this is probably that, as the tongue moved from the palatal consonant to the vowel, it passed momentarily through the [j] position, so that instead of *e* (< [a]) we had [jE], and instead of [ej] (< [e] *ē*) we had a triphthong [jEj] which, as in words like *lit* > *lĕctum* (**4.8.5**) was reduced to [i].

In MidFr the [j] of [jE] was absorbed into a previous [ʃ], [ʒ], [ʎ] or [ɲ]: *chier* > *cher*, *chief* > *chef*, *chievre* > *chèvre*, *vengier* > *venger*, *veillier* > *veiller*, *deignier* > *daigner*. Elsewhere it remains (*pitié, moitié*), except where it has been eliminated by analogy (e.g. *laissier* > *laisser*, see **16.1.2** (b)).

4.8.7. The results in late OFr of the principal vowel changes that had been influenced by palatalization can be tabulated and exemplified as follows:

factum > fait	[a] + yod > [aj] > [ε]	
tēctum > toit	[e] + yod > [ej]	
vōcem > voix	[o] + yod > [oj]	[ɔj] > [wε]
carum > chier	Palatal + [a]	> [jE]
lĕctum > lit	[ε] + yod	
cēra > cire	Palatal + [e]	*[jEj] > [i]
frūctum > fruit	[u] + yod	
nŏctem > nuit	[ɔ] + yod > *[wεj]	[yj] > [ɥi]

[14] For the uncertainty as to the pronunciation of this *e* in OFr, see **4.5.4.**4.

4.9. *Oral vowels in late Old French.*

4.9.1. The development of vowels from VL to the end of the OFr period is characterized by two dominant trends:

(a) the reduction of unstressed vowels: this has continued into ModFr in the case of the vowel [ə] (see **4.12**);
(b) the creation of diphthongs and triphthongs (as a result of the development of tonic free vowels, vocalization of [l] and palatalization) many of which were reduced in later OFr to simple vowels.

The period of diphthongization and reduction of diphthongs is what we have referred to (**4.5.2**) as Stage 1. Stage 2 is characterized by the tendency to prefer close vowels ([e], [o], [ø]) in open syllables and open vowels ([ɛ], [ɔ], [œ]) in closed syllables (see **4.13**). There is a substantial overlap of the two periods, particularly in that (i) the reduction of [aw] to [o] is not completed until the 15th or 16th century, and (ii) the opening of [e] to [ɛ] in closed syllables took place as early as the 13th century (*mĭttere* > *metre* [metrə] > [mɛtrə]). With these exceptions, the end of Stage 1 coincides broadly speaking with the end of the OFr period.

4.9.2. In late OFr, i.e. c.1300, the language probably had the following oral vowels and diphthongs:[15]

a	e	ɛ	ə	i	ɔ	u	y	Ö
	jE	wɛ		ɥi				
aw								

This is very far removed from the VL vowel system, and the elements of the ModFr system are already in existence, in particular the vowel [ə] and the characteristic front rounded vowels [y] and [Ö], all of which mark off ModFr from most other Romance languages (with the notable exception of its near neighbour, Occitan).

We may note in particular:

(a) that the series of rounded front vowels, [y] and [Ö], is an innovation;
(b) that the only vowel deriving solely from the corresponding vowel in Latin is [a];[16]

[15] [əaw] < [ɛaw] is here considered not as a triphthong but as a succession of the vowel [ə] and the diphthong [aw].
[16] [a] also occurred in certain borrowings from other languages, in particular from Germanic.

(c) that [e] and [u] do not continue the [e] and [u] of Latin: [e] derives from tonic free [a], and [u] derives both from Latin [o] and [ɔ] in certain positions and from the reduction of the diphthongs [ɔw] < [ɔl] and [ow] < [ol];

(d) that there was no [o]; for the circumstances in which [o] was reintroduced into the French vowel system, see **4.13.2**.

4.9.3. The main topics in the development of oral vowels from OFr onwards that we shall deal with are:

(a) the development of [wɛ] to [wa] or [ɛ] (**4.10**),
(b) the introduction of the new phoneme /ɑ/ (**4.11**),
(c) the fate of /ə/ (**4.12**),
(d) the new basis of distinction between open and close vowels (**4.13**).

4.10. *The further development of* **oi** [wɛ]. By the end of the OFr period, the diphthong [ɔj] deriving from various sources (e.g. *tela > toile, tectum > toit, vocem > voix*) had become [wɛ] (**4.5.4.**3 and **4.8.2**) and there was already a tendency in some dialects for this to be reduced to [ɛ]: this conclusion can be drawn from spellings such as *crere* for *croire* in the late 13th century. On the other hand, there was a tendency in popular speech in the MidFr period for [wɛ] to become [wa].

In the 16th century, the pronunciation of *oi* was one of the issues to which grammarians devoted their attention. The pronunciation they advocated was [wɛ]. However, [ɛ] was frequent even in court circles in the 16th and 17th centuries and came to be accepted in a number of words, including the endings of the imperfect and conditional tenses (*habebat > avoit > avait*, etc., see **15.3.4**) and the following:

cognoscere > connoistre > connaître; cf. paraître, etc.
moneta > monnoie > monnaie   tonĭtrum > tonoire > tonnerre
creta > croie > craie   vĭtrum > voire > verre

There are relics of such hesitation in usage in the modern forms of *seta* which has given both *soie* 'silk', 'pig's bristle' and *saie* 'pig's-bristle brush used by goldsmiths', and in the existence of the personal name *François* beside the adjective *français*.

The spelling *oi* was retained for [ɛ] until the 19th century: though the spelling *ai* had been suggested in the late 17th century, it was not until 1835 that the Académie Française recognized it in its dictionary.

74

Meanwhile, the pronunciation [wa], stigmatized as 'vulgar' in the 16th and 17th centuries, was gaining ground. It seems to have begun to creep even into the pronunciation of Court circles in the late 17th century, but [wɛ] remained the generally accepted pronunciation until the abolition of the monarchy and the dispersal of the Court in 1793, after which the popular pronunciation [wa] in words such as *toile, soie, croire, avoir, noir, toit, voix* became finally established.

4.11. *The new phoneme* /ɑ/. The ModFr phoneme /ɑ/—the velar *a* of *pas*, etc.—probably originated in OFr as an allophone of /a/ before [s] and [z], and became phonemic when the affricate [ts] was simplified to [s], giving pairs such as the following which were differentiated only by the opposition /a/ ∼ /ɑ/:

chace [tʃatsə] > (il) chasse [ʃas(ə)] ∼ châsse [ʃɑːs(ə)].

The majority of words having /ɑ/ in ModFr are those in which the vowel was or still is followed by [s] or [z]:

masle > mâle [mɑːl]   aspre > âpre [ɑːpr]   haste > hâte [ɑːt]
bas [bɑ], cas, gras, las, pas, tas, etc.
basse [bɑːs], grasse, lasse, (il) passe, (la) tasse, etc.
(la) base (bɑːz), phrase, vase, etc.

Other words having /ɑ/ in ModFr include *sable* [sɑːbl], *paille* (pɑːj), *flamme* (flɑːm); there is fluctuation in *bataille* [batɑːj, -aj], *gare* [gɑːr, gaːr], *voix* [vwɑ, vwa] and many others.[17] At the present time, /ɑ/ has altogether disappeared in the speech of many members of the younger generation who make no distinction between, for example, *bas* and *bat* which are both [ba], and *pâte* and *patte* which are both [pat].[18]

[17] For a full discussion of the distribution of /ɑ/ and /a/ see P. Fouché, *Traité* . . ., 56–63.
[18] A. Martinet, *Éléments de linguistique générale*, Paris, 1960, 35, reports that whereas the opposition /ɑ/ ∼ /a/ is constant amongst Parisians born before 1920, very many of those born after 1940 make no distinction between for example *pâte* and *patte*. See also Ruth Reichstein's article 'Étude des variations sociales et géographiques des faits linguistiques', in *Word*, 13 (1960), pp. 55–95. Martinet returns to the subject in his article, 'Les deux *a* du français' (in *The French Language: Studies presented to Lewis Charles Harmer*, London, 1970, 115–22) in which he concludes that an increasing number of young Parisians fail to distinguish between /ɑ/ and /a/ and that one need no longer advise learners of the language to observe the distinction.

4.12. *The fate of /ə/.*

4.12.1. The majority of Latin unstressed vowels had disappeared before the OFr period. [ə] however remained, either as a reflex of unstressed *a*, as in *porte* < *porta*, *sairement* < *sacramentum* (**4.3.2.** (a)), or as a supporting vowel, as in *tendre* etc. (**4.3.3**). [ə] also remained in open initial syllables, principally as the reflex of [e] and [ɛ] (*venir* < *vĕnire*, etc., see **4.4.4**), but also as the reflex of [a] (i) after a palatal (*caballum, capillum* > *cheval, cheveu*) or (ii) when an intervocalic consonant disappeared, leaving the vowel in hiatus with a following tonic vowel (*maturum* > *mëur* [məyr] > *mûr*, **habutum* > *eu* [əy] > [y]).

4.12.2. The tendency for unstressed vowels to disappear has continued into ModFr, with the result that [ə] in its turn has disappeared in many circumstances, though the *e* that represented it usually remains in spelling.

The process seems to have begun about the 13th or 14th century, particularly where the vowel was in hiatus with a preceding or following vowel. When [ə] in hiatus disappeared, it has in most cases left no trace in spelling or at most is recalled by a circumflex accent:

videre > Early OFr vedeir > vēeir > vēoir [vɔɔjr] > voir
*habutum > ëu [əy] > eu [y]   maturum > mēur > mûr
*debutum > dĕu > dû   securum > sēur > sûr

Between consonants, [ə] has disappeared in such words as *vrai* < *verai* (which gives English *very*) < *veracem*, *soupçon* < *sospeçon* < *suspectionem* and *serment* < *sairement* < *sacramentum*.

4.12.3. Final [ə]—as in *il parle, la porte, une grande maison*—was perhaps sometimes dropped during the MidFr period,[19] but in the speech of educated Parisians was probably generally maintained at least until the end of the 16th century.

4.12.4. In ModFr, /ə/ is a phoneme that has two allophones, [ə] and ⦰ (zero); that is to say, it is sometimes pronounced and sometimes not. The circumstances governing the distribution of these allophones are far too complicated to be dealt with adequately here. The reader is referred to P. Fouché, *Traité* . . . , 91–139.

[19] Before a word beginning with a vowel, final [ə] was already elided in early OFr.

The following remarks, which relate to normal Parisian conversational usage, represent a considerable over-simplification:

(a) /ə/ is *not* pronounced (that is, we have the Ɋ allophone) at the end of a word-group, i.e. before a pause: *il parle* [parl], *où dois-je les mettre*? [mɛtr], *la chambre* [ʃɑ̃ːbr̥];

(b) /ə/ is *not* pronounced in hiatus with a preceding vowel: *j'étudierai* [ʒetydire], *nous jouerons* [ʒurɔ̃], *la scierie* [siri];

(c) in the initial syllable of a word-group, /ə/ is *always pronounced* (that is, we have the allophone [ə]) if preceded by two consonants (e.g. *Prenez-les!* [prənele]): it *may* be pronounced if preceded by only one consonant[20] (e.g. *je vous écris* [ʒə vuz ekri] or [ʒvuz ekri], *ce tableau* [sə tablo] or [stablo], *chemin faisant* [ʃəmɛ̃ fəzɑ̃] or [ʃmɛ̃ fəzɑ̃]);

(d) between consonants within a word or group, the tendency— but there are many exceptions—is to *pronounce* the /ə/ if it is preceded by two or more pronounced consonants but *not* to pronounce it if it is preceded by only one consonant:

/ə/ pronounced (preceded by two consonants):

il parle bien [il parlə bjɛ̃]	un appartement [apartəmɑ̃]
le parlement [parləmɑ̃]	il tournera [turnəra]
lourdement [lurdəmɑ̃]	je pars demain [ʒə par dəmɛ̃]

/ə/ not pronounced (preceded by only one consonant):

une grande maison [yn grɑ̃d mɛzɔ̃]

appeler [aple]	la leçon [la lsɔ̃]
la bijouterie [biʒutri]	il a reçu [il a rsy]
l'empereur [lɑ̃prœːr]	il viendra demain [il vjɛ̃dra dmɛ̃]
le jurement [ʒyrmɑ̃]	nous le voyons [nu lvwajɔ̃]
il chantera [ʃɑ̃tra]	pas de pain [pɑdpɛ̃]
un genou [œ̃ ʒnu]	la fenêtre [la fnɛtr]

The rules or tendencies that apply when /ə/ occurs in two or more successive syllables are extremely complicated (see Fouché), and we shall not embark on a discussion of them here.

In the above paragraphs, we have referred always to the position of /ə/ in a *word-group*, not in a *word*. The pronunciation of a given word having /ə/ in its first or last syllable may vary

[20] For an explanation of the circumstances in which [ə] *is* pronounced even when preceded by only one consonant—e.g. *ce ruisseau* [sə rɥiso], *Que casses-tu là?* [kə kastyla]—see Fouché, *Traité* .., pp. 121–2.

according to what precedes or follows: e.g. *la fenêtre* is [la fnɛtr], but *la grande fenêtre* is [la grãd fənɛtr] ([ə] is preceded by two consonants, [df]), and *il parle*, standing alone, is [il parl], but *il parle très haut* is [il parlə trɛ o] (see above).

4.12.5. Note that [ə] can never be stressed. Consequently, the pronoun *le* when stressed, i.e. after an imperative when no other pronoun follows, is pronounced [lø] e.g. *dites-le* [dit lø](but *dites-le-moi* [dit lə mwa]).

4.13. *The new basis of distinction between open and close vowels.*

4.13.1. The first examples appear in OFr of a tendency that has had far-reaching consequences in French on both the phonetic and the phonemic levels, namely the tendency to use close vowels ([e], [ø], [o]) in open syllables and open vowels ([ɛ], [œ], [ɔ]) in closed syllables. This can most conveniently be discussed by taking each pair of vowels separately and limiting our study mainly to tonic vowels.

4.13.2. /o/ ∼ /ɔ/. OFr seems at one stage to have had only [ɔ]; the sound [o] developed from [ɔ] in late OFr and MidFr in the following circumstances:

(a) before [z] and [v]: *rose* [rɔzə] > [rozə], *povre* [pɔvrə] > [povrə] (*pauvre*), *chose*, *oser*, etc.; this development in itself would not confer phonemic status on [o] and [ɔ] which, in these circumstances, would be merely allophones of a phoneme /O/, the distinction between them being determined solely by their phonetic circumstances;
(b) as a result of lengthening when preconsonantal and final *s* disappeared: *tost* [tɔst] > [toːt] (now *tôt*), *gros*;
(c) as a result of the reduction of the diphthong [aw] to [o] (see **4.7**(d) and (e)).
The result of (b) and (c) was to introduce a phonemic opposition /o/ ∼ /ɔ/ that remains in ModFr in closed syllables:

coste > côte [koːt]	cotte [kɔt]
saute [soːt]	sotte [sɔt]
paume [poːm]	pomme [pɔm]
heaume [oːm]	homme [ɔm]

In these circumstances, the phonemic status of /o/ and /ɔ/ in

ModFr is indisputable. In open syllables, however, the opposition has been neutralized as a result of the tendency to prefer close vowels in such syllables; so, whereas the opposition /o/ ∼ /ɔ/ exists in *saute* [soːt] ∼ *:otte* [sɔt], it does not exist in (*le*) *saut* [so] ∼ *sot* [so], the original [ɔ] of *sot* having closed to [o].

The situation in ModFr can be summarized briefly as follows:

(a) in final closed syllables, the distinction between /o/ and /ɔ/ is phonemic;
(b) in final open syllables, the opposition has been neutralized and the pronunciation is always [o];
(c) in other syllables, the pronunciation may be either [o] or [ɔ], depending on a variety of factors, and in many words there is hesitation between the two; where the opposition /o/ ∼ /ɔ/ exists, this is a reflection of a similar opposition in the final syllable in related words (e.g. the opposition *botté* [bɔte] ∼ *beauté* [bote] reflects the opposition *botte* [bɔt] ∼ *beau* [bo]).

For a full descriptive treatment of the distribution of [o] and [ɔ] in contemporary French, see Fouché, *Traité* . . . , 51–54 and 75–80.

4.13.3. /ø/ ∼ /œ/. As we have seen, OFr /Ö/ arose both from tonic free *ō* (**4.5.4.**3) and from tonic free *ŏ* (**4.5.4.**2), and also from other sources (e.g. *illos* > *eux*). It is not at all certain what the pronunciation of this phoneme was in OFr, or even whether both [ø] and [œ] existed as allophones of it. In ModFr, the distinction between the two sounds has to be considered phonemic, but on the basis of two pairs of words:

jeûne [ʒøːn] ∼ jeune [ʒœn]
veule [vøːl] ∼ veulent [vœl]

Elsewhere, the two are in complementary distribution:

(a) In final open syllables, the pronunciation is always [ø]: *bœufs* [bø], *jeu*, *heureux*, *nœud*, etc.
(b) In final closed syllables the pronunciation is in most cases [œ]: *bœuf* [bœf], *neuf*, *pleure*, etc., but [ø] before [z] and in a few other words: *heureuse* [œrøːz], *meute* [møːt] *feutre* [føːtr], etc.
(c) In non-final syllables, the pronunciation depends in most cases on that of a corresponding final syllable (e.g. [ø] in *pleuvoir*, *deuxième* corresponding to *pleut* [plø], *deux* [dø], but [œ] in *jeunesse*, *pleurer* corresponding to *jeune* [ʒœn], *pleure* [plœːr]); for further details, see Fouché, *Traité* . . . , 54–56 and 80–83.

79

If *jeûne, veule* come to be pronounced [ʒœn, vœl],[21] the number of phonemes in ModFr will be reduced by one and we shall have a single phoneme /Ö/with two allophones [ø] and [œ].

4.13.4. /e/ ~ /ɛ/. In discussing the opposition /e/ ~ /ɛ/, we shall consider only the following cases:

(a) OFr [e] < tonic blocked *ē, ĭ* (*sĭccum* > *sec*, etc.; see **4.5.3**)
(b) OFr [jE] < tonic free *ĕ* (*hĕri* > *hier*, etc.; see **4.5.4.***2*)
(c) OFr *e* < tonic free *a* (*mare* > *mer*, etc.; see **4.5.4.***4*)
(d) OFr *ai* in tonic syllables (**4.8.3**)

(a) As early as the 12th century, OFr [e] < tonic blocked *ē, ĭ* became [ɛ]:
mĭttere > metre [metrə] > [mɛtrə]   sĭccum > sec [sek] > [sɛk]
Also: *ĭlla* > *ele, crĭsta* > *creste* (> *crête*), *vĭridem* > *vert, debita* > *dete* (> *dette*) etc.; the result was that pairs such as *ele* < *ĭlla* and *bele* < *bĕlla, creste* < *crĭsta* and *teste* < *tĕsta* henceforward rhymed.
(b) and (c) Opinions differ as to whether OFr [jE] *ie* was [je] or [jɛ], and, as we have seen (**4.5.4.***4*), it is uncertain how OFr *e* < tonic free *a* was pronounced. However, in late OFr we find the beginnings of a tendency that was not finally accepted until the 17th or 18th century, namely to prefer [je], [e] in open syllables but [jɛ], [ɛ] in closed syllables. (N.B. in words such as *pierre, père*, an originally open syllable—[pje-rə], [pe-rə]—became closed when the final *e* ceased to be pronounced: [pjɛːr], [pɛːr]). We therefore have in ModFr:

[je]		[jɛ]
pĕdem > pied	hĕri > hier	lĕporem > lièvre
sĕdet > sied	pĕtra > pierre	fĕbrem > fièvre

[e]	[ɛ]
natum > né	mare > mer
pratum > pré	amarum > amer
cantatum > chanté	patrem > père
cantare > chanter	labra > lèvre
fata > fée	ala > OFr ele > aile

[21] In *La prononciation du français contemporain*, Paris, 1945, based on a survey of the pronunciation of officers in a prisoner-of-war camp, A. Martinet reports that 15% of his northern French subjects did not in fact distinguish between *jeune* and *jeûne*.

(d) The diphthong [aj] became [ɛ] in OFr (**4.8.3**), except in verb endings where it became [e] (*j'ai* [e], *je porterai* [pɔrtəre]).

The situation in ModFr is as follows:

(i) In closed syllables, the pronunciation, whatever the origin, is [ɛ]:

from *ē, ĭ*: *dette, elle, mettre, sec, vert, crête*
from OFr *ie*: *hier, pierre, lièvre, fièvre*
from *a*: *mer, amer, père, lèvre, fève*
from OFr *ai*: *faite, (il) laisse, (il) traite*

To these must be added [ɛ] < Latin tonic blocked *ĕ* that has remained [ɛ] since VL: *belle, fête, tête, fer, sept, terre, herbe, hiver, perdre*.

The opposition /e/ ∼ /ɛ/ is therefore neutralized in this position and there is no possibility of oppositions between close and open vowels similar to the one we have between *saute* [soːt] ∼ *sotte* [sɔt], etc.

(ii) In open syllables, the situation is far from simple. Whereas in this position the opposition /o/ ∼ /ɔ/ is neutralized and only [o] is possible (**4.13.2**), oppositions such as *pré* [pre] ∼ *prêt* [prɛ] are possible. There is a tendency to prefer [e], but [ɛ] is found in certain circumstances, and in particular:

(1) when the spelling is *-ai-* (except in the verb ending *-ai—j'ai* [e], *je chanterai* [ʃɑ̃tre], etc.):
fait [fɛ], *laid* [lɛ], *palais* [palɛ], *français* [frɑ̃sɛ], *balai* [balɛ], *vrai* [vrɛ], *(je) parlais* [parlɛ], *(il) paie* [pɛ], etc.;
(2) when the spelling is *-ès, -et, -êt, -ect, -est*:
après [aprɛ], *sujet* [syʒɛ], *billet* [bijɛ], *forêt* [fɔrɛ], *respect* [rɛspɛ], *est* [ɛ], etc.

For a full discussion of this problem, see Fouché, *Traité* . . . , 48–50.

It is always dangerous in linguistics to speculate about what *might* have been. However, since the oppositions /ø/ ∼ /œ/ and /o/ ∼ /ɔ/ have been neutralized in this position, only [ø] and [o] being found, one is tempted to suggest that, but for the influence of grammarians, the opposition /e/ ∼ /ɛ/ would likewise have disappeared. There is both historical and contemporary evidence to support this:

(A) We know that 17th-century grammarians advocated the pronunciation [ɛ] for the spelling *ai* and endings such as *-et, -êt,* etc., in the face of a growing tendency to use [e] (*forêt*, for example, was pronounced [fɔre] in the 17th century).

(B) Many French speakers fail to observe the recommendation to pronounce *-et*, *-ait*, as [ɛ]; Martinet, for example, in his *Prononciation du français moderne*, records that 10% of his subjects made no distinction between *piqué*, *piquet* and *piquait* and that, of the rest, the majority pronounced *piquet* like *piqué* [pike] not like *piquait* [pikɛ].

4.13.5. We can summarize the main points made in the preceding paragraphs by saying that there is a tendency—whose beginnings can be observed in late OFr—to prefer [ø], [o], [e] in open syllables, [œ], [ɔ], [ɛ] in closed syllables. Were this tendency to be uniformly adopted, as has almost happened in the case of [ø] ~ [œ], we should then have three phonemes instead of the present six, viz. /Ö/, /O/ and /E/, each having two principal allophones, a close variety and an open one. As it is, in the case of [o] ~ [ɔ] the opposition is neutralized in open syllables but not in closed (*paume* ~ *pomme*, etc.), as a consequence of the comparatively late reduction of [aw] to [o], whilst in the case of [e] ~ [ɛ] the opposition is neutralized in closed syllables but not in open (*pré* ~ *prêt*, *fée* ~ *fait*, etc.), probably because in the latter position the open vowel has been preserved as a result of the efforts of successive generations of grammarians.

4.14. *Nasal vowels.*

4.14.1. One striking respect in which the phonemic system of French differs from that of Latin is that French has four phonemic nasal vowels, /ɛ̃/, /œ̃/, /ɔ̃/ and /ɑ̃/.

4.14.2. Nasal consonants such as [m], [n] [ɲ], [ŋ] are characterized by the fact that though the flow of air through the mouth is blocked at some point, the velum and uvula are lowered and the air is allowed to escape through the nose. The difference between [d] and [n] in French is illustrated by the diagrams on p. 83.

The difference between such pairs as [b] and [m], [d'] and [ɲ], [g] and [ŋ] is of a similar nature.

As we have seen when, for example, discussing palatalization, there is a constant tendency in language to anticipate following sounds. One consequence of this is that if, when uttering a vowel, we allow the uvula to drop and open the nasal passage in anticipation of a following nasal consonant, some air will escape through the nose whilst we are pronouncing the vowel which will thereby become to some extent nasalized. In English, for example,

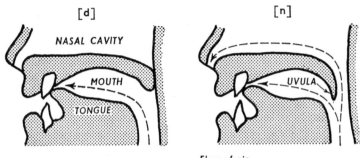

[d]   [n]

NASAL CAVITY

MOUTH   UVULA

TONGUE

◄ ‒ ‒ ‒ ‒ = Flow of air

the *a* of *can* is slightly nasalized and so, to that extent, differs from the *a* of *cat*. In English, the difference is merely between allophones and indeed is generally not noticed, but in French the four nasal vowels have phonemic status.

The history of nasalization and its consequences in French is a complicated one, and we shall here concentrate on some of the principal aspects. It is uncertain when many of the developments discussed took place, and so the datings we suggest are often only tentative.

4.14.3. Before nasalization of the vowel took place, the two vowels [ɛ] and [ɔ] were raised to [e] and [o] before a nasal consonant, (e.g. *vĕntum* > [vento], *pŏntem* > [ponte]). In practice, therefore, we have five vowels to consider, [a], [e], [i], [o], [y]. Any vowel can be nasalized, and at various stages in its history French has had nasal vowels that have now disappeared. ([~] over the symbol for any vowel indicates the corresponding nasal vowel.)

4.14.4. *Vowels in closed syllables, tonic and initial.*

4.14.4.1. Starting with [a] in about the 10th century and finishing with [i] and [y] in about the 13th century, all five vowels successively became nasalized. At first the nasal consonant remained, as [m] before a labial consonant, [n] before a dental consonant, [ŋ] before a velar consonant:

campum, cantare, Germanic *blank > [tʃãmp], [tʃãnter], [blãŋk]
vĕntum, tĕmplum, vēndere, lingua > [vẽnt], [tẽmplə], [vẽndrə], [lẽŋgwə]
pŏntem, cŏmputare, mŏntem > [põnt], [kõnter], [mõnt]
quinque (>V.L. [kinkwe]) > [tsĩŋk] > [sĩŋk]
*lunis die > [lỹnsdi]

83

The lowering of the velum combined with the raising of the tongue meant that the air passage through the mouth was somewhat restricted. In the case of each of the nasal vowels except [ã] (in which the tongue was at its lowest), this narrowing of the oral passage seems to have been compensated for by a lowering of the tongue—or rather by a failure to raise the tongue as high as would be needed to produce the original vowel sound. The result is a modification of the timbre of the vowel: more precisely, [ẽ], [õ], [ĩ] and [ỹ] were successively, over a period of some centuries, lowered to [ã], [ɔ̃], [ɛ̃] and [œ̃] respectively.[22]

4.14.4.2. A further development was that in MidFr the nasal consonant ceased to be pronounced. It may be that a lengthening of the nasal vowel in compensation for the loss of the nasal consonant is the reason why [ã] became [ɑ̃], which seems to be a comparatively recent development.

4.14.4.3. The developments discussed above can be tabulated as follows:

Latin	Old French	Modern French
campum	[tʃãmp]	[ʃɑ̃] champ
sĕntire	[sẽntir]	[sɑ̃tiːr] sentir
lĭngua	[lẽŋgwə]	[lɑ̃ːg] langue
pŏntem	[põnt]	[pɔ̃] pont
quinque	[sĩŋk]	[sɛ̃ːk] cinq
*lunis die	[lỹndi]	[lœ̃di] lundi

4.14.4.4. In ModFr, words such as *flamme, année*, i.e. words in which a vowel is followed by a nasal consonant—which is, or was until the loss of final [ə], intervocalic—have no nasal vowel. In OFr, however, nasalization took place here as elsewhere, e.g. *flamma, *annata* > [flãmə] [ãneə]. In such cases, the nasal consonant, being intervocalic, did not disappear and in the 16th and 17th centuries the vowel denasalized: [e.g. [flãmə] > [flam], [ãneə] > [ane], *flamme, année*.[23] Long before this time, [ẽ] had

---

[22] The lowering of [ẽ] to [ã] seems to have taken place by the early 12th century, to judge by the evidence of the *Roland* in which words such as *gent, vent, cent, fierement* assonate with *tant, blanc, grant, camp*, etc. On the other hand [i] and [y] did not nasalize till long after this and the lowering of [ĩ] and [ỹ] to [ẽ] and [œ̃] respectively may not have become fully established until MidFr or later.

[23] The fact that the vowel denasalized to [a] and not to [ɑ] is the reason why it is suggested that the change [ã] > [ɑ̃] in those words where the nasal vowel remains is fairly recent; i.e. later than the period of denasalization. The reason

VOWELS

lowered to [ã] and [õ] had lowered to [ɔ̃]; consequently, these denasalized to [a] and [ɔ] respectively. This is the explanation of the pronunciation [a] in *femme*, in spite of the archaic spelling in -*e*-: *femina* > [fẽmə] *feme* > [fãmə] > [fam]. Similarly, *sŭmma* > [sõmə] > [sɔ̃mə] > [sɔm] *somme*, *hom(i)nem* > [õmə] [ɔ̃mə] > [ɔm] *homme*.

4.14.5. *Initial open syllables.* The only initial open syllables that are known to have nasalized were those containing [o] (< *ō, ŭ, ŏ*), which developed like tonic free [o] (*donat* > *donne*, etc.) :

dōnare > [dõner] > [dɔne] donner ‑ sŏnare > sonner

4.14.6. *Tonic open syllables.*

4.14.6.*1*. The following table compares the results in OFr of tonic free vowels (i) before a nasal consonant and (ii) elsewhere (excluding cases where the vowel was modified under the influence of palatals) :

	+ *nasal*	*Elsewhere*
a	manum > main [mãjn]	mare > mer
ē, ĭ	plenum > plein [plẽjn]	me > mei > moi
ĕ	bĕne > bien [bjẽn]	pedem > pie [pje]
ō, ŭ	donum > don [dõn]	florem > flour > fleur
ŏ	bonum > buen [bwẽn]	ovum > uef > œuf
ī	finem > fin [fĩn]	vita > vie
ū	unum > un [ỹn]	nudum > nu

The following points call for comment:

(a) The *ai* of the nasalized vowel may indicate that tonic free *a* elsewhere went through the stage [aj] before becoming *e* (as in *mare* > *mer*).

(b) *ō, ŭ* did not diphthongize when followed by a nasal; according to some authorities the pronunciation of *don*, etc. in OFr was [dŭn], etc.

(c) No words remain in ModFr showing the development of

for denasalization is, according to Pope (§ 440) and others, that the nasal vowel was dissimilated from the following nasal consonant. Fouché (*Phonétique* . . . , II, 386), putting it rather differently, argues that the tendency to anticipate the nasal consonant—which, in the circumstances in question, was in a different syllable from the vowel, e.g. *bonne* [bõ-nə], *année* [ã-neə]—weakened, with the result that the vowel lost its nasal quality.

tonic free *ŏ* + nasal; *bon* < *bŏnum* appears to show the development of the word in an unstressed position.

4.14.6.2. The later development of nasalized diphthongs is complicated and we shall do no more here than show what they have become in ModFr after undergoing the processes of simplification (reduction to simple vowels), lowering and, where appropriate (i.e. when an intervocalic nasal consonant remained, see **4.14.4.4**), denasalization:

No denasalization	*Denasalization*
[ãj] > [ɛ̃]	[ãj] > [ɛ̃] > [ɛ]
manum > main [mɛ̃]	amat > aime [ɛm]
vanum > vain	vana > vaine
famem > faim	lana > laine
planum > plain	plana > plaine
[ẽj] > [ɛ̃j] > [ɛ̃]	[ẽj] > [ɛ̃j] > [ɛ]
plēnum > plein [plɛ̃]	plēna > pleine [plɛn]
frēnum > frein	frēnat > (il) freine
sĭnum > sein	
[jẽ] > [jɛ̃]	[jẽ] > [jɛ̃] > [jɛ]
bĕne > bien [bjɛ̃]	tĕnent > tiennent [tjɛn]
tĕnet > tient	

ŏ, *ŭ*, as we have seen above, did not diphthongize before a nasal:

[õ] > [ɔ̃]	[õ] > [ɔ̃] > [ɔ]
donum > don [dɔ̃]	donat > donne [dɔn]
	poma > pomme
	persona > personne
	corona > couronne

The nasal vowels [ĩ] and [ỹ] lowered, as elsewhere, to [ɛ̃] and [œ̃] in:

fīnem > [fĩn] > [fɛ̃]   ūnum > [ỹn] > [œ̃]
vicinum > voisin   vinum > vin   Germanic *brūn > brun

No lowering took place, however, in those words in which there was denasalization:

fine [fin]	une [yn]	lune
voisine	brune	plume
lime	(il) fume	

which probably indicates that [i] and [y] were only slightly nasalized in this position and that they were not only the last to nasalize but also perhaps the first to denasalize, doing so before lowering had taken place.[24]

4.14.6.3. We saw in **4.8.6** that, after a palatal, tonic free *a* and *e* became *ie* and *i* respectively (*carum > chier, cera > cire*). When followed by a nasal, these became [jẽ] and [ẽ]; e.g. *canem > chien, racemum > raisin*.

4.14.7. The history of those vowels that were followed in OFr by a palatal element as well as by a nasal consonant, and were consequently affected by the processes *both* of nasalization *and* of palatalization, is too complicated to trace in any detail here. We shall say merely that the various nasal diphthongs or vowels produced were all reduced to [ẽ] (sometimes preceded by a semi-consonant) or, in appropriate circumstances, denasalized:

No denasalization	*Denasalization*
sanctum > saint [sãjnt] > [sẽ]	montanea > montagne
fĭngere > feindre [fẽjndrə] > [fẽːdr]	insĭgnia > enseigne
pŭnctum > point [põjnt] > [pwẽ]	verecŭndia > vergogne
junium > juing [dʒɣ̃jɲ] > juin [ʒɥẽ]	linea > ligne

4.14.8. In place of the great variety of OFr nasal vowels and diphthongs, ModFr has only the four nasal vowels [ẽ], [œ̃], [ɔ̃] and [ɑ̃], and one of these, [œ̃], has virtually disappeared in the speech of many speakers, having become assimilated to [ẽ]: so, *un, brun, humble, lundi*, etc. are pronounced [ẽ], [brẽ], [ẽːbl], [lẽdi]. The reason for this is doubtless that [œ̃] occurs in comparatively few words and that its functional yield is exceptionally low, i.e. the cases in which it serves to make a phonemic distinction are very few. There are in common use only two cases of a phonemic opposition between [œ̃] and [ẽ], viz. [brœ̃] *brun* ~ [brẽ] *brin*, and [œ̃] *un* ~ [ẽ] *hein*.[25]

[24] Close vowels such as [i], [y] and [u] are less liable to nasalization than more open vowels, for the reason that, as they involve raising the tongue almost to the maximum height possible without causing friction and so producing a consonant, the air passage through the mouth is already restricted and there is less 'room for manœuvre' for the lowering of the velum in anticipation of a following nasal consonant.

[25] A very few other cases are also possible, e.g. [defœ̃] *défunt* ~ [defẽ] *des fins*, [ɑ̃prœ̃ːt] (*il*) *emprunte* ~ [ɑ̃prẽːt] *empreinte*. On the loss of /œ̃/, see T. Akamatsu, 'Quelques statistiques sur la fréquence d'utilisation des voyelles nasales françaises,' in *La linguistique*, 1967, 75–80.

4.15. *Vowel length.*

4.15.1. On the phonetic level, ModFr has both short vowels (e.g. *blanc* [blã], *coq* [kɔk]) and long vowels (e.g. *blanche* [blãːʃ],[26] *corps* [kɔːr]). The rules governing length of vowels as stated by Fouché, *Traité* . . . , pp. xxxvii–xlii, can be summed up very briefly:

(a) Unstressed vowels are always short.[27]

(b) Stressed vowels are always short in open syllables: il est *grand* [il ɛ grã], je ne sais *pas* [ʒən se pɑ], cet *été* [sɛt ete].

(c) All stressed vowels are long in closed syllables when followed by [r], [z], [ʒ], [v] or [vr]:[28] finir [finiːr], fer [fɛːr], part [paːr], chaise [ʃɛːz], creuse [krøːz], épouse [epuːz], ange [ãːʒ], neige [nɛːʒ], éloge [elɔːʒ], grève [grɛːv], fleuve [flœːv], ivre [iːvr], ouvre [uːvr].

(d) In closed syllables before any other consonant or consonants:

(i) the vowels [ɛ̃], [œ̃], [ɔ̃], [ã], [ø], [o] and [ɑ] are long: mince [mɛ̃ːs], peintre [pɛ̃ːtr], (il) emprunte [ãprœ̃ːt], longue [lɔ̃ːg], ongle [ɔ̃ːgl], blanche [blãːʃ], banque [bãːk], émeute [emøːt], jeûne [ʒøːn], chaude [ʃoːd], jaune [ʒoːn], (il) passe [pɑːs], âpre [ɑːpr];

(ii) all other vowels are short: guide [gid], tigre [tigr], chaîne [ʃɛn], faible [fɛbl], hache [aʃ], calme [kalm], globe [glɔb], école [ekɔl], douce [dus], coudre [kudr], tube [tyb], muscle [myskl], bœuf [bœf], jeune [ʒœn], peuple [pœpl].

4.15.2. Length therefore depends on one or other—or, in some cases, both—of two factors:

(a) the nature of the following consonant, viz. [r], [z], [ʒ], [v], [vr]: it is probably significant that these are all voiced fricatives;

---

[26] [ː] indicates that the preceding vowel is long.

[27] It is important to remember that ModFr has a group-stress not a word-stress, and that only the final syllable of a group is stressed. Consequently a given syllable may, in the same word, be stressed or unstressed according to the context: e.g. *grande* is stressed in *elle est grande* [ɛl ɛ grãːd], but unstressed in *la grande armée* [la grãd arme]; similarly *je crois qu'il part* [ʒə krwa kil paːr] but *il part déjà* [il par deʒa].

[28] Some authorities add [j] to this list, e.g. *fille* [fiːj], *travail* [travaːj], *feuille* [fœːj], etc.; Fouché however recommends [fij], [travaj], [fœj], etc.

(b) the nature of the vowel; here, length is generally speaking the result of various historical factors:

(i) the length of nasal vowels is a result of compensatory lengthening when the nasal consonant was lost (**4.14.4**): e.g. [mɔ̃ntə] > [mɔ̃ːt] *monte*;

(ii) the long [o] of *chaude, paume, haute, sauf, heaume* is the result of the reduction of the diphthong [aw] (**4.7**(d) and (e));

(iii) the long vowel of *hâte, pâte, hôte, côte*, etc., is a result of compensatory lengthening when the *s* of *haste, paste, oste, coste*, etc., disappeared in OFr;

(iv) [s] seems to have exercised a lengthening influence on [ɔ] (> [oː]) and [a] (> [ɑː]) in MidFr, giving the long vowel of *basse, grasse, passe, grosse, fosse*, etc.

The explanation of the length of the vowel in many other words is uncertain, e.g. *meute* [møːt], *neutre, feutre*.

4.15.3. If Fouché's analysis is accepted, then vowel length in modern French is not phonemic; whether or not a vowel is long is determined solely by phonetic circumstances, and there is no possibility of having a pair of words differentiated solely by vowel quantity. However, it is argued by some that such pairs do exist. Lilias Armstrong, for example, claims (Armstrong, 17) that an opposition [ɛ] ~ [ɛː] exists in the following pairs:

[ɛ]	[ɛː]	[ɛ]	[ɛː]
mettre [mɛtr]	maître [mɛːtr]	faite [fɛt]	fête [fɛːt]
lettre	l'être	laide	l'aide
saine	scène	paresse	paraisse

On the other hand, M. Grammont in his *Traité pratique de prononciation française*, Paris, 1914, 38, gives [ɛ] as long in both *faite* and *fête*, *saine* and *scène*, and many other words, including *tête, chaîne*, etc.

In his *Studies in French and Comparative Phonetics*, The Hague, 1966, P. Delattre comments (106) that *maître* is 'souvent prononcé plus long que dans *mètre* ou *mettre*' and lists other pairs including (in addition to some of those listed by Armstrong) *tette* [tɛt] ~ *tête* [tɛːt], *bette* ~ *bête*, *elle* ~ *aile* and *renne* ~ *reine*. He comments however, with reference to [ɛː] in such pairs, that 'en général, cette durée additionnelle est fort instable. La majorité des Français ne l'observent que dans l'énonciation soignée'.

89

The most one can say is that in the speech of anyone who consistently observes a distinction between *mettre* [mɛtr] and *maître* [mɛːtr], etc., vowel length is, for the one vowel [ɛ], phonemic, but that in the speech of most people it probably is not. Vowel length is not phonemic in the case of other vowels.

5 Semi-consonants (or semi-vowels)

5.1. *The three semi-consonants.* French has three semi-consonants,[1] two of which, [ɥ] and [w], occur only before vowels:

huit [ɥit]	lueur [lɥœːr]	menuet [mənɥɛ]
nuance [nɥɑ̃ːs]	persuader [pɛrsɥade]	juin [ʒɥɛ̃]
oui [wi]	loi [lwa]	joueur [ʒwœːr]
ouest [wɛst]	louange [lwɑ̃ːʒ]	avoué [avwe]

The third, [j], occurs both before and after vowels, and intervocalically:

hier [jeːr]	fille [fij]	payer [pɛje]
fiacre [fjakr]	oreille [ɔrɛj]	fillette [fijɛt]
milieu [miljø]	paille [pɑːj]	ailleurs [ajœːr]
rien [rjɛ̃]	grenouille [grənuj]	maillot [majo]
viande [vjɑ̃ːd]	feuille [fœj]	voyant [vwajɑ̃]

5.2. *The phonemic status of the semi-consonants.* Opinions differ as to whether or not the semi-consonants are to be regarded as independent phonemes. [ɥ] and [w] at least are in complementary distribution with [y] and [u]—for example, after consonant clusters consisting of stop + [l] or [r],[2] we have [y], [u], as in *cruel* [kryɛl], (nous) *excluons* [ɛ ksklyɔ̃], *clouer* [klue], *éblouir* [ebluiːr], but elsewhere [ɥ], [w], as in *duel* [dɥɛl], *persuader* [pɛrsɥade], *louer* [lwe], *jouir* [ʒwiːr]—and pairs of words distinguished solely by the opposition [y] ~ [ɥ] or [u] ~ [w] are impossible. [ɥ] and [w] must therefore be considered as prevocalic allophones of the phonemes /y/ and /u/ respectively.[3]

Pre-vocalic [j] is likewise in complementary distribution with [i]: *crier* [krie], *peuplier* [pœplie], *triomphe* [triɔ̃ːf], but *pied* [pje], *soulier* [sulje], *bastion* [bastjɔ̃], etc. However, it is argued that [j]

---

[1] For a full discussion of the French semi-consonants, or semi-vowels, see Alf Lombard, *Le rôle des semi-voyelles et leur concurrence avec les voyelles correspondantes dans la prononciation parisienne*, Lund, 1964.

[2] *-ui-* however is always pronounced [ɥi], e.g. *pluie, truie, construire*.

[3] Consequently, certain verbs have an allophonic variation of the type (*je*) *tue* [ty] ~ (*nous*) *tuons* [tɥɔ̃], (je) *joue* [ʒu] ~ (*nous*) *jouons* [ʒwɔ̃], and similarly, with [i] ~ [j], (*je*) *lie* [li] ~ (*nous*) *lions* [ljɔ̃].

and [i] nevertheless count as separate phonemes since post-vocalically a few oppositions of the type *haï* [ai] ~ *ail* [aj], *pays* [pɛi] ~ *paye* [pɛj], *abbaye* [abɛi] ~ *abeille* [abɛj] are possible. Against this, one could argue that the basis of the distinction here is not an opposition [i] ~ [j] but the syllabic division, [ai] and [ɛi] each forming two syllables, [aj] and [ɛj] only one; in this case, [j] would still count as an allophone of the phoneme /i/. Either view seems defensible.

5.3. *Sources of the semi-consonants.* Some of the principal sources of the semi-consonants have been discussed in Chs. 3 and 4. See in particular:

[ɥ]: < *ū*, *ŏ* + a palatal, **4.8.4.** and **4.8.5.**;
[w]: in [wa] *oi* < [ɔj],[oj] < various sources, **4.8.2** and **4.10**;
[j]: < intervocalic [k], [g] in some circumstances, **3.4.3** (c);
     < OFr [λ], **3.9.4** (b) and **3.9.5**;
     < tonic free *ĕ*, **4.5.4.**2;
     in [jø] < OFr [jew] and [wew], **4.7** (c);
     < tonic free *a* after a palatal, **4.8.6** and **4.14.6.**3.

In addition:

(a) [y], [u], [i] in initial syllables (except after stop + [l] or [r]) have become semi-consonants—and thereby lost their syllabic value—when in hiatus with a following vowel (see **4.4.6**);
(b) semi-consonants also occur in very many words that have either been borrowed from Latin or other languages or been formed in French by means of suffixes, e.g.

[ɥ]: suave, suicide, duel, contribuer, menuet, nuage
[w]: ouest, douane, pingouin, week-end, water-closet
[j]: dialecte, idiote, hiérarchie, piano, folio, fiord

ADDITIONAL BIBLIOGRAPHICAL NOTE
N. C. W. Spence, 'The French Semi-Vowels: a Fresh Angle?', *Lingua* 27 (1971), 198–215

6 Nouns and adjectives

6.1. *The case system.*

6.1.1. *Modern French.* ModFr nouns have only one form each in singular and plural, i.e. they do not vary in form according to their function in the sentence, as English *boy*, for example, has a special form to indicate the possessive function, viz. *boy's*. The word *jour*, for example, retains the same form whether it functions as subject (*le jour est arrivé*), as direct object (*j'attends le jour de son départ*), after a preposition (*du jour*) or in an adverbial expression (*il viendra un jour, je le vois chaque jour*).

6.1.2. *From five cases to two.*

6.1.2.1. Latin nouns, on the other hand, could have up to five different forms, known as *cases*, in the singular and up to four more in the plural (two cases, dative and ablative, being always identical in the plural) depending on the noun's function in the sentence, e.g.:

(a) **Pater** *venit* 'the father comes': *nominative* case serving as subject of the verb;

(b) **Patrem** *video* 'I see the father'; *contra* **patrem** 'against the father'; *accusative* case serving as direct object or after certain prepositions;

(c) *Liber* **patris** 'the father's book': *genitive* case serving primarily to indicate possession;

(d) *Da librum* **patri** 'give the book to the father': *dative* case serving as indirect object;

(e) *Pro* **patre** 'for the father': *ablative* case used after numerous prepositions and in a variety of other constructions.

The forms taken by some other Latin nouns, *murus* (m.) 'wall', *magister* (m.) 'master', *porta* (f.) 'door', *canis* (m.) 'dog', *fructus* (m.) 'fruit', are:

SINGULAR

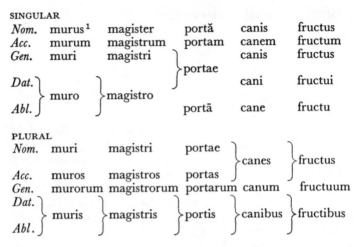

Nom.	murus[1]	magister	portă	canis	fructus
Acc.	murum	magistrum	portam	canem	fructum
Gen.	muri	magistri		canis	fructus
			portae		
Dat.				cani	fructui
	muro	magistro			
Abl.			portā	cane	fructu

PLURAL

Nom.	muri	magistri	portae		
				canes	fructus
Acc.	muros	magistros	portas		
Gen.	murorum	magistrorum	portarum	canum	fructuum
Dat.					
	muris	magistris	portis	canibus	fructibus
Abl.					

6.1.2.2. The cases were gradually reduced in number and only two remain in OFr, the nominative and another that is usually referred to as the 'oblique case'. The oblique case is generally considered as deriving from the Latin accusative, though it would perhaps be more accurate to consider it, at least in the singular, as representing a fusion of the accusative and the ablative. A number of factors combined to eliminate the other cases, among them the following:

(a) Phonetic factors blurred certain distinctions; e.g. the loss of final -*m* (**3.8.2**) and of the distinction between *ă* and *ā* (**4.1.2**) meant that *portă*, *portam* and *portā* all became *porta*; the loss of -*m* and the falling together of *ŭ* and *ō* (**4.1.2**) abolished the distinction between *murŭm* and *murō* (both becoming *muro*) and between *canem* and *cane*.

(b) There was a growing tendency to use prepositions, e.g. *de* 'from' in the sense of 'of' instead of the genitive (**liber de patre* for *liber patris*) and *ad* 'to' instead of the dative (**da librum ad patrem* for *da librum patri*).

The relationship of Latin and OFr forms is most clearly shown by words of the *murus* type:

	LATIN		OFR	
	Sing.	*Plural*	*Sing.*	*Plural*
Nom.	murus	muri	murs	mur
Acc.	murum	muros	mur	murs

[1] Nouns of the *murus* type also had a vocative case used when addressing someone (e.g. the vocative of *dominus* is *domine* 'Lord!').

94

(Note that *murs*—with an *s*—is nominative *singular*, and *mur*—without an *s*—is nominative *plural*).

Other types of nouns, which had an *s* in both nom. and acc. plur. in Latin, had been influenced by the *mur* ∼ *murs* type and so had no -*s* in the nom. plur. in OFr:

	LATIN		OFR	
	Sing.	*Plural*	*Sing.*	*Plural*
Nom.	pater	patres	pere	pere
Acc.	patrem	patres	pere	peres
Nom.	imperátor	imperatóres	emperére	emperĕór
Acc.	imperatórem	imperatóres	emperĕór	emperĕórs

In *imperátor* ∼ *imperatórem*, etc., note that the main stress in the nom. sing. falls on a different syllable from that in the other forms, and that this is reflected in OFr; other parallel examples are *peccátor* ∼ *peccatórem* > *pechiére* ∼ *pechëór, ínfans* ∼ *infántem* > *énfes* ∼ *enfánt*; a similar, but not identical, state of affairs is seen in *hómo* ∼ *hóminem* > *uem* (or *on*) ∼ *ome* (> *homme*) in which the number of syllables varies in Latin but the accent remains on the same syllable.

The influence of the *murs* ∼ *mur* type sometimes resulted in a remodelling of the other nouns in the nom. sing. so that we find patterns such as the following:

	Sing.	*Plural*
Nom.	peres, empereres	pere, emperëor
Obl.	pere, emperëor	peres, emperëors

In the fem. sing., *porta* and *portam* fell together when the -*m* was lost; there is also evidence that, in VL, the fem. plural ending -*as* of the accusative came to be used instead of the nominative -*ae*, so we have the following patterns:

	CLLAT		VL		OFR	
	Sing.	*Plural*	*Sing.*	*Plural*	*Sing.*	*Plural*
Nom.	porta	portae	porta	portas	porte	portes
Acc.	portam	portas				

i.e. nouns of this type had no case system in OFr. Fem. nouns not ending in -*e* followed a similar pattern, though, as in masculines

95

such as *pere*, an analogical -*s* is sometimes found in the nom. sing., e.g.:

	LATIN		OFr	
	Sing.	*Plural*	*Sing.*	*Plural*
Nom.	flos	flores	flor(s)	flors
Acc.	florem	flores	flor	flors

Masc. and fem. nouns having a stem ending in -*s* or -*z* [ts]—e.g. *pas* < *passum*, *mois* < *mensem*, *voiz* (*voix*) < *vocem*—were invariable in OFr:

	Sing.	*Plural*
Nom.	pas, mois, voiz	pas, mois, voiz
Obl.	pas, mois, voiz	pas, mois, voiz

6.1.3. *From two cases to one.*

6.1.3.*1.* In OFr there are numerous instances of the use of the inappropriate case, and especially of the use of the oblique where the nominative might have been expected. In the *Roland* we find, for example, '*Dreiz emperere,*' *dist Rollant le* **barun**, which occurs in a *laisse*[2] having the assonance *u* with other lines ending in such words as *reproverunt, bastun, plurt*—the oblique *le barun*, used as the subject of a verb, cannot be amended to the 'correct' nominative *li ber* which would not fit; *barun* must therefore have been what the author intended.

From an early period, then, there are indications that the OFr two-case system was breaking down. It has been suggested, indeed, that it may have been somewhat artificially maintained in the literary language and not have been characteristic of the spoken language. By the end of the OFr period it was on the verge of collapse.

6.1.3.*2.* Of the two OFr cases, it is generally speaking the oblique that has remained. There are perhaps two main reasons for this: (a) the oblique case was more frequently used than the nominative and had a wider range of functions, being used:

(i) after all prepositions;
(ii) as the direct object;
(iii) occasionally as indirect object (e.g. *Li nums Joiuse* **l'espée**

[2] In the OFr epics, a *laisse* is a sequence of assonating lines (for assonance, see Ch. 4, note 11): e.g. in the *Roland*, lines 761–5, assonating in [a], form one *laisse*, 766–73 in [o] another and 774–82 in [y] another.

fut dunét 'The name of Joyeuse was given *to the sword*'; *Di* **ton nevo** 'Tell your nephew');

(iv) with certain nouns, especially personal names, titles (*Dieu, seigneur, roi*, etc.) and nouns relating to family relationships, as a possessive (e.g. *li filz* **Marie** 'the son of Mary', *la niece* **le duc** 'the duke's niece', *li chevaus* **le roi** 'the king's horse', *la meson* **son pere** 'his father's house')[3]

(v) in numerous adverbial functions (e.g. **chascun jor** 'each day', *Li chevaliers s'en part* **les granz galos** 'the knight sets off at a great gallop', *E vint i Carlemaignes* **tut un antif sentier** 'Charlemagne came [along] an ancient path', **quatre sols** *vaut* 'it is worth four sous')

(vi) in exclamations, e.g. **Quel pecié** (='péché')! 'What a pity!'

On the other hand, the nominative functioned only as the subject of the verb and as a mode of address, i.e. as a vocative, e.g. *Roland: U estes vos, bels nies*? 'Where are you, my fine nephew?' —*nies* (<népos) is the nom. sing. of *nevot* (<nepótem) >*neveu*. The oblique case therefore was a 'neutral' or 'unmarked' form indicating no particular function, whereas the nominative was a 'special' or 'marked' form indicating certain specific functions. (Similarly, in English, one might consider *child* to be an unmarked form and *child's* a marked form indicating possession.) If this is so, any pressure on the system would be likely to result in the disappearance of the marked rather than of the unmarked form;

(b) in the oblique case, the relation between singular and plural was constant—no *s* in the singular ~ *s* in the plural:

Sing.	Plural	Sing.	Plural
mur	~ murs	ome	~ omes
pere	~ peres	porte	~ portes
emperëor	~ emperëors	flor	~ flors

In the nominative, on the contrary, there was no constant relationship:

murs	~ mur	uem, om	~ ome
pere(s)	~ pere	porte	~ portes
emperere(s)	~ emperëor	flor(s)	~ flors

[3] There are some relics of this construction in such expressions as *hôtel-Dieu* (literally 'God's hospice') and numerous place names, e.g. *Bourg-la-Reine*, *Pont-l'Évêque*.

97

Here again, any pressure on the system would lead to a preference for the case offering a constant relationship between singular and plural.

What pressures might have tended to weaken the system and lead to a generalization of one case at the expense of the other? No sure answer can be given, but the following points deserve mention:

(1) the majority of feminine nouns had no case-system;
(2) there was a growing tendency to adopt certain fixed word-orders (see **20.3** to **20.5**), with the result that the function of a noun in the sentence was well enough indicated by its position.

We can therefore conclude that the maintenance of a two-case system for masculine nouns was not structurally necessary but something of a redundancy.

6.1.3.3. There are, however, some survivals of the nominative in Mod. Fr.[3a] e.g.

OFr Nom.	OFr Obl.	ModFr.
prestre	provoire[4]	prêtre
ancestre	ancessor	ancêtre
peintre	peintor	peintre
traître	traïtor	traître
suer[5]	seror	sœur

Occasionally, both forms remain, as completely distinct words:

OFr Nom.	ModFr.	OFr Obl.	ModFr.
compain	copain	compaignon	compagnon
garz	gars	garçon	garçon
sire	sire	seignor	seigneur

There is a relic of the nominative use of *om* in the pronoun *on*, which can still be used only as the subject of the verb, beside *homme* (< OFr obl. *ome*).

6.1.4. *The fate of the Latin neuter.* In **6.1.2** and **6.1.3** we have discussed only masculine and feminine nouns. Latin also had a

---

[3a] See N. Spence's article, 'La survivance en français moderne des formes du nominatif latin', in *Actes du Xe Congrès International de Linguistique et Philologie Romanes* (1962), Paris, 1965, 231–43.

[4] This form remains in the name of a Paris street, *rue des Prouvaires*.

[5] *Suer ~ serór*, reflecting Latin *sóror ~ sorórem*, is one of the very few fem. nouns having distinct nom. and obl. forms in OFr on the *emperére ~ emperëór* pattern.

third gender, the neuter. The declension of some typical neuter nouns can be illustrated by *vinum* 'wine' and *cor* 'heart':

	Singular		Plural	
Nom.	vinum	cor	vina	corda
Acc.	vinum	cor	vina	corda
Gen.	vini	cordis	vinorum	cordum
Dat.		cordi		
	vino		vinis	cordibus
Ab.		corde		

In the singular, the *vinum* type differs from the *murus* type only in the nominative. There was already a tendency in VL to create analogical nominatives such as *vinus, castellus, collus* for *vinum, castellum* amd *collum*; by the time these nouns appear in French, they had abandoned their original plurals and nouns of the *cor* type had also been remodelled, so we have in OFr, corresponding to Latin *vinum ~ vina, castellum ~ castella, cor ~ corda, nomen ~ nomina*, and many others, nouns of the *mur* type:

Nom. sing.	vins	chasteaus	cuers	noms
Obl. sing.	vin	chastel	cuer	nom
Nom. pl.	vin	chastel	cuer	nom
Obl. pl.	vins	chasteaus	cuers	noms

There are however some relics of the neuter plurals in *-a*. In some words in which the plural could be taken in a collective sense, these plural forms in *-a* were assimilated to fem. sing. nouns in *-a* of the *porta* type: for example, *folia*, the plural of *folium*, has given *la feuille* (now 'leaf' but probably used earlier in a collective sense, i.e. 'foliage'). Likewise, *labra, festa, gaudia, opera, vela* (the plurals of *labrum, festum, gaudium, opus, velum*) have become *lèvre, fête, joie, œuvre*, and *(la) voile*. There are a number of instances in which both singular and plural exist in ModFr, as masc. and fem. singulars respectively,[6] e.g.

cerebellum > cervel > cerveau	*cerebella > cervelle*
vascellum > vaisseau	*vascella > vaisselle*
granum > grain	*grana > graine*

[6] Beside *fueille* (*feuille*) < *folia*, OFr also had *fueil* < *folium*, which remains in *chèvrefeuil*.

6.1.5. The OFr case-system also applied to adjectives, e.g.

LATIN

	M. sing.	F. sing.	M. pl.	F. pl.
Nom.	durus	dura	duri	durae
Acc.	durum	duram	duros	duras

OFr

Nom.	durs	dur	
Obl.	dur	durs	

(Nom. durs / Obl. dur) } dure   (Nom. dur / Obl. durs) } dures

LATIN

Nom.	viridis	viridis	virides	virides
Acc.	viridem	viridem	virides	virides

OFr

Nom.	verz	vert
Obl.	vert	verz

(Nom. verz / Obl. vert) } vert   (Nom. vert / Obl. verz) } verz $(z=[ts])$

These illustrate various types of remodelling of the same kind
as we have seen in nouns—e.g. the use of *dures* (like *portes*) in the
nominative plural and the introduction of an opposition $\emptyset \sim s$
in the masc. plural of *vert* (like *pere ~ peres*). (N.B. $\emptyset$ = zero.)

The relationship between singular and plural forms of nouns
and adjectives is discussed further in **6.2** and that between masc.
and fem. forms of adjectives in **6.3**.

6.2. *Singular and plural.*

6.2.1. *Singular and plural in modern French.*

6.2.1.1. The majority of ModFr nouns and adjectives are ac-
counted for by the following statements:

(a) In the written language, the plural is formed by adding *s* to
the singular form:

mur ~ murs	père ~ pères	vif ~ vifs
sac ~ sacs	fleur ~ fleurs	naval ~ navals
cou ~ cous	porte ~ portes	seul ~ seuls
bal ~ bals	dur ~ durs	belle ~ belles
hôtel ~ hôtels	vert ~ verts	heureuse ~ heureuses

100

but words ending in *eau*, and some words ending in *eu* or *ou*, have a plural in *x*, and words in *-s*, *-x*, or *-z* are invariable:

château ~ châteaux	cheveu ~ cheveux	pas–pas
beau ~ beaux	genou ~ genoux	voix–voix

(b) In the spoken language, there is no difference (except in liaison forms: e.g. *un grand homme* [œ̃ grɑ̃t ɔm] ~ *les grands hommes* [le grɑ̃z ɔm]) between singular and plural. This is true of, for example, all the words quoted in (a) above, e.g.

mur [myːr] ~ murs [myːr]	vif [vif] ~ vifs [vif]
sac [sak] ~ sacs [sak]	belle [bɛl] ~ belles [bɛl]
bal [bal] ~ bals [bal]	beau [bo] ~ beaux [bo]
porte [pɔrt] ~ portes[pɔrt]	cheveu [ʃəvø] ~ cheveux [ʃəvø]

6.2.1.*2*. A distinction between singular and plural is, however, made in both the spoken and the written language, in (a) most nouns and adjectives in *-al*,[7] (b) some nouns in *-ail*,[7] (c) a few other words in *-l* that have both a 'regular' and an 'irregular' plural,[8] e.g.

(a) cheval [ʃəval] ~ chevaux [ʃəvo]
    journal [ʒurnal] ~ journaux [ʒurno]
    loyal [lwajal] ~ loyaux [lwajo]
(b) travail [travaj] ~ travaux [travo]
    vitrail [vitraj] ~ vitraux [vitro]
(c) aïeul [ajœl] aïeuls aïeux [ajø]   ciel [sjɛl] ciels cieux [sjø]
    œil [œj] œils yeux [jø]

6.2.1.*3*. A further small group is formed by those nouns that are 'regular' in the written language but not in the spoken language, viz. *œuf*, *bœuf*, *os*, which in the plural, *œufs*, *bœufs*, *os*, lose the final consonant that is pronounced in the singular: [ø] [bø] [o].

6.2.2. *The history of the singular ~ plural relationship.*

6.2.2.*1*. We have four main categories of plurals to discuss:

(a) those which are both descriptively and historically 'regular' (**6.2.2.2**);

---

[7] For a discussion of the plural of nouns and adjectives in *-al* and nouns in *-ail* in ModFr see for example Grevisse, §§ 278, 280, 358.
[8] For a full discussion of these, see Grevisse, §§ 282–6.

(b) those which distinguish between singular and plural in both the spoken and the written language (**6.2.2.3**);
(c) those which are now 'regular' but have undergone some remodelling (**6.2.2.4**);
(d) *œuf*, *bœuf*, *os* (**6.2.2.5**).

6.2.2.2. In the oblique case there was in OFr a constant relationship between singular and plural:

singular, no *s* ∼ plural, *s*

a state of affairs that was inherited from the Latin accusative case:

LATIN	OFR
murum ∼ muros	mur ∼ murs
patrem ∼ patres	pere ∼ peres
portam ∼ portas	porte ∼ portes
florem ∼ flores	flor ∼ flors
imperatorem ∼ imperatores	emperĕor ∼ emperĕors

In ModFr, the *s*—like other final consonants—has long since ceased to be pronounced (**3.8.4**), with the result that, in the majority of nouns, the two forms are now identical in speech. In spelling, however, the *s* remains as the sign of the plural.

6.2.2.3. In OFr, *l* before a consonant vocalized to [w] (**3.5.6**). Consequently, a further phonetic difference in addition to the presence of a final [s] was introduced into the singular ∼ plural opposition in nouns and adjectives ending in *l*:

cheval [tʃəval] ∼ chevals > chevaus [tʃəvaws]

The later loss of final *s* and the reduction of the diphthong [aw] to [o] (**4.7** (d)) gave rise to the modern opposition [al] ∼ [o] *-al* ∼ *-aux*. Nouns in *-ail* [aλ] underwent a similar development:

travail ∼ travailz[9] > travauz > travaux
[travaλ] > [travaj] ∼ [travaλts] > [travawts] > [travo]

---

[9] A [t] developed as a glide-consonant between [λ] and the following [s]: [λ] then probably became [ɫ] before vocalizing to [w].

Other examples: *journal ~ journaux*, *mal ~ maux*, *vitrail ~ vitraux*, *émail ~ émaux*.[10]

6.2.2.4. *Regularity due to analogical remodelling.*

(a) In OFr, the results of the vocalization of *l* resulted in such singular ~ plural oppositions as the following:
-el ~ -eus [el] ~ [ews]:

chevel ~ chevels > cheveus	ostel ~ osteus
cruel ~ crueus	mortel ~ morteus
quel ~ queus	tel ~ teus

-el ~ -eaus [ɛl] ~ [ɛaws]:

chastel ~ chastels > chasteaus	chapel ~ chapels > chapeaus
bel ~ bels > beaus	novel ~ novels > noveaus

-eul ~ -eus [ewl] ~ [ews]:
   seul ~ seus   filleul ~ filleus
-ol ~ -ous [ɔl] ~ [ɔws]:
   sol ~ sols > sous   mol ~ mols > mous
   chol ~ chols > chous   fol ~ fols > fous   col ~ cols > cous
-eil ~ -euz [eλ] ~ [ewts]:
   conseil ~ conseuz > conseus   vieil ~ vieuz > vieus
   pareil ~ pareuz > pareus
-oil ~ -ouz [oλ] ~ [owts]:
   genoil ~ genouz > genous

Had such words as these undergone a regular phonetic development into ModFr, we would have had a situation like that of *cheval ~ chevaux*, i.e. pairs like **châtel ~ châteaux*, **chol ~ choux*, *conseil ~* *conseus, etc. However, analogical remodelling has brought these words into line with the majority of words in which, in speech, there is no distinction between singular and plural. The remodelling can be in either direction:

(i) a new plural is formed on the basis of the singular, e.g.

hôtel ~ hôtels	seul ~ seuls	pareil ~ pareils
quel ~ quels	filleul ~ filleuls	conseil ~ conseils

[10] The *-x* of these plurals calls for explanation. Medieval scribes used a character similar to an *x* as an abbreviation for *us*: so, the plural of *cheval* could be written *chevaus* or *chevax*. Later, as a result of a contamination of these two forms, the spelling *chevaux* came into use. Similarly, *cheveus/chevex > cheveux*, *beaus/beax > beaux*, *travaux*, *vieux*, *genoux*, *cieux*, etc. The *x* was not, however, adopted in *sous*, *fous*, *mous*.

This is the explanation of the dual plurals of *aïeul*, *ciel* and *œil*, the forms *aïeux*, *cieux*, *yeux* being regular phonetic developments of the OFr forms, and *aïeuls*, *ciels*, *œils* being analogical; in each of these words, there is a distinction in meaning between the two plural forms;[11]
(ii) a new singular is formed on the basis of the plural, e.g.

cheveu ∼ cheveux	château ∼ châteaux	beau ∼ beaux
chou ∼ choux	genou ∼ genoux	sou ∼ sous
mou ∼ mous	vieux ∼ vieux	

There are however a number of relics of the OFr singulars:

(1) in the 'liaison' forms *bel*, *nouvel*, *mol*, *fol*, *vieil* beside *beau*, *nouveau*, *mou*, *fou*, *vieux*;
(2) in place names such as *Neuchâtel* (cf. *Châteauneuf*) and *Châtellerault*).

Further, as a result of analogy having worked both ways, *col ∼ cous* has produced the two words *col ∼ cols* and *cou ∼ cous*.

A number of words in -*al* and -*ail* also have remodelled plurals, e.g.

bals ∼ bals	éventail ∼ éventails
naval ∼ navals	épouvantail ∼ épouvantails

In popular speech, the tendency to have a single form in both singular and plural has been carried further than in the standard language. Such oppositions as *animal ∼ animaux*, *cheval ∼ chevaux*, for example, have been eliminated by the creation of new singulars, *un animau*, *un chevau* (i.e. the process that gave rise to *cheveu*, *château*, *chou*, etc., has operated in the case of -*al* nouns as well).

(b) One consequence of the tendency in OFr to simplify consonant clusters was to eliminate the final consonant of an uninflected form of a noun before the *s* of the plural (or of the nom. sing.). This affected in particular the consonants [p], [k] and [f]. The full declension of *drap*, for example, was:

	Sing.	Plural
Nom.	dras	drap
Obl.	drap	dras

[11] See Grevisse, §§ 282–5.

Other examples—which we quote only in the oblique—are:

coc ~ cos	coup ~ cous	chief ~ chiés
sac ~ sas	clef ~ clés	vif ~ vis
blanc ~ blans	buef ('bœuf') ~ bués	
sec ~ ses	nuef ('neuf') ~ nués	

In the MidFr period the vanished final consonant was restored in spelling in the plural under the influence of the singular:

drap ~ draps	coup ~ coups	blanc ~ blancs
clef ~ clefs (also *clé ~ clés*)		

In these words in which this final consonant, that was in danger of disappearing, was restored in pronunciation in the singular, it usually came to be pronounced in the plural too, e.g.

sac ~ sas [sas] > [sa] > sacs [sak]
sec ~ ses > secs [sɛk]
vif ~ vis [vis] > [vi] > vifs [vif]

6.2.2.5. In the words *bœuf ~ bœufs* and *œuf ~ œufs*, which are pronounced [bœf] [œf] in the singular, the pronunciation of the plural is still [bø], [ø]. A similar example is provided by *un os* [ɔs] ~ *des os* [o].

6.2.2.6. In conclusion we can say that the fact that, for phonetic reasons (viz. the loss of final *s* in pronunciation), the great majority of French nouns and adjectives have (except in liaison) no special plural forms has led to a marked tendency to make other nouns invariable also by creating either a new singular by analogy with the plural (*cheveu, beau, chou,* etc.) or a new plural on the basis of the singular (*seuls, conseils, hôtels, bals, sacs,* etc.). In popular speech this often affects those nouns that still distinguish between singular and plural in higher speech registers—the pronunciation of the plurals *bœufs, œufs, os* like the singular and, at an even more popular level, the creation of singulars like *chevau, animau.*

6.3. *Masculine and feminine adjectives.*

6.3.1. The relationship between the singular and the plural of adjectives is covered by section **6.2** above. In this section we con-

105

sider only the singular. A full descriptive statement of the relationship between masc. and fem. forms would be very long and involved. Our discussion is therefore selective.

6.3.2. *The written language.* In modern written French, the fem. of the adjective is formed from the masc. by adding -*e*[12] (unless the masc. already ends in -*e*, e.g. *rouge, triste*), with, in many cases, a modification to the preceding consonant and/or vowel, as in *vif* ~ *vive, premier* ~ *première*, or a modification to the vowel and the addition of a consonant, as in *beau* ~ *belle*.

6.3.3. *The spoken language.*

6.3.3.1. There is no constant relationship between the masc. and fem. forms of adjectives in contemporary spoken French. We shall merely mention the main types of relationship that exist and not attempt an exhaustive descriptive statement accounting for every adjective.[13]

6.3.3.2. In the spoken language, the fem. form of the adjective may be:
(a) identical with the masc., e.g.

[vrɛ] vrai ~ vraie	[dirɛkt] direct ~ directe	
[ʃeːr] cher ~ chère	[naval] naval ~ navale	
[fɛrm] ferme	[ʃoːv] chauve	[ruːʒ] rouge

(b) formed from the masc. by the addition of a consonant:

[grɑ̃] grand ~ [grɑ̃ːd] grande	[lɔ̃] long ~ [lɔ̃ːg] longue
[o] haut ~ [oːt] haute	[blɑ̃] blanc ~ [blɑ̃ːʃ] blanche
[vɛːr] vert ~ [vɛrt] verte	[œrø] heureux ~ [œrøːz] heureuse
[fo] faux ~ [foːs] fausse	[ʒɑ̃ti] gentil ~ [ʒɑ̃tij] gentille

(c) formed from the masc. by changing the final consonant:

[sɛk] sec ~ [sɛʃ] sèche   [vif] vif ~ [viːv] vive

---

[12] For some rare exceptions, e.g. *chic* and *kaki*, see Grevisse, § 351.
[13] For fairly full descriptive statements see for example Nyrop, II, §§ 446–50; G. Gougenheim, *Système* . . . , 51–4; J. Dubois, I, 69–72.

(d) formed from the masc. by changing the vowel and adding a consonant, e.g.

[so] sot ~ [sɔt] sotte	[leʒe] léger ~ [leʒeːr] légère
[fu] fou ~ [fɔl] folle	[fɛ̃] fin ~ [fin] fine
[bɔ̃] bon ~ [bɔn] bonne	[brœ̃] brun ~ [bryn] brune
	[peizɑ̃] paysan ~ [peizan] paysanne

6.3.4. *The history of the masculine ~ feminine relationship.*

6.3.4.1. The relationship between masc. and fem. adjectives in Latin was simple and regular. To quote only the accusative singular forms, which are at the origin of the French forms, there are only two types of relationship:

(a) opposition *-um ~ -am*: *durum ~ duram, asperum ~ asperam*[13a]
(b) complete identity: *fortem—fortem, pauperem—pauperem*[13b]

The factors that have led from this to the complicated system of relationships in ModFr are of two kinds, *phonetic* and *analogical*.

By OFr, these factors, that are discussed at greater length below, had led to a three-fold relationship:

(i) both masc. and fem. in *-e* [ə]: *rouge, tendre, âpre*, in which the *-e* in the masc. is a supporting vowel (**4.3.3.**);
(ii) masc. without *-e* ~ fem. in *-e* [ə]: [dyr] *dur* ~ [dyrə] *dure*; these are a continuation of the Latin *durum ~ duram* type; in some of these, phonetic development had led to a consonantal alternation, e.g. [vif] *vif* ~ [vivə] *vive*;
(iii) neither masc. nor fem. in *-e*: [fɔrt] *fort—fort*; these are a continuation of the Latin *fortem—fortem* type.

The ModFr system is, as we have seen, much more complicated.

6.3.4.2. *The origins of the final -e.*
(a) As a general rule, the only final unstressed vowel of Latin that left any trace in OFr was *-a*, which remained as [ə], written *e*. This in itself is sufficient explanation for the opposition Ǫ ~ *e*

[13a] These correspond to two different types of opposition in the nominative, viz. *durus ~ dura, asper ~ aspera*.
[13b] The corresponding nominative forms are *fortis-fortis, pauper-pauper*; some adjectives of this type have a masc. ~ fem. opposition in the nominative, e.g. *acer ~ acris/acrem-acrem*.

in the masc. and fem. of many French adjectives. In the following examples we quote only the accusative (oblique) case:

LATIN		OLD FRENCH	
masc.	*fem.*	*masc.*	*fem.*
durum	~ duram	dur	~ dure
bellum	~ bellam	bel	~ bele
bonum	~ bonam	bon	~ bone
falsum	~ falsam	faus	~ fause
sanum	~ sanam	sain	~ saine
siccum	~ siccam	sec	~ seche
vetulum	~ vetulam	vieil	~ vieille
vivum	~ vivam	vif	~ vive

(b) Many Latin adjectives, however, had only one form for both masc. and fem., e.g. *grandem, fortem, viridem, mortalem, crudelem, talem, qualem,* and in OFr their reflexes *grant, fort, vert, mortel, cruel, tel, quel* were both masc. and fem.; e.g. we find such fem. forms as *grant perte, en quel mesure, mortel vie, plus cruel chose, de tel parole, la fort cité,* etc. Very early, however, there was a tendency to bring these adjectives into line with the *dur ~ dure* type by creating new, analogical fem. forms in *-e*. In the *Vie de St Alexis* (11th century) we find *Ne vus sai dirre cum lur ledece est* **grande**, 'I cannot tell you how great is their joy', and in the *Roland* there are further examples of *grande* and of *l'herbe verte*. Nevertheless, though the original fem. forms are gradually supplanted by the analogical ones *grande, forte, verte, mortelle, cruelle, tele* (> *telle*), *quele* (> *quelle*) etc. during the OFr and MidFr periods, *grant* etc. occasionally occur as late as the 16th century.

There are some relics of the original fem. forms:

(i) in words such as *grand-mère, grand-rue, pas grand-chose,* etc., where the adjective has lost its separate identity and become fused with the noun (*une grand-mère* and *la Grand-Rue* are not the same thing as *une grande mère* and *la grande rue*);

(ii) in place-names like *Grandville, Rochefort* and *Villefort* (cf. *une ville forte,* etc.).

(c) Some masc. adjectives ended in [ə] for phonetic reasons, the [ə] having developed as a supporting vowel after certain consonant groups (**4.3.3**). Amongst these were:

álterum > altre > autre flébilem > foible > faible
ásperum > aspre > âpre ténerum > tendre
páuperem > povre > pauvre rŭbeum > *[robdʒə] > rouge

Here, there was no distinction between masc. and fem. Certain other adjectives were fitted analogically into this pattern. *Largum*, for instance, gave masc. *larc* in OFr, but the form that occurs most frequently is *large* (=fem. *large* < *larga*). Amongst others that were remodelled on the basis of the fem. in the course of OFr and MidFr were:

firmum > OFr ferm > ferme rigidum > OFr roit > roide, raide

calvum > OFr chauf > chauve[14] *vocitum > OFr vuit > vuide > vide

6.3.4.3. Phonetic factors.

(a) The simplest type is illustrated by *durum ~ duram*; as intervocalic [r] remained unchanged, this became OFr [dyr] ~ [dyrə], which, with the loss of final [ə], gave ModFr [dyːr] in both genders, *dur ~ dure*; other examples are *carum ~ caram* > [ʃeːr]*cher ~ chère*, *amarum ~ amaram* > [amɛːr]*amer ~ amère* and, with [l], *nullum ~ nullam* > [nyl] *nul ~ nulle*.

(b) When the final consonant of the masc. did not remain (as in *dur*, etc.), this produced an opposition Ø ~ consonant: *bassum ~ bassam* > OFr [bas] ~ [basə] > ModFr [bɑ] ~ [bɑːs] *bas ~ basse*; similarly:

grossum ~ grossam > [gro] ~ [groːs] gros ~ grosse
altum ~ altam > [o] ~ [oːt] haut ~ haute
sanctum ~ sanctam > [sɛ̃] ~ [sɛ̃ːt] saint ~ sainte
curtum ~ curtam > [kuːr] ~ [kurt] court ~ courte
satullum ~ satullam > [su] ~ [sul] soûl ~ soûle

and with the added opposition [e] ~ [ɛ]:[15]

primarium ~ primariam > [prəmje] ~ [prəmjeːr] premier ~ première
*leviarium ~ leviariam > [leʒe] ~ [leʒɛːr] léger ~ légère

[14] Baldness being a male characteristic, it is surprising that the fem. form should have triumphed in the case of this particular adjective; could it perhaps be the influence of the expression *tête chauve* that has brought this about?
[15] A similar opposition [o] ~ [ɔ] is found in [so] *sot ~* [sɔt] *sotte* < OFr [sɔt] ~ [sɔtə], of unknown origin.

109

(c) The relationship is further complicated by the fact that consonants could develop differently in different positions; one particularly important factor is the unvoicing of consonants when they became final (**3.8.3**), which results in such forms as *vivum ~ vivam* > [vif]*vif* ~ [viːv]*vive, salvum ~ salvam* > *sauf ~ sauve, novum ~ novam* > *neuf ~ neuve*. With the loss of the final consonant in the masc., some oppositions of this type have been replaced by one of the *bas ~ basse* type, e.g. *cal(i)dum ~ cal(i)dam* > OFr [tʃawt]*chaut* ~ [tʃawdə]*chaude* > [ʃo]*chaud*[16] ~ [ʃoːd]*chaude; sŭrdum ~ sŭrdam* > OFr *sourt ~ sourde* > [suːr] *sourd*[16] ~ [surd] *sourde; rotundum ~ -am* > *rëont ~ rëonde* > *rond*[16] *~ ronde*.

A similar situation arose from the voicing of intervocalic consonants, but the loss of the final consonant in the masc. has now brought these into the *bas ~ basse* category: *clausum ~ clausam* > OFr [klɔs] ~ [klɔzə] > [klo] *clos ~* [kloːz] *close;* similarly the Latin endings *-osum ~ -osa* > [ø] *-eux ~* [øːz] *-euse* (as in *joyeux ~ joyeuse,* etc.).

(d) The fact that [k] before [a] became [tʃ] and later [ʃ] (**3.9.2** (b)) has given the opposition *siccum ~ siccam* > [sɛk]*sec ~* [sɛʃ] *sèche;* in two words of Germanic origin, a similar opposition has been replaced by the *bas ~ basse* type with the loss of the final consonant in the masc.; [blɑ̃] *blanc ~* [blɑ̃ːʃ] *blanche, franc ~ franche;* similarly, the fact that [g] before [a] likewise became [dʒ] > [ʒ] gave OFr [lɔ̃ŋk] *lonc ~* [lɔ̃ndʒə] *longe <* Latin *longum ~ longam,* but the fem. form has now been replaced by analogical [lɔ̃ːg] *longue.*[17]

(e) Oppositions such as [peizɑ̃] *paysan ~* [peizan] *paysanne,* [plɛ̃] *plein ~* [plɛn] *pleine,* [fɛ̃] *fin ~* [fin] *fine,* [bɔ̃] *bon ~* [bɔn] *bonne,* [brœ̃] *brun ~* [bryn] *brune* are explained by various developments discussed in the section on nasalization etc., viz. lowering, the loss of final nasal consonants after a nasal vowel, and denasalization (see **4.14**).

6.3.4.4. *Analogical factors.*

(a) We have seen (**6.3.4.2.** (b)) that a masc. ~ fem. opposition has been introduced in those adjectives that, historically, had no [ə] *e* in the fem., e.g. Latin masc. and fem. *grandem* > OFr *grant* > ModFr *grand ~ grande,* etc.; in some words, the loss of fem. [ə] has eliminated the opposition again in speech, e.g. *mortalem* > *mortel ~*

---

[16] The *-d* of *chaud, sourd* and *rond* is merely a matter of spelling and has no bearing on pronunciation.

[17] *Longe,* however, remains as a noun = 'halter'.

analogical *mortelle*, both giving [mɔrtɛl], *crudelem > cruel ~ cruelle*
[kryɛl], etc.

(b) The replacement of an original masc. form by an original fem.
form has, on the other hand, eliminated the opposition in such
adjectives as *large, chauve, raide* (see **6.3.4.2** (c)).

(c) Some adjectives that had the *dur ~ dure* type opposition in
OFr now have a more highly differentiated opposition as a
result of the creation of new masc. sing. forms on the analogy of
the masc. plural (**6.2.2.4** (a)):

LATIN	OFR	MODFR
bellum ~ bellam	bel ~ bele	beau ~ belle
novellum ~ novellam	novel ~ novele	nouveau ~ nouvelle
vetulum ~ vetulam	vieil ~ vieille	vieux ~ vieille

The adjectives deriving from Latin *mollem* and *follem* (originally
a noun) have twice been remodelled analogically: the type of
analogy that we saw in *fortem > fort ~ forte* gave *mol ~ mole* and
fol ~ folle, which have since been replaced by [mu] *mou ~* [mɔl]
molle and *fou ~ folle*.

6.3.4.5. Analogical changes have the effect of increasing morphological regularity, i.e. of making the relationship between
given linguistic forms conform to a pattern to which it had
previously not conformed. However, the establishment of one
pattern may lead to the destruction of another. So, although the
creation of analogical masculines like *large, raide, chauve*, etc.,
made for uniformity between the two genders, on the other
hand:

(a) identity between the masc. and fem. forms was sacrificed to a
more widespread pattern—Q ~ [ə]—when *fort—fort* etc. became
fort ~ forte, etc.

(b) this Q ~ [ə] *e* pattern was itself sacrificed in the interests of a
regular relationship between masc. sing. and masc. plural when
bel ~ bele, mol ~ mole, vieil ~ vieille, etc., were replaced by *beau ~
belle, mou ~ molle, vieux ~ vieille*, etc. (the new sing. ~ plural relationship being *beau ~ beaux*, etc., in place of the earlier *bel ~ beaus*,
etc.).

In popular speech, the tendency to have one invariable form
for both genders and both numbers that is characteristic of such
adjectives as [ruːʒ] *rouge(s)*, [dyːr] *dur(e)(s)*, sometimes results in
the use of masc. forms for fem. (*une femme maladif, elle est furieux,*

111

elle est tout petit) or in the use of *sèche, sauve*, etc. in the masc. (like *chauve*, etc.), or in the abandonment of plurals in *-aux* (e.g. *des experts médicals*).[18]

6.3.4.6. It remains to be mentioned:

(a) that the final [ə] *e* can reappear in certain circumstances, e.g. [yn fɔrtə tãdãːs] *une forte tendance* (see **4.12.4** (d)), and

(b) that those masc. adjectives that had a final pronounced consonant in OFr but have lost it in most circumstances, retain it as a 'latent consonant' that can reappear in *liaison*; in these circumstances, the liaison form is sometimes identical in pronunciation with the fem.—[fɔrt ɛmabl] *fort aimable*, [ã plɛn ɛːr] *en plein air*, [ʒwajøz ãfã] *joyeux enfant*, etc.—and sometimes different—[œ̃ groz efɔːr] *un gros effort* (cf. [groːs] *grosse*), [œ̃ grãt ɔm] *un grand homme*[19] (cf. [grãːd] *grande*), [œ̃ lɔ̃k ivɛːr] *un long hiver*[19] (cf. [lɔ̃ːg] *longue*); the OFr forms *bel, nouvel, mol, fol, vieil* are also retained as liaison forms. It is noteworthy, however, that in popular speech there is a tendency for the masc. adjective to remain invariable, and forms like [ã plɛ̃ ɛːr] *en plein air*, [œ̃ gro aʃa] *un gro(s) achat*, [œ̃ bo edifis] *un beau édifice* can be heard.

6.4. *Comparative and superlative.*

6.4.1. The comparative and superlative of adjectives were formed in Latin, as in English adjectives of the *hard—harder—hardest* type, by means of suffixes, i.e. 'synthetically'. The comparative and superlative of *durus* 'hard', for example, were as follows (for simplicity, we give only the accusative forms, and omit the neuter):

Masc. sing.	Fem. sing.	Masc. plur.	Fem. plur.	
duriorem	duriorem	duriores	duriores	'harder'
durissimum	durissimam	durissimos	durissimas	'hardest'

In French, on the other hand, the comparative and superlative are formed 'analytically', by means of the adverb *plus* (as in English *difficult* ∼ *more difficult* ∼ *most difficult*): *dur* ∼ *plus dur* ∼ *le plus dur*.

---

[18] See H. Frei, 192, and H. Bauche, 85–6.

[19] Although the OFr spelling *grant, lonc* has been replaced by *grand, long*, the voiceless consonant [t], [k], remains in pronunciation in the liaison forms.

6.4.2. Some Latin adjectives, however, mainly those ending in
-*ius* such as *dubius* 'doubtful', formed their comparative and
superlative 'analytically' by means of the adverbs *magis* 'more'
and *maxime* 'most':

dubius ~ magis dubius ~ maxime dubius.

The use of *magis* spread to other adjectives and is now, in its
modern forms, the adverb normally used to form the comparative
in some Romance languages: Spanish *duro* 'hard' ~ *más duro*
'harder', Rumanian *bun* 'good' ~ *mai bun* 'better'. In VL *plus*
also was used as the equivalent of *magis* and has been generalized
in French, *dur* ~ *plus dur*, and Italian, *duro* ~ *piú duro*.

The superlative differs from the comparative in French only in
the use of the definite article: *ce livre est plus difficile* 'this book is
more difficult', *le livre le plus difficile* 'the most difficult book'.

6.4.3. A few Latin synthetic comparatives survived. We quote
them here in their Latin and OFr forms, but for simplicity only
in the masc. (the fem. forms are the same as the masc. in the
comparative, both in Latin and in OFr):

	LATIN		OLD FRENCH	
	Positive	*Comparative*	*Comparative*	
Nom.	bonus	mélior	miéudre	'better'
Acc.	bonum	meliórem	MEILLÓR	
Nom.	malus	péior	PÍRE	'worse'
Acc.	malum	peiórem	peiór	
Nom.	parvus	mínor	MENDRE	'smaller'
Acc.	parvum	minórem	menór	

The forms printed in small capitals are those that survive in
ModFr:

bon ~ *meilleur* ~ *le meilleur*: < *mĕliorem*
mauvais ~ *pire* ~ *le pire*: < *péior*
petit ~ *moindre* ~ *le moindre*[20]: < *mínor*

Note:

(a) that these were all already irregular in Latin; the adjectives in

---

[20] *Moindre* is not a regular phonetic development of *mendre* but has been influenced by *moins* < *minus*. ModFr *mineur* is a 14th-century borrowing from
minor.

question are among the commonest in the language and it is a common feature of language that frequently used forms are, for one reason or another, irregular;[21]

(b) that the Latin synthetic comparitives had the same alternation between nom. and acc. that we have seen in nouns like *imperátor ~ imperatórem* (**6.1.2.**2); two of the three ModFr relics listed above (viz. *pire, moindre*) in fact continue the Latin and OFr nominative;

(c) that the surviving synthetic comparatives are also used as superlatives (*le meilleur* 'the best' etc.);[22]

(d) though (*le*) *meilleur* is still the normal comparative of *bon*, *pire* undergoes strong competition from *plus mauvais*, and *moindre* as the comparative and superlative of *petit* can only be used figuratively (*de moindre importance* 'of less importance', *sans le moindre danger* 'without the least danger', but *il est plus petit que son frère* 'he is smaller than his brother').

Some other Latin synthetic comparatives survived in OFr but not, as adjectives, in ModFr, though two of the nominative forms remain as nouns:

Latin	Old French	Modern French
maior 'bigger'	maire	maire 'mayor'
iunior 'younger'	joindre	gindre 'baker's boy'

[21] Cf. *good ~ better ~ best, bad ~ worse ~ worst* in English.
[22] The Latin superlatives (e.g. **durissimus**, *parvus ~* **minimus**, *magnus; ~* **maximus**) all disappeared. ModFr *maximum* and *minimum* are borrowings from written Latin and the *-issime* of *richissime* etc. a borrowing from either Latin or Italian (or both).

ADDITIONAL BIBLIOGRAPHICAL NOTE

B. A. Woledge, 'Noun declension in twelfth-century French', *Transactions of the Philological Society* (1973), 75–97
Q. I. M. Mok, *Contribution à l'étude des catégories morphologiques du genre et du nombre dans le français parlé actuel*, The Hague–Paris, 1968

7 The articles

7.1. *Introduction.* ModFr has three articles. (i) the definite article *le*, *la*, *les*, (ii) the partitive article *du*, *de la*, (iii) the indefinite article *un*, *une*, *des*. ClLat, however, had no articles—and those Romans who could make a comparison with Greek were aware of the fact: *Noster sermo articulos non desiderat* 'Our language has no need of articles', says Quintilian.

7.2. *The definite article.*

7.2.1. The def. art. in most Romance languages, including French, derives from the Latin demonstrative *ille* 'that'.[1] Already in some late Latin texts, the use of *ille* and *ipse* (which has given the def. art. in, for example, Sardinian and some Catalan dialects) is frequent enough for one to assume that their demonstrative value was much weakened and that they were well on the way to becoming articles.

7.2.2. The forms of the def. art. in OFr are:

	SINGULAR		PLURAL	
	masc.	*fem.*	*masc.*	*fem.*
Nom.	li		li	
		la		les
Obl.	lo, le		les	

When the prepositions *a*, *de*, *en* preceded *le* (*lo*) or *les*, the following contractions occurred:

	à	*de*	*en*
le, lo	al	del	el
les	as	des	es

Before consonants, the *l* of *al*, *del* and *el* vocalized (**3.5.6**), giving *au*, *deu* or *dou* (which later became *du*) and *eu* or *ou*. *Ou*

[1] The def. art. in Greek and the Germanic languages also originates in the demonstratives. Insofar as it singles out a particular individual or individuals for attention—as in English—it still retains a certain demonstrative value. In French, as we shall see (**7.2.4**), the def. art. has taken on additional functions.

remained until the 16th century when its functions were taken over by *au*, so that we now sometimes find *au* corresponding to *en +* article, e.g. **en** *mon nom et* **au** *vôtre. Es* has disappeared except in the expressions *licence ès lettres, licence ès sciences, docteur ès lettres*, etc. *As* has been replaced by *aux*, formed on the analogy of *au*.

7.2.3. In OFr the 'definite' article merits the name: it 'defines' or specifies a particular individual or individuals:

'la gentiz damme a le conte appellé'[2] (*Ami et Amile*, c. 1200)

If the noun refers to something that is unique of its kind, the def. art. would be superfluous and so is sometimes lacking in OFr —e.g. with reference to geographical names, specific social groups, etc., e.g.

'Passet Girunde'[3] (*Roland*)
'Franceis murrunt e France en ert hunie'[4] (*Roland*)
'Paien unt tort e chrestïens unt dreit'[5] (*Roland*)

There are relics of this in the use of *Dieu* without an article and of *Noël* beside *la Noël*.

7.2.4. In late OFr, the def. art. began to be used in contexts where it no longer 'defined' a particular individual. Consequently by ModFr it has assumed a functional in addition to a semantic role: it serves as one of the characteristic 'markers' by which, except in certain constructions, some of which are referred to later, French nouns are regularly accompanied (*le pain, un pain, du pain, mon pain, ce pain, quel pain*, etc.). In ModFr, therefore, the def. art. occurs with nouns used in a completely general sense, in which case the term 'definite' article is something of a misnomer:

L'homme est mortel ('Man' as a species)
J'aime le fromage ('cheese' in general)
Les femmes sont toutes pareilles ('women' in general)
la beauté, le bonheur, la nature, la mort, etc.

In OFr, however, the article, being truly a 'definite' article,

[2] 'The noble lady called the count.'
[3] 'He crosses the Gironde' (but N.B. in the same text *sur le Rosne* 'on the Rhône').
[4] 'The French will die and France will be shamed'.
[5] 'Pagans are wrong and Christians are right.'

was not used in such contexts, and abstract nouns occur without the article as late as the 17th century:

'Femmes se ressemblent assez' (Marie de France, 12th cent.)
'Ne li faut chose . . . mais que santez' [6] (*Ami et Amile*)
'Jusques mort me consume' (Villon)
'Avarice est cause de beaucoup de maux' (Nicolas de Troyes, 16th cent.)
'Pensée fait la grandeur de l'homme' (Pascal)

There are relics of the OFr usage in expressions like *noblesse oblige, pauvreté n'est pas vice, blanc comme neige, lâcher pied, fermer boutique, par terre, après déjeuner.*

7.3. *The partitive article.*

7.3.1. In contexts such as 'to buy bread', 'to drink wine', etc., OFr—like modern English—used no article, and the construction can still occur in MidFr:

'Si mengierent pain et burent cervoise' [7] (*Queste del Graal*, 13th cent.)
'Aucuns ('some') y mettent beurre' (*Ménagier de Paris*, c. 1393)

Even with expressions of quantity (*assez*, etc.) the noun was normally used without *de* in OFr:

'Asez i ad reliques' [8] (*Roland*)

However, an alternative construction was to use *de*. This occurs in late Latin, especially with verbs of eating and drinking, but occasionally with others, e.g. in the Vulgate *comede de venatura mea* (Genesis 27, 19) (cf. English 'eat of my venison'), *tulit de fructu illius* (Genesis 3, 6) 'she took of the fruit thereof'. In OFr too *de* occurs mainly with verbs of eating and drinking:

'Mieldre convers ne puet de pain mangier' [9] (*Couronnement de Louis*)

Later examples:

'Jehan de Paris envoya . . . de viande toute chaulde' (15th cent.)
'A mesure qu'on a de lumiere . . .' (Pascal)

[6] 'He lacks nothing but health.'   [7] 'They ate bread and drank beer.'
[8] 'There are a lot of relics.'   [9] 'A better convert cannot eat bread.'

117

7.3.2. Examples having the same formal structure as in ModFr (*boire du vin*, etc.) occur in OFr, but with a different value in that the def. art. here too retains its specifying value: so, *boivre del vin* means 'to drink some of the [particular] wine', e.g.:

'But del vin k'il a el champ trové'[10] (*Chanson de Guillaume*)

As the def. art. takes on a general in addition to a specific value (**7.2.4**), the part. art. also comes to be used in a general sense. The modern usage is more or less established by the 16th century, though in literary usage *de* alone still occurs today if an adjective precedes a plural noun: *de jolies fleurs*—but in the singular the type *du bon vin* seems to be well established.

7.3.3. Relics of the OFr construction remain in such verbal or prepositional expressions as *faire attention, faire peur, porter secours, chercher fortune, avoir faim/soif/peur, par malheur, sans argent, avec difficulté*, etc. The opposition ∅ ~ part. art. sometimes corresponds to a semantic difference, as in *avec patience* 'patiently' *avec de la patience* 'by exercising patience'.

7.3.4. The use of *de/des* is formally parallel to that of *de/du/de la*, but functionally *de/des* serve as the plural of the indefinite rather than of the partitive article and so are discussed in **7.4.4** below.

7.4. *The indefinite article.*

7.4.1. The indef. art. singular in all the Romance languages derives from Latin *unus* 'one'. The OFr forms *uns* (masc. nom.), *un* (masc. obl.), *une* (fem.) retain something of the value of *unus* in that they serve to identify a particular individual[11]—'a certain one'—and are not generally used to mean 'any one'. The distinction is well illustrated by two examples from the *Vie de St Alexis*: a childless couple pray for a child, saying to God *Enfant nos done* 'Give us a child'—no article is used; when their prayer is granted we are told *Un fil lor donet* 'He gives them a son'—the reference is now to a particular individual and the article is used. Other examples of the non-use of the article, all from *Ami et Amile* (c. 1200) are:

'Veïz tu home qui me puist resambler?'[12]
'Hom qui tort a combatre ne se doit'[13]

[10] 'He drank some of the wine he found in the field.'
[11] Whereas the OFr def. art. refers to an individual previously mentioned or implied, the indef. art. singles out an individual not already so indicated.
[12] 'Have you seen a man (='any man') who looks like me?'
[13] 'A man who is in the wrong ought not to fight.'

'Qui plus blanche est que serainne ne fee'[14]
'Si faitement com fame a son mari'[15]
'N'i a evesque ne face a mon talent'[16]

Constructions of the type *Jamais* **histoire** *n'a été plus exacte* (Taine)
are a relic of this usage.

The noun is also frequently used in a general sense:

(a) as direct object of the verb, e.g. in *prêter serment* ('to engage in
the act of oath-taking' rather than 'to take a [particular] oath');
numerous such expressions remain, e.g. *donner congé, livrer bataille,
prendre place, tirer parti, trouver moyen*;
(b) in various prepositional phrases, many of which remain,
e.g. *à cheval, sans fin, sous clef*.

Even when a particular individual is referred to, the OFr
noun frequently lacks an accompanying article if qualified by an
adjective, e.g.

'Bel nom li mistrent'[17] (*Vie de St Alexis*)

No article was used when the noun characterized rather than
individualized the subject, i.e. when it had something of an
adjectival value, e.g.

'Riches hom fut'[18] (*Vie de St Alexis*)

This usage remains with reference to occupations: *je suis
professeur, il est soldat.*

7.4.2. Gradually, the indef. art. came to be used in a general as
well as in a particular sense, and ModFr has lost the distinction
that OFr made between the constructions *enfant* 'a child = any
child' and *un enfant* 'a [particular] child'. The indef. art., like
the def. art. and the part. art., has now become one of the
characteristic 'markers' of the noun.

7.4.3. In the plural, OFr generally used no article, even in a particularizing sense:

'encontra un garson qui gardoit bestes'[19] (*Ami et Amile*)

However, *un* had a plural form *uns, unes* that was used with
nouns that either denoted things going in pairs (e.g. *uns guanz*

---

[14] 'Who is whiter than a siren or a fairy.'
[15] 'Like a woman with her husband.'
[16] 'There is not a bishop who will not do what I want.'
[17] 'A fine name they gave him.'   [18] 'A rich man he was.'
[19] 'He met a boy who was looking after some [particular] animals.'

'gloves', *uns esperons* 'spurs', *unes brayes* 'breeches', *unes joes* 'cheeks'—this usage occurs as late as the 16th century, e.g. *uns ciseaulx* 'scissors') or were used in a collective sense (e.g. *uns dras* [= 'draps'] 'clothes', *unes novelles* 'news').

7.4.4. The use of *de/des* developed in OFr and MidFr as a plural indef. art. in the way in which *de/del/de la* were used as partitives, *des* being first used in a particularizing sense. The *Roland*, for example, mentions the following in a list of relics:

' La dent seint Perre et del sanc seint Basilie
E des chevels mun seignur seint Denise '[20]

As in the singular, modern literary usage prefers *de* to *des* when an adjective precedes the noun (*de jolies fleurs*—but *des jolies fleurs* occurs in speech). *Des*, however, is frequent in OFr and MidFr and as late as the 17th century:

'il eurent akaté des nouveles viandes'[21] (Robert de Clari, early 13th cent.)
'Et faisoient souvent . . . des hardies emprises, des belles chevauchies' (14th cent.)
'Des grandes et très utiles victoires' (Montaigne)
'Des grosses larmes' (Sévigné)
   On the other hand, *de* is found without an adjective:
'et aucunefois y a de cops donnés' (15th cent.)

[20] 'St. Peter's tooth, some of St. Basil's blood, and some of St. Denis's hairs.'
[21] 'They had bought fresh supplies of food.'

8 The demonstratives

8.1. *Introduction.* Standard English has a two-term system of demonstratives, *this ∼ that*, the two terms indicating nearness and distance respectively.[1] This is not by any means the only possible system. The dialects of parts of the north of England and northeast Scotland, for example, have a three-term system: *this ∼ that ∼ yon*, in which *that* and *yon* indicate different degrees of remoteness. Latin likewise had a three-term system, *hic* 'this' indicating something near or associated with the speaker (*hic liber* 'this book') ∼ *iste* corresponding to the person spoken to (*iste liber* 'that book [that you have]') ∼ *ille* to something associated with neither the speaker nor the person being addressed (*ille liber* 'that book [over there]'). On the other hand, though in ModFr the demonstrative pronouns form a two-term system (*celui-ci* 'this one' ∼ *celui-là* 'that one'), the adjectives form a one-term system (*ce livre* 'this book' or 'that book').[2]

OFr occupied a position midway between that of Latin and ModFr in that it had a two term system similar to that of English:[3] *cest* 'this' ∼ *cel* 'that' (we quote them in the forms of the masc. sing. oblique).

[1] The distinction between *this* = 'nearness' and *that* = 'distance' is a subjective not an objective one: it is fundamentally one of nearness or remoteness of interest. I may well say *Who's this?* rather than *Who's that?* of someone who is some distance away, *this* implying that I consider the person as having some relationship to myself (e.g. that he is coming towards me); on the other hand, noticing a stain on my sleeve I may say either *What's this stain?* or *What's that stain?*, the difference between the demonstratives reflecting a difference in my attitude.
[2] This may of course be converted into a two-term system by means of the particles *ci* and *là* (*ce livre-ci* 'this book' ∼ *ce livre-là* 'that book'). Nevertheless, whereas in the case of the pronouns the speaker is *obliged* to choose between *celui-ci* and *celui-là*, in the case of the adjectives the choice remains optional. Fundamentally, therefore, the adjectives form a one-term system.
[3] The fact that two languages each have a two-term or a three-term system does not necessarily mean that the functions of the corresponding forms are the same in each language. Though German *dieser* and *jener*, for example, correspond in general to English *this* and *that*, German uses *dieser* in many contexts where English uses *that*.

121

These systems can be tabulated as follows:

Latin	Dialectal English	Standard English	Old French	Modern French (adjectives)
hic	this	this	cest	
iste	that	that	cel	ce
ille	yon			

8.2. *From Latin to Old French.*

8.2.1. Latin *hic* gradually went out of use and its place was taken by *iste* (cf. Spanish *esta casa* 'this house') whose original functions were taken over by *ille*, so that the distinction 'that-of-yours' ~ 'that-over-there' was lost: i.e. the language now had a two-term system of demonstratives.[4]

8.2.2. *Iste* and *ille* were reinforced in some areas, including the north of Gaul, by a deictic particle *ecce* 'lo! behold!'.

These reinforced forms, *ecce iste* and *ecce ille*, gave the following series in OFr,[4a] (only the commoner forms are given in this table):

		SINGULAR		PLURAL	
		m.	f.	m.	f.
ecce iste	nom.	cist		cist	
			ceste		cestes
	obl.	cest, cestui		cez	
ecce ille	nom.	cil		cil	
			cele		celes
	obl.	cel, celui		cels	

[4] In some areas, such as Spain, when *iste* replaced *hic* it was itself replaced by *ipse*—which originally meant 'oneself'—e.g. Spanish *ese libro* 'that book (of yours)' < *ipsum librum*, and so a three-term system was maintained.

[4a] Each reflex of *ecce* + a form of *iste* or *ille* exists in OFr in two forms, one in *c*- and one in *ic*-, viz. *cist/icist*, *cele/icele*, *cez/icez*, etc. There is no apparent syntactical difference between the two forms. The last remaining *ic*- forms went out of current use in the 16th century, though *icelui*, *icelle*, *iceux*, *icelles* still occasionally occur in legal language. Note that both forms of the demonstrative adverb *ci/ici* still exist, the former only as a bound form (*ce livre-ci*, etc.) the latter as a free form, *ici* 'here'.

The forms *cestui*, *celui* derive from VL dative forms **istui*, **illui*, for ClLat *isti*, *illi*.

8.3. *From Old French to Modern French.*

8.3.1. There are two profound differences between the OFr demonstrative system and the ModFr system:

(a) OFr has a two-term system whereas ModFr has a one-term system for adjectives; ModFr has, indeed, a two-term system for the demonstrative pronouns (*celui-ci* ~ *celui-là*, etc.), but this does not continue the OFr system as it depends on the use of the particles *ci* and *là* and not on an opposition between reflexes of the OFr *cest* and *cel* series.

(b) Like English *this, these* ~ *that, those*, each OFr form of either series could function either as an adjective (cf. English **this** *pencil*, **those** *books*) or as a pronoun (cf. English **this** *is my pencil*, *I'll take* **those**): e.g. the *Roland* has **ceste** *bataille* and *ki* **ceste** *fait* '(celui) qui fait celle-ci', **cele** *place* and *en* **cele** 'en celle-là'. In ModFr, on the other hand, there is a distinction in function between the adjectival forms *ce*,[5] *cet, cette, ces* and the pronominal forms *celui, celle, ceux, celles*.

8.3.2. In ModFr, the forms *celui, celle, ceux, celles*, though originally demonstratives, are *not* now demonstratives but determinatives, i.e. the equivalent of English 'the one, the ones': *Quel livre?* **Celui** *que j'ai acheté ce matin* 'Which book? The one I bought this morning'; *Mes livres et* **ceux** *de mon frère* 'My books and my brother's' (= 'the ones/those of my brother').

These determinative pronouns are transformed into demonstratives by means of the particles *ci* and *là* (*celui-ci, ceux-là*, etc.), i.e. the demonstrative function as well as the function of differentiating between nearness and distance is carried solely by the particles and not by the pronouns.[6]

8.3.3. How is this transformation of the French demonstrative system to be explained? It is sometimes suggested that there was a tendency in OFr to prefer the *cest* series as adjectives and the *cel* series as pronouns. Even if this is true—which is doubtful—it is no explanation to say that the situation we are trying to explain arose not in, say, MidFr but in OFr: the problem remains the

---

[5] The pronoun *ce* (as in *c'est, sur ce,* etc.) is a different word from this adjective *ce* (as in *ce livre*) (see **8.4**).

[6] In *ce livre-ci, ce livre-là,* etc., on the other hand, the particles, which are optional, serve only to express the opposition nearness ~ distance, the demonstrative function being still expressed by *ce*.

THE FRENCH LANGUAGE: PRESENT AND PAST

same. Indeed, the idea that the *cest* forms *as a series* became adjectives and the *cel* forms *as a series* became pronouns assumes that things happened more systematically than they did. It so happened (i) that certain forms became specialized in an adjectival or pronominal function long before others of the same series, and (ii) that, though in literary French there is an apparent regularity (*cest* forms = adjectives, *cel* forms = pronouns), in the various French patois confusion reigns, with an apparently arbitrary choice of forms from amongst those of the two series.[7]

8.3.4. In what follows, we shall consider only the forms of the oblique case, the only one that remains. The principal forms in OFr were:

SINGULAR		PLURAL	
Masc.	*Fem.*	*Masc.*	*Fem.*
cest, cestui	ceste	cez	cestes
cel, celui	cele	cels	celes

8.3.5. As we have said, each of these forms could originally function either as an adjective or as a pronoun. However, as early as the 12th century one very important development took place: in the plural, *cels* ceased almost completely to function as an adjective and was replaced by *cez*, which also largely but not entirely took over the adjectival functions of *cestes* and *celes*. The reasons for this are not fully clear, but it may have been due to the influence of such forms as *les, des, mes, tes, ses*. Whatever the reason, we have, for the adjectives, the following situation (we omit *cestui* and *celui* which were used as pronouns rather than as adjectives):

SINGULAR		PLURAL	
Masc.	*Fem.*	*Masc.*	*Fem.*
cest	ceste	cez	cez
cel	cele		

The great significance of this development is that the opposition nearness ~ distance was no longer expressed in the plural.

[7] To quote only one example, in Picardy *chel* (= *cel*) is an adjective, *chetti* (= *cestui*) a pronoun, and *chelle* (= *celle*) both an adjective and a pronoun. For further details, see S. Krayer-Schmitt, *Die Demonstrativ-Pronomina in den französischen Mundarten*, Bâle, 1953.

During the OFr period, there was a further significant development, in that both *cest* and *cel* gave way to *ce* before a consonant (though they remained before vowels: *cest arbre, cel arbre*), giving the following situation:

Masc. sing. +consonant	Masc. sing. +vowel	Fem. sing.	Plural
	cest	ceste	
ce			ces
	cel	cele	

(The origin of this *ce* is not certain. It has often been considered to be a development of *cest* only, but it seems more probable that in fact it represents a phonetic development of both *cest* and *cel*.)

The opposition nearness ~ distance was therefore now seriously undermined in the singular as well. In these circumstances, it was almost inevitable that a distinction that had ceased to be observed in the masc. sing. (except before vowels) and in the plural should disappear also in the fem. sing. and in the masc. sing. before a vowel. One member or other of each of the pairs *cest ~ cel* and *ceste ~ cele* was doomed to give way to the other. It so happens that, for reasons which are not understood, *cest* and *ceste* remained, as *cet* and *cette*, in the dialect of the Paris area, but in certain other dialects forms of the *cel* series remain as adjectives.

8.3.6. There remains the problem of why the opposition nearness ~ distance disappeared in the case of the pronouns as well. The most frequently used pronominal forms were:

SINGULAR		PLURAL	
Masc.	Fem.	Masc.	Fem.
cest, cestui	ceste	cez	cestes
cel, celui	cele	cels	celes

(*Cez* occurs less frequently than the other forms, but examples of its use as a pronoun are found throughout the OFr period.) Here, there seems on the face of it no reason why the two series should not have remained as distinct as, say, *questo* and *quello* in Italian. The reason is probably the weakening and eventual obliteration of the distinction in the adjectives. The transformation of the adjectival system could well have had repercussions on the pronominal system even if the two systems had been formally distinct: it is unlikely that the language, having abandoned

125

a two-term system for the demonstratives, would have maintained it for the pronouns. In fact, the two systems were not formally distinct but, even at a comparatively late date, had some forms in common—in particular *ceste* and *cest*. From the time when these forms ceased to enter into an opposition with *cele* and *cel* as adjectives, it is almost inconceivable that they could have entered into such an opposition as pronouns.

If we accept that, in the circumstances, the semantic opposition between the two series, and with it some of the forms that expressed that opposition, was doomed to disappear, we still have to account for the fact that it is the forms of the *cel* series (*celui*, *celle*, *ceux* < *cels*, *celles*) that remain. Theoretically, one might have expected the influence of the adjectival forms *ceste* and *cest* to have operated in favour of these—and perhaps others of the same series—as pronouns, and indeed this may be the reason why in many modern dialects, in Champagne and Burgundy for example, it is largely forms of this series that function both as adjectives and as pronouns. On the other hand, forms of the *cel* series were widely used as determinative pronouns (see **8.3.2**), and this probably militated in favour of their retention as demonstrative pronouns.

8.3.7. As the old semantic opposition between the *cest* and *cel* series disappeared, the language resorted to another means of making this distinction where necessary. The adverbs *ci* (an alternative form of *ici*) and *là* came to be increasingly used in association with demonstratives. But it is a clear indication that the demonstratives had lost their function of expressing the nearness ~ distance opposition when in late OFr and MidFr we find *ci* 'here' used with the *cel* series: the 14th-century chronicler Froissart, for example, uses such forms as *cil ci* 'ceux-ci' and *cel endroit chi* 'cet endroit-ci' (*chi* is a Picard variant of *ci*); *là* with the *cest* series appears rather later, e.g. *ceste là* in the 15th-century chronicler, Commynes.

In ModFr, the use of the particles *ci* and *là* remains optional with the demonstratives, but is now compulsory with the pronouns which, without the particles, function as we have seen only as determinatives.

8.3.8. The transformation of the demonstrative system in French is an instructive illustration of the way in which, in the course of time and as the result of the combined operation of phonetic and analogical factors, a given grammatical system can be completely

126

re-structured. The elements of the ModFr system are all Latin in origin—the deictic particle *ecce*, forms of the Latin demonstratives *iste* and *ille*, and the adverbs *ci* (< *ecce hic* 'lo here!') and *là* (< *illac* 'there')—but the system itself is a wholly French creation owing nothing to Latin.[8]

8.3.9. In spoken French, the fact that *là* is tending to take over the functions of *ici* (e.g. *Je suis là* 'I'm here') has had the effect of obliterating anew the opposition nearness ∼ distance, since *ce train-là*, *celui-là*, can now mean 'this train, this one' as well as 'that train, that one'. In practice, the meaning is often clear from the context, but where necessary a distinction can be made between *celui-là* 'this one' and *celui-là-bas* 'that one', *ce train-là* and *ce train-là-bas*, etc.

8.4. *The neuter demonstrative pronoun* **ce**. French has a neuter demonstrative pronoun *ce*, which has now become semantically weakened to the point where it is approximately equivalent to the English 'it': *c'est difficile* 'it is difficult'. It survives as a determinative in the constructions *ce qui, ce que, ce dont*, etc. (*je ne comprends pas ce que vous dites* 'I don't understand *what* [lit. 'that which'] you say'), and there are some relics of its fully demonstrative value in such faintly archaic expressions as *sur ce* 'thereupon', *ce faisant* and *pour ce faire*.

This pronoun *ce* represents almost the only survival in French—and one of the very few in any Romance language—of the Latin demonstrative *hic* 'this'; more precisely, it derives from *ecce* + *hoc* (the neuter form of *hic*): *ecce hoc* > OFr *ço* > *ce*.[9]

As a demonstrative, the simple pronoun *ce* has been almost entirely displaced by the compound forms *ceci* (< *ce* + *ci*) and *cela* (< *ce* + *là*). (In speech, *cela* is usually reduced to *ça*, which is tending to go the way of *ce* and be weakened to 'it', e.g. *ça pleut* for *il pleut* 'it's raining'.)

ADDITIONAL BIBLIOGRAPHICAL NOTE

A. Dees, *Étude sur l'évolution des démonstratifs en ancièn et en moyen français*, Groningen, 1971

[8] For a more detailed study of the history of the demonstratives in French, see my article 'La transformation du système français des démonstratifs' in *Zeitschrift für romanische Philologie*, 85 (1969), 489–505.

[9] There are other relics of *hoc* in *oui* < OFr *oil* < *hoc ille* and *avec* < OFr *avuec* < *ab hoc* or *apud hoc*.

9 The possessives

9.1. *The three persons singular.*

9.1.1. Corresponding to the three persons singular, Latin had the following forms (we quote only the nominative and accusative cases, masc. and fem.) (NB *meus* etc. = 'my', *tuus* etc. = 'thy', *suus* etc. = 'his, her'):[1]

	SINGULAR		PLURAL	
	Masc.	*Fem.*	*Masc.*	*Fem.*
Nom.	meus	mea	mei	meae
	tuus	tua	tui	tuae
	suus	sua	sui	suae
Acc.	meum	meam	meos	meas
	tuum	tuam	tuos	tuas
	suum	suam	suos	suas

These forms served both as adjectives (as in English **my** *book*) and as pronouns (as in English **mine** *is red*).

9.1.2. ModFr has two distinct series of possessives, one unstressed (*mon, ma, mes*, etc.), the other stressed (*mien*, etc.). The existence of an unstressed series is first referred to by a 5th-century grammarian from Gaul, Virgilius Maro, who quotes such forms as *mus, mum, mi, mos, ma, mas, tus* for *meus, meum, mei, meos, mea, meas, tuus*. These unstressed forms became in OFr:

	SINGULAR		PLURAL	
	Masc.	*Fem.*	*Masc.*	*Fem.*
Nom.	mes		mi	
		ma		mes
Obl.	mon		mes	

(and likewise *tes, ton* and *ses, son*, etc.). The obl. forms give ModFr *mon, ma, mes; ton, ta, tes; son, sa, ses*. There is one relic of the OFr

---

[1] *Suus* also means 'their' (see **9.4.1**)

masc. sing. nom. *mes* in the word *messire*, used as a title of honour
('My Lord').

Just as *la > l'* before vowels, so *ma, ta, sa > m', t', s'* in OFr (e.g.
m'ame 'my soul', *s'espee* 'his sword'), but already in OFr these
began to be replaced by the masc. forms *mon, ton, son* which became
general in the 14th century: *mon ame, son espee*, etc.[2] Relics of the
old usage are found in *ma mie* (resulting from a misinterpretation
of *m'amie*) and in *faire des mamours à quelqu'un* (*mamour = m'amour*—
the word *amour* used to be feminine).

9.1.3. The stressed forms in OFr were:

	SINGULAR		PLURAL	
	Masc.	*Fem.*	*Masc.*	*Fem.*
Nom.	miens		mien	
		MOIE		MOIES
Obl.	MIEN		miens	
Nom.	tuens, suens		tuen, suen	
		TOUE, SOUE		TOUES, SOUES
Obl.	TUEN, SUEN		tuens, suens	

The forms in small capitals, MIEN, etc., go back to Latin (to VL
not ClLat in the case of *moie, moies, tuen* and *suen*),[3] the others are
analogical: *meus, mei, meos* etc. cannot give *mien, miens* which are
based on *mien < meum* (the only Latin form ending in a nasal
consonant)—*tuens, suens* and plural *tuen, suen* are likewise based
on masc. sing. obl. *tuen < tuum* and *suen < suum*. Of these OFr
forms, only *mien, miens* remain. As early as the 13th century,
tien and *sien* are found, modelled on *mien*, and soon after new
feminine forms arose based on these—*mienne(s), tienne(s), sienne(s)*[4]

[2] The reasons why *mon, ton, son* came to be used in the fem. are uncertain. The
topic has been much discussed, most recently by P. Rickard in his article 'The
rivalry of *m(a), t(a), s(a)*, and *mon, ton, son* before feminine nouns in Old and
Middle French' (in *Archivum Linguisticum*, XI, 1959, 21–47 and 115–147),
which includes a survey of previous work. Rickard concludes that the decisive
factor was the numerical predominance of masc. words beginning with a vowel
over the corresponding fem. words.
[3] The tonic vowel of *moie* presupposes a Latin *mēa (tonic free *ē > oi*, 4.5.4.3)
and that of *tuen, suen*, presupposes a Latin *ŏ* (tonic free *ŏ > ue*, 4.5.4.2), whereas
ClLat in fact had *mĕa, tŭum sŭum*; there must therefore have been some
remodelling in VL.
[4] Other analogical forms, *toie* and *soie*, based on *moie*, also occurred in OFr.

—and these finally prevailed in MidFr. So the ModFr forms are:

	SINGULAR		PLURAL	
	Masc.	*Fem.*	*Masc.*	*Fem.*
'my'	MIEN	**mienne**	**miens**	**miennes**
'your (thy)'	**tien**	**tienne**	**tiens**	**tiennes**
'his, her'	**sien**	**sienne**	**siens**	**siennes**

The forms in bold type are all analogical and are modelled directly or indirectly on *mien*.

Here again, as in the case of the demonstratives (see **8.3.8**), we have a system that is a wholly French creation, owing to Latin nothing but the one form *mien*.

9.2. *1st and 2nd persons plural*. The Latin possessive adjective and pronoun *noster* 'our' was declined as follows (we give only the nom. and acc. forms and omit the neuter):

	SINGULAR		PLURAL	
	Masc.	*Fem.*	*Masc.*	*Fem.*
Nom.	noster	nostra	nostri	nostrae
Acc.	nostrum	nostram	nostros	nostras

Similarly, corresponding to the second person plural was *vester*, *vestra*, etc. 'your'. It is clear from the evidence of the Romance languages that in VL these forms were replaced by **voster*, **vostra*, etc., modelled on *noster* (cf. French *notre/votre*, Italian *nostro/vostro*, Rumanian *nostru/vostru*, etc.).

As in the case of the three persons singular, these have both unstressed and stressed forms in OFr (unstressed *nostre*, *noz*,[5] stressed *nostre*; likewise *vostre* and *voz*) which have come down into ModFr in the following forms, without any distinction of gender:

	SINGULAR	PLURAL
Unstressed:	notre [nɔtr], votre	nos, vos
Stressed:	nôtre [noːtr], vôtre	nôtres, vôtres

9.3. *3rd person plural*. *Leur* 'their' derives from the Latin genitive plural pronoun *illorum* 'of them'. It is not clear whether OFr had both unstressed and stressed forms (the usual spellings—*lor*,

---

[5] The forms *noz*, *voz* (> *nos*, *vos*) were originally only masc.; they replaced unstressed fem. plural *nostres*, *vostres*, in the same way as *cez* (> *ces*) replaced *cestes* (**8.3.5**).

lour—could represent either), but the only form remaining in ModFr, *leur*, must have been originally a stressed form (*ō* > [œ] only when tonic and free) which at some stage has taken over the functions of an unstressed form also. As *illorum* did not vary for gender and number (*mater illorum* 'their mother', *fratres illorum* 'their brothers'), its reflexes *lor* etc. continue to be invariable in OFr, e.g. *leur mains*; the form *leurs* is first found in the 13th century, but plural *leur* occasionally occurs as late as the 17th century; *leur* has not developed a specifically fem. form, so we still have *leur mère*, etc.

9.4. *The syntax of the possessives.*

9.4.1. *3rd person possessives.* Latin *suus* meant 'his own, her own, their own', e.g. *suum librum videt* 'he sees his (own) book', *suum librum vident* 'they see their (own) book'; 'his, her, their' referring to someone else were expressed by pronouns meaning 'of him, of her, of them', e.g. *librum eius video* 'I see the book of him (=his book)', *librum illorum video* 'I see the book of them (= their book)'. Whereas in Spanish the *suus* construction took over all the functions of the other type in both singular and plural (e.g. *veo su libro* 'I see his/her/their book'), in French (and Italian) relics of both constructions exist, but are redistributed on an entirely different basis from in Latin:

(a) *suus* remains only in the singular but has enlarged its scope to take on the functions of *eius*: *je vois son livre*;
(b) in the plural, *leur* < *illorum* 'of them' has also taken on the meaning 'their own' and so has completely displaced *suus*: *je vois leur livre, ils voient leur livre* ('their [own] book').

9.4.2. *Pronouns and adjectives.* The unstressed forms are used only as adjectives (*mon livre, nos amis*) and the stressed forms, generally speaking, only as pronouns (*cette maison est plus grande que la mienne/la nôtre/la leur*, etc.). In OFr the stressed forms also functioned as adjectives, e.g. *un mien ami* 'a friend of mine', *ce tien ami* 'this friend of yours'; ModFr has lost this usage except as an occasional archaism in the literary language (Verlaine, for example, refers to *ce mien livre*) and is the poorer thereby (*un mien ami* is much neater than *un ami à moi* or *un de mes amis*).

The existence of two sets of forms, one set functioning as adjectives and the other as pronouns, is, here as in the case of the demonstratives (*ce-cet-cette-ces* ~ *celui-celle-ceux-celles*), an example of the way in which French has used elements that are inherited from Latin but has re-structured them into a non-Latin type of system.

131

10 Relatives and interrogatives

10.1. *Introduction.* The French systems of relative and interrogative pronouns are based on the following forms, many of which are common to both systems:

(a) *qui, que, quoi*
(b) *dont* (relative only)
(c) *quel*, etc. (interrogative only)
(d) *lequel*, etc.
(e) *qu'est-ce qui*, etc. (interrogative only).

10.2. Qui, que, quoi.

10.2.1. Latin had a whole battery of relative and interrogative pronouns, varying according to gender, number and case. In the following table, where two forms are given (e.g. *qui ~ quis*) the first is relative, the second interrogative; where only one form is given, it served as both relative and interrogative:

	Masc.	*Fem.*	*Neuter*
		SINGULAR	
Nom.	QUI ~ quis	quae ~ quis	quod ~ QUID
Acc.	QUEM	quam	
Gen.	cuius	cuius	cuius
Dat.	CUI	CUI	CUI
Abl.	quo	qua	quo
		PLURAL	
Nom.	QUI	quae	quae
Acc.	quos	quas	
Gen.	quorum	quarum	quorum
Dat.	quibus	quibus	quibus
Abl.			

Only the forms printed in small capitals have survived.

10.2.2. The drastic process of simplification that eliminated so

132

many of the Latin forms began in VL. Three important consequences of this process were:

(a) The elimination of distinctions based on gender and number in the relative pronouns:

> as subject of the verb, *qui* took over the functions of *quae* and is now used in masc. and fem., singular and plural (*l'homme/la femme **qui** arrive, les hommes/les femmes **qui** arrivent*);
> as object of the verb, *que* (< *quem* and < *quid* which took over the function of *quod*) replaced *quam, quos, quas*: *l'homme/la femme/les hommes/les femmes **que** je vois*.[1]

(b) The assimilation of relative and interrogative forms: the relative *qui* took over the functions of the interrogative *quis* 'who?', and on the other hand the neuter relative *quod* was replaced by the original interrogative *quid*; there is consequently no formal distinction in French between ***Qui** vient?* and *l'homme **qui** vient* or between ***Que** faites-vous?* and *le travail **que** vous faites*.

(c) The falling together in OFr of *qui* and *cui*, both now spelt *qui* and pronounced [ki]:[2] *qui* < *cui* remains, with reference to persons but not to things, as a relative pronoun after prepositions (*l'homme avec qui je suis venu*) and as an interrogative after prepositions and as direct object of the verb (*Avec **qui** êtes-vous venu? **Qui** voyez-vous?*).

10.2.3. In contrast to the falling together or elimination of various forms that we have considered in **10.2.2**, the one Latin form *quid* has given two forms in French according to whether or not it was stressed:

quid (stressed) > quoi   quid (unstressed) > que

The syntax of *quoi* and *que* is briefly discussed in **10.7**.

10.2.4. The relationship between Latin and French relative and interrogative forms as outlined above can be tabulated thus:

<hr>

[1] As an illustration of the beginnings of this loss of gender and number in VL, here is an extract from a 5th-century inscription, in which *qui* is used instead of the fem. *quae*: *puella **qui** vitam suam prout proposuerat gessit* 'a girl who lived her life as she had decided to'.

[2] *qui* [kwi] > OFr *qui* [ki]; *cui* [kui] > OFr *cui/qui* [kyi] > [ki] in the 12th century.

10.3. Dont. The relative pronoun *dont* derives from Latin *de unde* 'from whence'. *Unde* alone meant 'whence' in ClLat but lost the idea of '*from* a given place' and came to be used as the equivalent of *ubi* 'where, *at* a given place' (cf. Rumanian *unde*, Portuguese *onde*, 'where'); so, to express the idea of 'whence', the preposition *de* 'from' was prefixed to it. In French, the resulting *dont* extended its meaning to take on those of 'of whom, whose, of which', etc. (*l'homme dont je connais le fils* 'the man whose son I know'). *Dont* eventually lost its interrogative meaning (though it still retained it in OFr: *Dont estes vous?* 'Where are you from?') and has now largely though not entirely lost its meaning of 'whence' even as a relative (as an archaism, one still occasionally comes across examples such as *la chambre **dont** Justin se retirait* (Duhamel)): nowadays, *d'où* replaces *dont* in these constructions (*D'où êtes-vous? la chambre d'où* . . .).

The syntax of *dont* is briefly discussed further in **10.7** and **10.8**.

10.4. Quel and **lequel.** In Latin *qualis* was an interrogative meaning 'what kind of?', but in the Romance languages it came to mean 'which?', i.e. it enquired about the identity rather than about the nature of something or someone (*Quel est votre nom? Quel livre désirez-vous?*).

The OFr forms of *quel* in the oblique case (corresponding to *qualem* m. and f. sing., *quales* m. and f. plural) were: sing. *quel*, plural *queus*. The form *quelle* is analogical (cf. *grant > grande*, **6.3.4.**2 (b)), as also is the plural *quels* (**6.2.2.4** (a)).

In OFr, examples are found in which *quel* is accompanied, first as a pronoun and later as an adjective, by the definite article, e.g. *Il ne sevent **li quels** d'els la veintrat (Roland)* 'They do not know which of them will win it [the battle]'; the following example indicates that there was apparently no difference in function between *quel* and *lequel*: *Mais ço ne set, **li quels** veint ne **quels** nun* (Roland) 'He does not know which is winning and which not'. In later OFr, *lequel* appears also as a relative and becomes very frequent in MidFr, e.g. *Jakemes d'Artevelle, li quel i vint liement* (Froissart) 'J. d'A, who came joyfully'.

In OFr and MidFr *quel* and *lequel* were each used both as adjectives and as pronouns (*quel* only as an interrogative, *lequel* as both interrogative and relative). Since the 16th century, however, *quel* has been used almost exclusively as an adjective (except with *être*: e.g. *Quel est son nom?*) and *lequel* mainly as a pronoun.[3] The syntax of *lequel* is discussed more fully in **10.8**.

[3] For some examples of *quel* pronoun in poetic style in ModFr, see Nyrop,

10.5. Qu'est-ce qui, etc.

10.5.1. In OFr one occasionally finds expressions of the type *Qu'est-ce que dit avez?* This was probably not the precise equivalent of *Qu'avez-vous dit?* 'What did you say?'; each element is to be given its full value, so the example we have quoted would be better translated 'What was it you said?'. In the course of time, however, the emphatic value of such constructions weakened and in MidFr they became much more common. In ModFr, they are virtually the equivalents of the simple interrogative *qui*, etc. The constructions in question are:

(a) *Qu'est ce-qui?* 'What?' (subject) (e.g. *Qu'est-ce qui vous intéresse?* 'What interests you?')
(b) *Qu'est-ce que?* 'What?' (object) (*Qu'est-ce que vous voyez? = Que voyez-vous?*)
(c) *Qui est-ce qui?* 'Who?' (*Qui est-ce qui chante? = Qui chante?*)
(d) *Qui est-ce que?* 'Whom?' (*Qui est-ce que vous attendez? = Qui attendez-vous?*)

10.5.2. As subject of the verb with reference to things ('what?'), the periphrastic construction *qu'est-ce qui* is now the only one in general use: e.g. 'What is in the box?' and 'What's amusing him?' cannot be rendered other than by *Qu'est-ce qui est dans la boîte?* and *Qu'est-ce qui l'amuse?* The older construction with *qui* 'what?' suffered from the disadvantage that it did not distinguish between 'what?' and 'who?'; nevertheless, it survived until the 17th century (*Qui vous fait soupirer?* [Corneille] 'What makes you sigh?') and still remains in the literary language in one or two archaisms such as *Qui vous amène?* 'What brings you here?'.

The other periphrastic constructions are little more than stylistic variations on *qui* and *que*. Originally more expressive than *qui* or *que*, they have now lost all expressive value and in familiar speech may be considered as the usual construction (*Qu'est-ce qu'il dit?* rather than *Que dit-il?* etc.).

10.6. *Syntax: introduction.* The syntax of the relative and interrogative pronouns in ModFr is far too complex a subject to be discussed in detail here. We shall therefore consider only a few basic

V, § 366, and Grevisse, § 577, *Hist.*, e.g. *Je vous livre un secret.—**Quel?** (Rostand). For *lequel* adjective, see Nyrop, V, § 335 and Grevisse, § 439, e.g. *Pendant que les regards des Alliés étaient fixés sur Pétrograd, contre **laquelle** capitale on croyait que les Allemands commençaient leur marche* (Proust).

constructions and, for the rest, refer the reader to a comprehensive grammar (e.g. Grevisse, §§ 536–577).[4]

10.7. *The syntax of* **qui, que, quoi, dont.**

10.7.1. These four words can be regarded as the basic relative and interrogative pronouns of French. As the table below shows, they can fulfil nearly all the functions that relative and interrogative pronouns are called on to perform. The other two series of pronouns—*lequel* etc. and *qu'est-ce que* etc.—are, with two important exceptions, little more than stylistic alternatives to *qui, que, quoi* and *dont.*

In discussing both relatives and interrogatives, it is necessary to distinguish between those referring to people and those referring to things. In discussing relatives, a further distinction must be made within the category 'things' between pronouns referring to nouns and those referring to what for want of a better term we shall call 'indefinites' (principally the word *chose*, the pronouns *ce* and *rien*, and occasionally a previously expressed idea).

10.7.2. The main relationships expressed by the French relatives are the subject of the verb, the object of the verb, prepositional (cf. English *with whom, for which/what*, etc.) and possessive (cf. English *whose, of which*).[5] The principal functions fulfilled by *qui, que, quoi*, and *dont* are summarized in the table below.

RELATIVES

Refers to:	*Subject*	*Direct Object*	*Prepositional*	*Possessive*
People	qui (1)	que (4)	(avec) qui (7)	dont, de qui (10)
Things	qui (2)	que (5)	Ø (8)	dont (11)
In-definites	qui (3)	que (6)	(avec) quoi (9)	dont (12)

[4] See also the article by H. Bonnard, 'Le système des pronoms *qui, que, quoi* en français,' in *Le français moderne*, 29 (1961), 168–82, 241–51.

[5] In OFr and MidFr, *cui* retained its original dative value, e.g. in Villehardouin *cil* **cui** *vos obeissez* (='à qui'), *Renier de Trit*, **cui** *l'empereres Baudoins l'ot donnée* ('... à qui l'empereur B. l'eut donnée'). It also had a possessive function similar to that of English 'whose': e.g. as a relative, *le roi de France* **cui** *cousin il ere* (Villehardouin) 'whose cousin he was', *as signours par* **cui** *conseil il estoient là venu* (Froissart) 'to the lords on whose advice they had come', and, as an interrogative, *il ne set pas tres bien* **cui** *filz il fu* (*Queste del Saint Graal*) 'He does not know whose son he was'.

Refers to:	Subject	Direct Object	Prepositional	Possessive
People	qui? (13)	qui? (15)	(avec) qui? (17)	de qui? (19)
Things	Ø (14)	(a) que? (16) (b) quoi?	(avec) quoi? (18)	de quoi? (20)

N.B. (a) Ø(=zero) indicates that (at least in normal usage) the function in question is not normally expressed by any of the four pronouns in question.

(b) The boxes are numbered and an illustration of each construction is given, numbered correspondingly, in **10.7.3.**

10.7.3. The following examples illustrate the functions of the relative and interrogative pronouns tabulated in **10.7.2**:

Relatives:

(1) L'homme **qui** vient.
(2) Le livre **qui** est sur la table.
(3) Ce **qui** me plaît.
(4) L'homme **que** je vois.
(5) Le livre **que** je vois.
(6) Ce **que** je fais.
(7) L'homme avec **qui** je suis venu.
(8) Quoi *was widely used up to the 18th century, and is nowadays to some extent being revived in literary usage*, e.g. une migraine **à quoi** elle n'attachait aucune importance (*Hermant*), la vide coupole **sous quoi** la mort continue une séance de parlement et d'institut (*Mallarmé*);[6] *normally, however, this function is fulfilled by* lequel, e.g. le papier **sur lequel** j'écris, la raison **pour laquelle** je viens, les arbres **derrière lesquels** ils se cachent.
(9) Ce à **quoi** je pense.
(10) L'homme **dont** le fils est mort; *less frequently* de qui, e.g. 'les personnes **de qui** les idées et les actes s'interrogent et se répondent' (*Valéry*)
(11) Une maison **dont** le toit est de chaume.
(12) Ce **dont** je parle.

---

[6] For further examples, see Nyrop, V, § 328, Grevisse, § 352.

Interrogatives:

(13) **Qui** chante?

(14) *As we have seen* (**10.5.2**), *the periphrastic form* Qu'est-ce qui *is now required*: **Qu'est ce qui** est tombé?

(15) **Qui** cherchez-vous?

(16) (a) **Que** cherchez-vous? (b) Quoi *is used with infinitives* (Quoi répondre? Pour quoi faire?) *and, in familiar speech, in the construction* Vous cherchez **quoi**? 'What is it you're looking for?'

(17) Avec **qui** voyagez-vous?

(18) Sur **quoi** travaillez-vous?

(19) De **qui** êtes-vous le fils?

(20) J'ai déjà écrit trois chapitres.—De **quoi**?

10.7.4. In our discussion above, we considered *que* only as a direct object. In fact it also has various other functions, in particular that of indicating 'time when', as in *Un jour qu'il faisait froid, la première fois que je l'ai vu*. In 17th-century French, it could also be used to express other relationships, e.g. *Me voyait-il de l'œil qu'il me voit aujourd'hui?* (='with which') (Racine, *Andromaque*).

In popular French, *que* is widely used as a 'generalized relative' that merely indicates in a vague and unspecific way the nature of the relationship between the relative clause and the antecedent. There are two possibilities:

either (a) *que* merely replaces other relatives, e.g. *la chose **que** j'ai besoin* (=*dont*), *c'est moi **qu'**a* (=*qui ai*),

or (b) the functions of the relative are divided, the general relationship being expressed by *que*, the more specific aspects of it in some other way, as the following examples show:

*C'est moi **qui** suis arrivé le premier*: here *qui* both (i) indicates that there is a relationship between the subordinate clause and the antecedent, and (ii) functions as subject of the subordinate clause; in the popular equivalent, *C'est moi **que je** suis arrivé le premier*, (i) is expressed by *que*, (ii) by *je*; cf. *C'est nous **qu'on** est* [=*qui sommes*] *les vainqueurs*;

*la personne à **qui** j'ai donné votre lettre*: pop. *la personne **que** je **lui** ai donné votre lettre*;

*la femme **dont** le mari est mort hier*: pop. *la femme **que son** mari est mort hier*.[7]

[7] For a fuller discussion and additional examples (including some from VL and OFr), see N. Susskind, 'The decumulated relative pronoun of popular French,' in *Studia Neophilologica*, 31 (1959), 195–201.

10.8. *The syntax of* **lequel**.

10.8.1. As mentioned above (**10.4**), *lequel*, relative and interrogative, functioned both as an adjective and as a pronoun in OFr and MidFr, but is now found only very occasionally as an adjective. The Latinizing writers of the 16th century made considerable use of it, but from the 17th century onwards the tendency has been to avoid it except after prepositions and where it is an aid to clarity. In most functions, it is an alternative to *qui, que, quoi, dont*.

10.8.2. The following examples illustrate the use of *lequel* in the functions listed and numbered in **10.7.2** (N.B. *lequel* does not refer to indefinites, so Nos. 3, 6, 9 and 12 are not applicable):

Relative:

(1) *and* (2) Lequel, *which has the advantage of marking distinctions of gender and number as* qui *does not, is used especially where* qui *could be ambiguous*: il y a une édition de ce livre **laquelle** se vend fort bon marché ('There is an edition of this book which [i.e. the edition] sells very cheaply').
(4) *and* (5) Lequel *is only rarely used as direct object* (= que): Gabriel, **lequel** j'avais veu [= 'vu'] en vision (*Pascal*).
(7) Lequel *is always used instead of* qui *after* parmi *and* entre: parmi lesquels, *but only infrequently after other prepositions*.
(8) *The use of* lequel *for* quoi *is virtually obligatory after prepositions*: les crayons **avec lesquels** j'écris (but see **10.7.3**).
(10) *and* (11) Duquel, *etc., are used instead of* dont *if the relative is the complement of a noun preceded by a preposition* (*i.e. where OFr would have used* par cui conseil, *etc.* 'on whose advice'): les amis pour le bonheur **desquels** [*or* **de qui**] je travaille ('for whose happiness'); le problème à l'étude **duquel** il a consacré sa vie.

Interrogative:

Whereas as a relative *lequel* is semantically the equivalent of *qui*, etc., there is a clear distinction in meaning between the two series as interrogatives. *Qui, que, quoi* mean 'who?', 'what?', *lequel* means 'which?'. The usage is the same whether *lequel* refers to people or to things:

(13) *and* (14) **lequel** de ces garçons est votre frère?
(15) *and* (16) **laquelle** de ces couleurs préférez-vous?

139

(17) *and* (18) Avec **lequel** de vos frères voyagez-vous?
(19) *and* (20) Voilà la voiture d'un de mes frères?—**Duquel?**

10.9. *The syntax of* **qu'est-ce qui,** *etc.* The use of *Qu'est-ce qui* is obligatory in function (14) in the interrogative table in **10.7.2**: *Qu'est-ce qui vous amuse?* The other periphrastic interrogatives are alternatives to *qui* and *que* (see **10.5**).

11 Personal pronouns

11.1. *The forms of the personal pronouns.* Whereas French has long since lost its declensional system for nouns, it has retained it for personal pronouns. The system of personal pronouns in ModFr allows for a maximum of three unstressed forms, serving as subject, direct object, and indirect object respectively, and one stressed form fulfilling these three functions and also occurring after all prepositions. In fact, only one pronoun, the 3rd person plural masculine, has as many as four forms, whereas at the other extreme the 1st and 2nd persons plural have a single form for all functions:

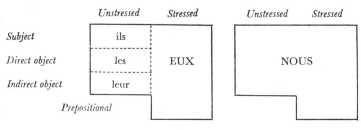

Similarly: VOUS

In between these four-form and one-form systems, there are various three-form systems:

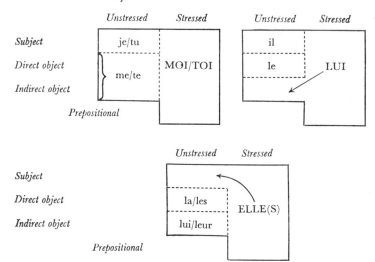

Between Latin and OFr, and again between OFr and ModFr, there has been a reduction in the number of forms, some forms taking over the functions of others.

11.2. *Subject pronouns.* The system that has changed least is that of the (now unstressed) subject forms:

LATIN	OFR	MODFR
ego	gié, jo, je	je
tu	tu	tu
ille (VL *illī)	il	il
illa	ele	elle
nos	nos	nous
vos	vos	vous
illi	il	ils
illae	eles	elles

The following points call for comment:

(a) In Latin these forms were always stressed; the OFr forms were probably both stressed and unstressed (see **11.4** and **11.5**).

(b) *il*, plural, in OFr had no *-s* in conformity with its Latin origin (*illi*); from the 14th century onwards, the analogical form *ils* appears.

(c) OFr *eles* derives not from the Latin nominative *illae* but from the accusative *illas*—compare the use of the accusative plural, *portas*, etc., of feminine nouns in place of the nominative (**6.1.2.**2).

(d) In popular spoken French, there is a tendency to reduce the number of forms in the 3rd person by using the masculine pronouns instead of the feminine, e.g. *Ils sont parti(e)s les jeunes filles*; *Ma femme il est venu(e)*.

(e) In familiar speech, *il* and *ils* are very frequently reduced to [i], e.g. *il vient* [i vjɛ̃], and *tu* becomes *t'* before a vowel, e.g. *t'as fini? t'es sûr?*

11.3. *Direct and indirect object.*

11.3.1. *Unstressed forms.* In the 1st and 2nd persons, singular and

142

plural, the Latin dative forms disappeared and their functions were taken over by the corresponding accusative forms:

	LATIN	FRENCH	
Acc.	me, te	me, te	⎫ Direct object and indirect
	nos, vos	nous, vous	⎬ object
Dat.	mihi, tibi	———	
	nobis, vobis	———	

In the 3rd person singular, both accusative and dative remain:

	LATIN	OFR	MODFR
Acc.	illum, illam	le (lo), la	le, la
Dat.	illi	li	lui

In ModFr, the OFr *li* has been replaced by *lui*, the original stressed form (**11.3.2**) deriving from VL *illui (which was presumably based on the form *cui*, the dative of the relative pronoun).

In the 3rd person plural, the original accusative remains but the dative has been replaced by a form *lor, leur* derived from the original genitive:

	LATIN	FRENCH
Acc.	illos, illas	les
Gen.	illorum	lor > leur (indirect object)
Dat.	illis	———

11.3.2. *Stressed forms.* The OFr stressed forms derived from the Latin accusative except the 3rd person singular, masc. and fem., which derived from the dative:

	LATIN	OFR	MODFR
Acc.	me, te	moi, toi	moi, toi
	nos, vos	nos, vos	nous, vous
	illos, illas	els > eus, eles	eux, elles
Dat.	illi > *illui	lui	lui
	illi > *illaei	li	ele

The following comments are necessary by way of explanation:

(a) *mē, tē* when unstressed developed like the initial syllables of words like *debere > devoir* (**4.4.4**) and give *me, te*; when stressed, they developed like the tonic free *ē* of *tēla > toile* (**4.5.4.***3*) and give *moi, toi.*

143

(b) OFr, *nos, vos* (which give ModFr *nous, vous*), though used as stressed forms, must originally have been unstressed; the stressed developments of Latin *nōs, vōs* would have been **neus, *veus*, which however never occur.

(c) The VL dative **illui* for *illi* was probably formed by analogy with the dative of the relative pronoun, *cui*; the corresponding feminine form **illaei* probably owes something to the dative of feminine nouns of the *porta* type, viz. *portae*.

(d) The OFr stressed form of the 3rd person fem. singular, *li* (e.g. *por li* 'for her') has been replaced by the original nominative, *elle*; the model for this is probably the feminine plural, *elles*, which in OFr functioned both as a nominative and as a stressed oblique form.

(e) In OFr, reflexes of *mihi* and *tibi* occur in some northern and north-eastern dialects as *mi, ti* which function as the equivalent of the stressed forms *moi, toi* (< *me, te*, see (a) above).

11.3.3. *The reflexive pronouns.* Just as *me, te* gave *me, te* when unstressed, *moi, toi* when stressed, so the accusative reflexive pronoun *se* gave French *se* and *soi*. The dative, *sibi*, disappeared and its functions were taken over by *se* (though a reflex of it, *si*, remains, like *mi* and *ti*—see **11.3.2** (e)—in some dialects as the equivalent of *soi*). (For the syntax of *soi*, see **11.7**).

11.4. *The syntax of the stressed forms.* In Latin, the subject personal pronouns are usually not expressed, as the form of the verb itself is sufficient to indicate whether the subject is 1st, 2nd or 3rd person, singular or plural: e.g. *video* 'I see', *videmus* 'we see', *vident* 'they see', etc. The pronouns are used to express emphasis: e.g. *Ego hoc volo* 'for myself, I wish this'; *tu Tarentum amisisti, ego recepi* 'You lost Tarentum, I retook it'; *et ego et tu manus sustulimus* 'both you and I raised our hands'.

In OFr, although the original subject pronouns were used very widely where there was no question of emphasis (**11.5**), they could also still be used in positions where there is a degree of emphasis, e.g.

(a) as one of two co-ordinate subjects: *e jo e vos i irum* 'both you and I will go' (*Roland*);

(b) when two subjects are contrasted: *tu es trop tendre e il trop dur* '*you* are too tender and *he* too hard';

(c) when separated from the verb: *et il, a toz ses oz . . . , s'en ala* (Villehardouin) 'and he, with his whole army, went away';

(d) when the verb is not expressed: *et qui i sera?—jou*[1] *et tu* 'who will be there?—You and I'; *et sarons liquelz est plus fors en ce pays, ou je ou vous* (Froissart) 'and we shall know which is stronger in this country, I or you';

(e) with *meïsmes* ('même'): *et il meismes mengierent ce que il porent trover* (Villehardouin) 'and they themselves ate what they could find'; also *je meïsmes* 'I myself', *tu meïsmes*, *il meïsmes*, etc.

Already in OFr, the original oblique stressed forms, *moi, toi, lui, li, eus, eles*, are sometimes found functioning as nominatives: e.g. in a 13th-century text *quant moi et li la mer passames* 'when she and I crossed the sea'; in MidFr these became more frequent, e.g. *eulz meismes*. The original subject forms, *je* etc., however, occasionally occur as stressed forms as late as the 16th century and there is still one relic of this construction in the formula *je soussigné* 'I the undersigned'.

Nowadays, *moi, toi* and stressed *nous, vous* cannot function as the grammatical subject of a verb but must be accompanied by the corresponding unstressed pronoun, *je*, etc: *moi je crois que* . . . '*I* believe that . . .', *vous, vous êtes Français mais nous, nous sommes Anglais* '*You* are French but *we* are English'. In the 3rd person, however, it is still possible in a literary style to write for example *Eux le sentaient vaguement, lui, plus nettement* (R. Bazin), *Lui ne bronchait toujours pas* (Simenon).

11.5. *The syntax of the unstressed subject forms.*

11.5.1. It is sometimes argued that some of the various OFr forms corresponding to *je*, e.g. *gié*, were stressed, and others, e.g. *je*, unstressed. The evidence for this is by no means certain. Elsewhere, one reads that the subject pronouns in OFr, as in Latin, were always stressed: the evidence contradicts this view.

As we have seen (**11.4**), there certainly are contexts where OFr *je, tu*, etc. must be considered as stressed. On the other hand, there are numerous cases where the subject pronouns cannot be considered as stressed without unduly forcing the sense of the passage. In between these two categories, there are many cases where the subject pronoun *may* be stressed, but not *necessarily* so: such examples should not of course be used as evidence either way.

11.5.2. The use of the unstressed subject pronoun in OFr depends mainly on the structure of the clause.

---

[1] *Jou* is a Picard form for *je*.

As we shall see when we discuss word order in Chapter 20, the three principal elements of the clause, **Subject**, **Verb**, and **Complement**[2] generally occur in OFr in one or other of these two orders (the use of square brackets [ ] indicates that the element in question may or may not be present):

(a) SV[C]
(b) CV[S]

It is true that there are numerous examples in verse texts in which the verb comes first (*Plurent lur filz* 'their sons weep') and that the order SCV also occurs, especially in subordinate clauses, and that CSV becomes increasingly frequent. Nevertheless, the principle that the verb tends to occupy the second position in the clause in OFr is, generally speaking, valid as far as prose texts are concerned.

Another factor to be mentioned is that, in OFr as in Latin, the form of the verb was in most cases sufficient to indicate whether the subject was 1st, 2nd or 3rd person, singular or plural.

11.5.3. Both of these factors, the tendency to place the verb in the second position and the possibility of dispensing with the subject pronoun, must be borne in mind if the use of unstressed subject pronouns in OFr is to be properly understood.

(a) CV[S]. In OFr, the subject pronoun is normally not inserted in these circumstances: e.g. *a Carlemagnes irez* 'you will go to Charlemagne', *Chrestïens ert* 'he will be a Christian', *Si grant doel ai* 'I have such great sorrow', *Perdut avum noz seignors* 'We have lost our lords' (all these examples are from the *Roland*).

(b) SV[C]. Though, as we have seen, there are exceptions, there was a strong tendency in OFr not to put the verb in first position in affirmative clauses. If there was no complement to occupy the first position and no other expressed subject (noun, demonstrative pronoun, relative pronoun, etc.), then this position was occupied by the appropriate subject personal pronoun: e.g. *je ne vus aim nient* 'I do not love you at all', *Vos en orrez noveles* 'you shall hear news of him'. *Il n'en set mot* 'He knows nothing of it',

---

[2] 'Complement' includes the direct object (**Branches d'olives** *en voz mains porterez*), the indirect object, adjectives (**Clere** *est la noit* 'clear is the night'), adverbs and adverbial expressions, infinitives (**Ademplir** *voeill vostre comande-ment* 'I am willing to carry out your command'), past participles (*fait m'avez un grant dun* 'you have made me a great gift'), etc. (these examples are from the *Roland*).

Nus le devuns ben fere 'We must do so' (examples from the *Roland*).
   Theoretically, then, the OFr system was:

(a) Subject pronoun not inserted if another element occupies the
first position, and the pronoun, if inserted, would therefore follow
the verb (order CV[S]);
(b) Subject pronoun inserted if there is no other introductory
element, and the pronoun consequently serves to prevent the
verb from falling in first position (order SV[C]).

In reality, this system is never found in its pure state. One
reason for this is that the main early literary texts are all in verse,
and metrical considerations probably account for the fact that
in these texts the verb not infrequently occupies first position. The
system is however seen functioning clearly in the early 13th-
century chronicle by Villehardouin. The following table gives the
approximate figures[2a] for the different constructions in the first
200 paragraphs of this text (N.B. Sp = 'subject pronoun inserted',
SpǬ = 'subject pronoun not inserted'):

SpV[C]	SpǬV[C]	CVSp	CVSpǬ
520	5	15	246

We see that the pronoun is almost invariably inserted if the verb
would otherwise occupy the first position in the clause, but that it
is only rarely inserted where there is an introductory complement,
i.e. where the pronoun if expressed would follow the verb.

11.5.4. It seems probable that the construction SpV was already
well-established in the pre-literary period and that the tendency
to use the pronoun in the construction CVSp was a later development. However, from the very beginnings of literary French,
examples are found of CVSp in circumstances in which the pronoun cannot be considered emphatic. By the 13th century, this
construction is already frequent in prose, and in some texts it
accounts for 25% to 60% of the cases of CV[Sp]. It is noteworthy
that in some of these texts CVSp is relatively more frequent in
conversational passages than in narrative passages, which seems to
indicate that literary usage was perhaps less advanced than the
spoken language in the extent to which it used CVSp. In the

[2a] The figures can only be approximate, as the interpretation of some examples
is doubtful.

147

Queste del Saint Graal, for example, the figures for the first 100 examples of CV[Sp] in narrative and conversation respectively are:

	CVSp	CVSpQ
Narrative	34	66
Conversation	58	42

Examples of CVSp: *a lui lais jo mes honurs e mes fieus* 'To him I leave my honours and my fiefs', *demi Espaigne vus durat il* 'He will give you half of Spain' (*Roland*); *lors oïrent il venir un escroiz de tonoire* 'then they heard a clap of thunder come' (*Queste del Saint Graal.*)

11.5.5. It is sometimes suggested that the growth of the use of the subject pronouns in French, a feature that differentiates French from other major Romance languages, in which the pronoun is little used except for purposes of clarity or emphasis (e.g. Spanish and Italian *vengo*, Rumanian *vin* 'I'm coming', but French *je viens*), is a consequence of the loss of the personal endings of the verb: i.e. when forms like (*je*) *voi*, (*tu*) *vois*, (*il*) *voit* and (*ils*) *voient*, or (*tu*) *chantes*, (*il*) *chante* and (*ils*) *chantent* came to be pronounced alike, the language had recourse to the subject pronouns to differentiate between the different persons of the verb. However, things were perhaps not as simple as this. The stages in the extension of the use of Sp were probably more or less as follows:

(a) Sp first came to be used in the construction Sp V, to prevent the verb from falling in first position; since the tendency to place the verb in second position is a feature of the Germanic languages but not of Latin or the other Romance languages, it may be that the Germanic-speaking Franks carried over this particular speech habit into the Romance speech they adopted in the north of Gaul.

(b) The fact that Sp could be used in the construction SpV without any particular emphasis led gradually to its adoption in other constructions also, and in particular in the construction CVSp; this construction occurs as early as the 10th century, and by the 13th century it seems to have been well established in the spoken language.

(c) The loss of the personal endings, though certainly not at the origin of the use of unemphatic Sp, can only have encouraged an

148

already well-established practice to have become an almost invariable one.[3]

11.5.6. The use of the unstressed subject pronoun has become so deeply rooted in the language that it is now found not only in conjunction with the stressed pronoun, where it adds nothing to the sense (e.g. *moi je dis* . . . , see **11.4**), but also, in the spoken language, where there is a noun that could serve as subject of the verb: *Mon frère il est venu; ils vont venir les garçons*, etc.

11.6. *The syntax of the oblique forms.*

11.6.1. In OFr, the stressed forms were used before the infinitive and the present participle, e.g. Villehardouin *pour lui traïr* ('pour le trahir'), *ala parler à l'empereor et lui veoir*. Occasional examples of the modern construction are found in OFr and become more frequent in MidFr; Froissart, for example, has *pour les garder, en la servant*, though here too the use of the stressed forms is usual: *pour moy aidier, en yaus assallant* ('en les assaillant'—*yaus* is a dialectal form of *eus*). The older construction still occurs in some 16th-century writers—e.g. Nicolas de Troyes *pour eulx veoir combatre, de toy marier*—and has left one relic in the expression *soi-disant* 'so-called'.

The stressed forms could also be used in OFr as direct or indirect object of a finite verb without necessarily being accompanied, as in ModFr, by the unstressed form: e.g. *Mes moi n'an porteras tu mie* (Chrestien de Troyes) 'mais tu ne m'emporteras pas moi', *et els en avint granz mesaventure* (Villehardouin) 'il leur arriva à eux un grand malheur'; ModFr: *Je ne le vois jamais lui; Moi, ça me donnait plutôt envie de rire* (Sartre).

11.6.2. In OFr, the direct pronoun always preceded the indirect: *Je le te comande*, . . . *qui le vous a dit, se Damedex le li consant* 'si Dieu le lui accorde'.[4] This is still true of two 3rd person pronouns (*je les lui donne*, etc.), but otherwise 1st and 2nd person pronouns (and *se*) precede 3rd person pronouns (*je vous le dis*, etc.). The

[3] In the 16th century, the pronoun is sometimes omitted where one would expect to find it, e.g. Rabelais *c'est raison que passes oultre* (='tu passes'), *à ce que verrez* (='vous verrez'), *le nombre me plaist et croy que* . . . (='je crois'). This is probably a Latinism and not a feature of the spoken language of the time.

[4] Examples of *le lui, le leur*, etc., are rare in OFr. The 3rd person direct object pronoun was usually not expressed before a 3rd person indirect object pronoun, e.g. *Li reis li dunet* = 'le roi la lui donne', *l'evesque lor rendy* = 'l'évêque la leur rendit'.

modern order *me le*, etc., is first found in the 15th century but the older construction still occurs occasionally in the early 17th century: *je les vous renvoie* (Malherbe), *on le m'a dit* (Voiture).

After imperatives, the order DIRECT OBJECT + INDIRECT OBJECT is still the usual one: *donnez-les-moi, dites-le-vous à vous-même.* Here too, however, in popular speech, the reverse order is found: *Chantez-vous-la* (Zola), *Donnez-moi-les, Rends-lui-le*, and this construction is accepted usage in the expression *Tenez-vous-le pour dit.*[4a]

11.6.3. When verbs such as *vouloir, pouvoir, devoir, aller, oser, falloir*, etc. were followed by an infinitive, the object pronouns in OFr preceded the modal verb, not as in ModFr the infinitive—i.e. though according to the sense they are the object of the infinitive, grammatically they are the object of the modal verb: *Je ne vos pois tenser* (*Roland*) 'Je ne peux vous protéger', *Notre gent les alerent ferir* (Villehardouin) 'Nos hommes allèrent les frapper', *il le faut faire* (Froissart). Similarly with *commencer, venir de*, etc.: *Si la commence a regarder* (Chrétien de Troyes) 'Il commence à la regarder'. In the 17th century, both constructions are current: Molière, for example, in *Le Bourgeois gentilhomme*, writes on the one hand *Vous l'allez entendre, Afin que vous me puissiez voir*, and on the other hand *Je ne puis pas m'expliquer*, etc. Other 17th-century examples of the older constructions are *Je ne l'ai pas voulu faire* (Fénelon), *Il me faut obéir* (Racine) 'Il faut m'obéir', *Je le viens de dépeindre* (Voiture).

The older construction is sometimes still found as a literary affectation: *Ils la peuvent apercevoir* (H. Bordeaux), *Si on la devait perdre* (R. Boylesve).

With such verbs as *voir, entendre, laisser, faire, envoyer* followed by an infinitive, the pronoun still precedes the main verb even though according to the sense it is the object of the infinitive: note the distinction between *Je le fais partir* 'I make him leave', *Je l'ai vu venir* 'I saw him come', etc., and *je le fais construire* 'I am having it built' (lit. 'I make [someone] build it'), *je l'ai vu tuer* 'I saw him killed' (lit. 'I saw [someone] kill him'), etc.; cf. *je l'enverrai chercher.*

11.6.4. In OFr, the unstressed oblique pronouns could not occur in the first position in the sentence. Consequently, if the verb was in the imperative and so there was no subject to introduce the

[4a] For a discussion of the reason why object pronouns follow the imperative, see **11.6.4.**

clause, the verb occupied first position and the pronouns followed:
*Secorez **moi**, Amenez **moi** mon palefroi, Alez **vos en**, Dites **le moi**,
Prenez **la**.* This construction has remained in ModFr.

However, if the imperative was preceded in OFr by some other
element, e.g. an adverb such as *or, si* or *ne* or another imperative,
then the same consideration did not apply: the object pronouns
could precede the imperative, just as they normally preceded
other forms of the verb, without occupying the first position in the
sentence: *Si **me** donnés de l'argent* 'Give me some money', *Par Deu
li dites que...* 'For God's sake tell him that...', *Or **te** haste*
'hâte-toi', *Ne **m'**oci* 'Don't kill me'. The original construction
remains with negative imperatives—*Ne me touche pas! Ne le lui
donnez pas!* Elsewhere, the order VERB + PRONOUN has been
generalized: *Téléphonez à votre frère et dites-**lui** que...* The order
PRONOUN + VERB was still regular with the second of two im-
imperatives in the 17th century: *Sèche tes pleurs, Sabine, ou **les**
cache à ma vue* (Corneille), *Apportez-moi mes pantoufles et **me** donnez
mon bonnet de nuit* (Molière). As late as the 19th century and even
occasionally in the 20th century, this construction is found as a
literary archaism: *Poète, prends ton luth, et **me** donne un baiser*
(Musset); *Taisez-vous et **m'**aimez* (Verlaine); *Faites venir vos bonnes
amies, madame, et **les** menez promener* (Anatole France).

11.7. *The syntax of* **soi**.

11.7.1. The stressed form of the reflexive pronoun, *soi*, has been
progressively losing ground to *lui, elle, eux* and *elles*.[5] In ModFr,
the use of *soi* is largely restricted, but not entirely (see **11.7.2**), to
the following circumstances:

(a) When the subject is a so-called 'indefinite' or 'indeterminate'
pronoun, particularly *on*: *on n'est jamais mieux que chez soi; on ne
peint bien que soi et les siens* (A. France).

After other 'indefinites', usage varies: *nul, en venant au monde,
n'apporte avec **soi** le droit de commander* (Lamennais); *tout le monde
rentra chez **soi**; personne maintenant ne pouvait rester chez **soi*** (Zola);
*ils sont retournés chacun chez **lui**; il n'est personne qui n'ait fait sur
lui-même cette expérience* (Guizot); however, except in the fixed
expression *chacun pour **soi***, there is a general preference for *lui*,
etc.

Similarly, nouns used in a general sense frequently take *soi*:
*un égoïste n'aime que **soi**; un avare n'amasse que pour **soi**.*

[5] For a historical survey, see G. Brandt, *La concurrence entre **soi** et **lui**, **eux**, **elle(s)**,*
Lund and Copenhagen, 1944.

(b) When there is no subject—here the use of *soi* is obligatory: *Il importe moins de ne pas mentir aux autres que de ne pas se mentir à **soi**-même* (Montherlant); *il ne faut pas toujours penser à **soi***; *l'obstacle c'est de s'imaginer qu'il n'y a que **soi*** (Colette); here belong also nouns such as *abnégation de **soi*** 'self-denial' and *amour de **soi***.

(c) in the expression *en soi*: *la guerre **en soi** est chose détestable; le concept de Dieu est possible **en soi***; and in *cela va **de soi***.

11.7.2. Though the use of *soi* with reference to 'definite' subjects was still widespread in OFr, there was already competition from *lui*, etc., e.g. *sa rereguarde avrat detrés **sei** mise* 'He will have positioned his rearguard behind him', but *desuz **lui** met s'espée* 'he puts his sword under himself' (*Roland*). In MidFr there is a good deal of fluctuation, some writers preferring *soi*, others *lui*, etc. There was a temporary increase in the use of *soi* in the work of some 16th-century writers such as Rabelais and Calvin—this is probably due at least in part to the influence of Latin. In the 17th century, however, the increase in the use of *lui*, etc. continues, and the modern usage, which prefers *lui* etc. with reference to 'definite' subjects, is more or less established. The normal construction nowadays therefore is: *il le fait pour **lui**-même, elle revint à **elle**, ils l'emmènent avec **eux***, etc.

However, in the literary language *soi* is, if only to a very modest degree, coming back into favour with reference to 'definite' subjects, both persons and things, e.g. *Il s'obligeait **soi**-même à ne jamais capituler devant eux* (Bremond); *Cet extraordinaire tableau ne ressemblait qu'à **soi**-même* (Duhamel); *Comme tous ceux qui ont devant **soi** un long avenir*.

11.8. *Pronominal ('reflexive') verbs.* The term 'reflexive verbs' is commonly used in English for what in French are more appropriately termed *verbes pronominaux*. These are of three types:

(a) true 'reflexive' verbs, i.e. those that indicate an action that the subject of the verb does to himself, e.g. *se laver* 'to wash oneself', *se faire mal* 'to hurt oneself';

(b) 'reciprocal' verbs, indicating an action which the persons referred to by the subject do to one another, e.g. *s'embrasser* 'to kiss one another', *s'envoyer des cadeaux* 'to send one another presents';

(c) what one might term 'pure pronominal verbs', in which the so-called 'reflexive' pronoun has a largely formal role with little or no semantic value, e.g. *s'écrier* 'to exclaim', *s'évader* 'to escape', *s'enfuir* 'to flee', *se réfugier* 'to take refuge', *se battre* 'to fight', *s'attendre à* 'to expect', *se méfier de* 'to mistrust', *se plaindre de* 'to complain of', *se moquer de* 'to make fun of', *se douter de* 'to suspect, surmise', *s'apercevoir de* 'to notice', *se rire de* 'to laugh at'.

Types (a) and (b) call for little comment. The problem of the precise value of the 'pure pronominal verbs' and their place within the structure of the French language has, however, given rise to considerable discussion. The author of the most recent lengthy treatment of the subject, J. Stefanini, acknowledges that he has not succeeded in arriving at a fully satisfactory classification of such verbs in OFr and in distinguishing them clearly from true reflexive verbs.[6] He suggests that both true reflexive verbs and 'pure pronominal verbs' evoke two images of a given process, one active and the other passive. These two images are quite clear in the case of true reflexive verbs: *il se lave* evokes at one and the same time the image of the subject's doing the washing and of his being washed. As for 'pure pronominal verbs', it seems that in OFr these served to express a number of different effects. There is always the danger that an interpretation of a given example may be too subjective, that we may read into it effects that were not intended by the author. We shall therefore, by way of illustration of the kinds of value that these verbs *may* have had in OFr, merely quote two examples from Stefanini with a summary of his comments:

(i) The verb *soi regarder* ('to look around'—we are not here concerned with the reflexive sense 'to look at oneself') differed from the simple verb *regarder* in that it conveyed not only the active idea of looking around but also the passive one of expecting one's gaze to be struck by something or other.
(ii) *soi mourir* added to the basic concept of 'dying' that of 'dying slowly'—a distinction that remains in ModFr (*mourir* 'to die', *se mourir* 'to be dying').

Many of the OFr verbs falling into this category (e.g. *soi regarder, soi partir, soi dormir, soi gésir*) have disappeared. Those that remain can be classified as follows:

(1) those that still express a different shade of meaning from the simple verb, e.g.

reposer ~ se reposer: *reposer* is used in such contexts as *la maison*

[6] J. Stefanini, *La voix pronominale en ancien et en moyen français*, Aix-en-Provence, 1962, 414.

153

repose sur le roc; *un bruit qui ne repose sur rien* 'is unfounded'; *se reposer* is 'to rest, to be resting'—with perhaps a trace of 'passive' value in the sense that one derives benefit from resting;

avancer ~ *s'avancer* and *approcher* ~ *s'approcher*: *s'avancer* and *s'approcher* convey an idea of deliberate intent that is absent from the simple verbs;

apercevoir ~ *s'apercevoir*: *apercevoir* refers to the objective act of catching sight of something, *s'apercevoir* to the mental process of realizing, becoming aware of something;

attendre 'to wait for' ~ *s'attendre à* 'to expect';

some verbs having *en* in the pronominal construction: *fuir* ~ *s'enfuir*, *dormir* ~ *s'endormir*, *voler* ~ *s'envoler*, *aller* ~ *s'en aller*;

(2) those that are now used only pronominally, e.g.

s'abstenir	s'évanouir	se moquer de
s'écrier	se lamenter	se raviser
s'efforcer	se méfier de	se réfugier
s'emparer de	se méprendre	se repentir

11.9. Y *and* en. *Y* and *en*, which function in French in exactly the same way as personal pronouns—*Il y pense, j'en ai trois*, etc.—derive from the Latin adverbs[7] *ibi* 'there' and *inde* 'thence', and retain their original values in, for example, *J'y vais* and *J'en viens*. Doubtless because they were the equivalent of expressions based on the use of the prepositions *à* and *de* respectively (*J'y vais/Je vais à Paris, J'en viens/ Je viens de Paris*), they came to be used as the equivalents of these prepositions + a pronoun even when the prepositions were used in a non-local sense. We therefore have in ModFr such equivalent patterns as the following:

Je pense **à** cela:	J'**y** pense
Je renonce **à** mon travail:	J'**y** renonce
Je prends trois **de** ces livres:	J'**en** prends trois
Je parle **de** ceci:	J'**en** parle

In ModFr, *y* and *en* do not often refer to people (except in partitive expressions of the type: *Il a vu plusieurs garçons/Il en a vu*

---

[7] *Y* and *en* are sometimes referred to as 'adverbial pronouns'.

plusieurs); *lui/à lui* etc. and *de lui,* etc. are generally speaking preferred, e.g.

People	*Things*
Je **lui** réponds	J'**y** réponds (= 'à la lettre')
Je pense **à lui**	J'**y** pense
Je parle **de lui**	J'**en** parle

In 17th-century French, however, *y* and *en* not infrequently refer to people: *J'y pense à tout moment* (= 'à lui') (Madame de Sévigné), *Un vieillard amoureux mérite qu'on en rie* (Corneille). Examples are indeed still found in literary French in the 19th and 20th centuries: *Trois fois la semaine elle en recevait une lettre* (i.e. 'from her daughter') (Flaubert), *Vous vous intéressez à lui? Je ne m'y intéresse pas* (Augier), and also occur in popular speech, e.g. *Nous en rêvons la nuit, nous y pensons le jour* (= 'd'elle, à elle') (the song *La Madelon*).

12 Adverbs, prepositions and conjunctions

12.1. *Adverbs of manner.*

12.1.1. In Latin, the majority of adverbs of manner were formed from the corresponding adjective by means of one or other of the suffixes *-e* or *-ter*:

dignus 'worthy'	*digne* 'worthily'
fortis 'strong'	*fortiter* 'strongly'

None of the *-ter* adverbs survive, but two common adverbs of the *-e* type remain: *bien* 'well' < *bene* (corresponding to *bonus*) and *mal* 'badly' < *male* (corresponding to *malus*).

12.1.2. French uses a number of adjectives as adverbs in certain fixed expressions: *parler* **haut/bas/fort**, *travailler* **dur/ferme**, *chanter* **faux**, *voir* **clair/net**, etc.

The usual adverbs corresponding to these and other adjectives are formed from the feminine form of the adjective and the suffix *-ment*: *hautement, bassement, fortement, durement, fermement, faussement, clairement, nettement, heureusement, premièrement, longuement, sèchement,* etc.

12.1.3. The origin of this adverbial formation, that has its parallels in all the western Romance languages but not in Rumanian, is the Latin noun *mens* 'mind'. The ablative case in Latin fulfilled a number of adverbial functions—it could, to mention only a few of these functions, express time (*septimā horā* 'at the seventh hour'), place (*terrā marique* [-*que* = 'and'] 'by land and sea'), manner (*summā diligentiā* 'with utmost care') and instrument (*gladio* 'with a sword'). When the ablative, *mente*, of the noun *mens* was used with an adjective to express manner, it indicated the state of mind in which someone performed a given action. The expression *obstinata mente* 'in a stubborn frame of mind', *mente placida* 'in a peaceful frame of mind' occur in classical Latin writers, and in later writers we find *bona mente, digna mente, devota* *mente, intrepida mente,* etc. Clearly, to say that one does something 'in a stubborn frame of mind' is much the same as saying one does it 'stubbornly'. Gradually, the original meaning of *mente* was forgotten and the construction ADJECTIVE + *mente* took on fully the role of an adverb of manner, with the result that *mente* (or *ment,* which it became in French) could be used when any idea of 'frame of mind' is completely excluded: e.g. *premièrement, nouvellement, longuement.* Though *ment* has lost both its meaning and its independent existence as a word and has been reduced to the role of a mere suffix, there is a purely formal reminder of the origin of the construction in the fact that it is the feminine form of the adjective that serves as the basis of the adverb, the noun *mens* having been feminine in gender.[1]

12.1.4. There are two groups of adverbs that, on the face of it, are exceptions to the rule that adverbs are formed on the basis of the feminine adjective. These are (a) those corresponding to adjectives in *-ant* and *-ent* and (b) those corresponding to adjectives ending in a vowel.

(a) The Latin present participle, like adjectives of the *fortem, grandem* type, made no formal distinction between masculine and feminine (e.g. the participle of *amare* 'to love' had, in both genders, nominative *amans,* accusative *amantem,* ablative *amante,* etc.). Though in Latin this *-antem* type of ending was characteristic only of the first conjugation (the other having *-entem* or *-ientem*), the ending *-ant* was used in OFr for all verbs. When the participle was used adjectivally, there was, in conformity with its origins, no distinction of gender so *vaillant,* for example, was both masculine and feminine, and the corresponding adverb was **vaillantment* which, with the simplification of the consonantal cluster *-ntm-,* became *vaillanment*[2] > ModFr *vaillamment;*[3] likewise, corresponding to *constant, savant, méchant,* etc., we have *constamment, savamment, méchamment.* When adjectives in *-ent,* e.g. *récent, prudent, ardent,* were borrowed from Latin (some in the OFr, some in the MidFr

---

[1] In OFr there is a further reminder of the origins of the construction in the fact that, where two adverbs are used together, the suffix *-ment* is sometimes added only to the second, e.g. *humeles e dulcement* 'humbly and gently' (*Roland*); this construction is still usual in Spanish, e.g. *clara y concisamente* 'clearly and concisely'.

[2] OFr likewise had the adverbs *grammment, forment* (< *fortment*), etc., corresponding to the feminine adjectives *grant, fort,* etc.; these later gave way to *grandement, fortement,* etc., formed on the basis of the new analogical feminine adjectives.

[3] The vowel [a] of the middle syllable, corresponding to [ã] of the adjective, is a consequence of denasalization (**4.14.4.4**).

period) they were equated with the existing forms in -*ant*, and so we have the corresponding adverbs *récemment, prudemment, ardemment*, etc. Forms such as *vaillantement, méchantement, prudentement, ardentement*, etc. are sometimes found in the 15th and 16th centuries, but only two of these, *présentement* and *véhémentement*, have survived.[4]

(b) Up until the MidFr period, adjectives ending in a vowel formed their adverbs quite regularly, on the basis of the feminine: *vrai—vraiement, aisé—aiséement, hardi—hardiement, éperdu—éperduement*. However, after the [ə] represented by *e* disappeared in pronunciation when it was in hiatus with another vowel, it disappeared from spelling too, and so we are left with the modern forms *vraiment, aisément, hardiment, éperdument*, etc. In a few cases, however, the lost *e* is recalled by a circumflex accent over the vowel: *assidu—assidûment, continu—continûment*, etc., and the adverb corresponding to *gai* has the two spellings *gaiement* (retaining the *e*) and *gaîment*.

12.1.5. *Comparative and superlative of adverbs.* Latin adverbs, like adjectives (**6.4**), formed their comparative and superlative synthetically:

	Comparative	*Superlative*
digne	dignius	dignissime
fortiter	fortius	fortissime

These have nearly all been replaced, as in the case of adjectives, by analytic forms (*durement—plus durement—le plus durement*) but a small number of irregular synthetic comparatives remain, and are also used as superlatives:[5]

melius 'better' > (le) *mieux*   *minus* 'less' > (le) *moins*
peius 'worse' > (le) *pis*   *plus* 'more' > (le) *plus*

12.2. *Other adverbs*

12.2.1. Very many Latin adverbs have disappeared, e.g. *hinc* 'hence' *huc* 'hither', *cras* 'tomorrow', *mox* 'soon', *semel* 'once', *paullum* 'little', *nimis* 'too much', *fere* 'almost', *vix* 'scarcely', *ita* 'thus'.

---

[4] *Lentement* is not a parallel example as *lent(e)* comes from Latin *lentum ∼ lentam*.
[5] *Magis*, the comparative of *magnopere* 'greatly', remains, not however as a comparative but as the conjunction *mais*.

Latin adverbs that have remained include:

illac > là	heri > hier	tarde > tard
tantum > tant	subinde > souvent	longe > loin
plus > plus	sic > si	non > non

Others remained in OFr, e.g. *unquam > onques* 'ever', *multum > mout*, *hodie > ui* (remaining in *aujourd'hui*), *iam > ja* (still in *déjà*, *jamais*), *magis > mais* (still in *jamais*). *Ibi* 'there' and *inde* 'thence' remain as the adverbial pronouns *y* and *en* (**11.9**).

12.2.2. Other French adverbs date from the VL period. Some derive from a syntagm PREPOSITION + ADVERB, e.g.

ad satis > assez   in simul > ensemble.

Others include *ecce hic > ici*, *paucum* (neuter adjective) *> peu*, *tostum* (neuter past participle) *> tôt*, *hora* (ablative case of *hora* 'hour') > OFr *ore > or*, *illa hora* 'at that hour' > OFr *lores > lors*;[6] **alid* (< *aliud* 'something else') + *sic > aussi*.

12.2.3. The adverbs *trop* and *guère* are of Germanic origin.

12.2.4. Many adverbs are of French formation. The following examples illustrate some of the main types:

(a) ADVERB + ADVERB: *plutôt* (< *plus* + *tôt*), *bientôt, aussitôt*;
(b) PREPOSITION + NOUN: *enfin* (< *en* + *fin*), *ensuite, parfois, davantage, autour*;
(c) ADJECTIVE + NOUN: *beaucoup* (< *beau* + *coup*), *longtemps, autrefois, toujours*;
(d) ADVERBIAL PHRASE: *naguère < n'a guère* (= 'il n'y a guère'), *dorénavant < d'or en avant*.

12.2.5. For forms serving both as adverbs and as prepositions, see **12.3.2.**

---

[6] A number of adverbs ended in an *-s* inherited from Latin, e.g. *plus < plus*, *mais < magis*, *sus < susum*. Consequently, *-s* came to be regarded as a marker of the adverb and was added to some adverbs that etymologically lacked it, e.g. *guères, oncques*. The *-s* remains in *lors, alors* and *volontiers < voluntarie*.

12.3. *Prepositions.*

12.3.1. Latin prepositions that have not survived in French include *ab* 'from, by', *ex* 'out of', *cum* 'with', *ob* 'on account of', *prae* 'in front of', *post* 'after', *sub* 'under', *circa* 'around'.

Latin prepositions that remain include:

ad > à	in > en	inter > entre	versus > vers
de > de	per > par	contra > contre	pro > pour

Sans and *sur* represent phonetically irregular developments of *sine* and *super* (or *supra*) respectively. In OFr, *apud* 'at, near' survives as *o* 'with'.

12.3.2. Many VL formations came into French both as adverbs and as prepositions (though some have since become specialized in one or other function), e.g.

ab hoc > avec	*postius > puis
ab ante > avant	ad pressum > après
de retro > derrière	foris > fors
de intus > dans	de foris > dehors
subtus > sous	susum > sus

Some of these combined with *de* in OFr, and so we have pairs such as the following, some forms remaining as adverbs, others as prepositions:

sous ~ dessous	dans ~ dedans
sus ~ dessus	puis ~ depuis

Other prepositions of VL origin include *dès < de + ex* and *chez <* (in) *casa* 'in the house (of)'.

12.3.3. Prepositions of French formation include *parmi < par + mi < per medium* 'through the middle' and *pendant*, originally a present participle (e.g. *le siège pendant* '[while] the siege [was] going on').

12.4. *Conjunctions.*

12.4.1. The great majority of Latin conjunctions have disappeared, e.g. *atque* 'and', *sed* 'but', *utrum* 'whether', *dum* 'while, until', *cum* 'when', *quoniam* 'since', *quamquam* 'although', *quamvis* 'although'.

12.4.2. The Latin conjunctions that have survived include:

et > OFr e > et	aut > ou	nec > OFr ne > ni[7]
si > OFr se > si[7]	quando > quant > *quand*	

and *que*, which appears to be a reflex of the three Latin conjunctions *quam* 'than', *quia* 'because' and *quod* 'because'.[8]

Also of ClLat origin are *mais* from the adverb *magis* 'more', and *car* and *comme* (OFr *com*) deriving from the syntagms *qua re* 'on which account' and *quo modo* 'by which means'.

12.4.3. The relationship between clauses was frequently not made as explicit in OFr as in ModFr. Indeed OFr—like modern English—sometimes dispensed with a conjunction altogether, e.g. in the *Roland*:

'Dunc ad tel doel, pur poi d'ire ne fent'[9] *and*
'Guardez de nos ne turnez le curage'[10]

Also, *que*—used alone—served to express a variety of relationships, e.g. in the *Couronnement de Louis*:

(a) *purpose*: 'A Looïs le covient enveier,
           Que il nos vieigne et secorre . . .'[11]
(b) *result*: 'Et dit soēf, **que** ne l'entendi on . . .'[12]
(c) *cause*: 'Li cuens s'abaisse, **que** paor a de mort'[13]
(d) *time*: 'Tresqu'al matin, **que** il fu ajourné . . .'[14]

This is still possible in certain circumstances, e.g. to express purpose after an imperative: *Viens **que** je t'embrasse* (A. France), and with the value of 'until' after *attendre*: *J'attendrai **que** vous ayez donné les ordres nécessaires* (Simenon); and where *que* is used to avoid repetition of *quand* or *si*:

[7] *Ni* and *si* derive from *n'i[l]* (< *ne + il*) and *s'i[l]* and finally triumphed over *ne* and *se* in the 16th century.
[8] Already in Late Latin, *quod* is found in the sense of 'that', e.g. in the Vulgate, Luke, 10, 24 *Dico enim vobis **quod** multae prophetae et reges voluerunt videre* . . . 'For I tell you, that many prophets and kings have desired to see . . .'
[9] 'Then he feels such grief [that] he nearly bursts with rage'
[10] 'Take care [that] you do not turn your hearts away from us'
[11] 'We must send him to Louis, so that he may come and help us'
[12] 'And he said softly, so that no-one heard him'
[13] 'The count bows his head, for he is mortally afraid'
[14] 'Until morning, when dawn had broken . . .'

'*Quand je regarde Auguste . . . et* **que** *vous reprochez à ma triste mémoire
. . .*' (Corneille), and
'*Si c'est une vérité et* **que** *je l'aie méconnue . . .*' (P. Bourget).

12.4.4. *Que* serves as the second element of a large number of
what are known in French as *locutions conjonctives,* the first element
consisting of an adverb (e.g. *tant que*), a prepositional phrase
(e.g. *de sorte que*), a preposition (e.g. *sans que*), a participle (e.g.
pourvu que) or, occasionally, a noun or pronoun (e.g. *faute que,
quoique*). Some of these that existed in OFr have survived, with
the same or a different meaning (e.g. *sans que, avant que; dès que =*
'after' in OFr). Others have disappeared, to be replaced by new
formations. The process of creating *locutions conjonctives* is a con-
tinuing one (cf. modern popular French *rapport que* 'because') and
the following list is far from exhaustive:

(a) Obsolete: *ainz que* 'before', *devant (ce) que* 'before', *tres que*
'until', *endementiers que* 'whilst', *mais que* 'provided that', *pour ce
que* 'because', *pour tant que* 'because', *combien que* 'although', *ja
soit ce que* 'although', *nonobstant que* 'although';
(b) extant: *avant que, après que, jusqu'à ce que, dès que, depuis que,
tant que* 'as long as', *aussitôt que, lorsque, au fur et à mesure que, bien
que, afin que, pour que, puisque, parce que, vu que, attendu que, étant
donné que, de sorte que, à moins que, pourvu que, à condition que, tandis
que, sans que.*

12.4.5. The origin and development of the *locutions conjonctives*
cannot be adequately discussed within a few pages, and here we
shall merely raise a few of the more important points.[15]
Not only does the first element vary greatly in nature (**12.4.4**)
but the value of the second element, *que,* is not always the same:

(a) In most cases, *que* is a conjunction, serving to introduce a
subordinate clause. This can be illustrated by the history of OFr
tant que 'until'. The following example from the *Roland*:

> '**Tant** chevalcherent e veies et chemins
> **Que** en Sarraguce descendent'

may legitimately be translated as 'they rode by roads and tracks

---

[15] For an overall coverage with ample illustration, see Sneyders de Vogel,
§§ 344–376 *bis*. For a full and penetrating discussion of some of the temporal
locutions conjonctives, see P. Imbs, *Les propositions temporelles en ancien français,*
Paris, 1956.

until they dismounted at Saragossa', though in fact *tant* is grammatically associated with *chevalcherent* and a literal translation would be 'they rode *so much . . . that . . .*'. Gradually, *tant* and *que* came to form a syntagm (Type: *il chevalcherent **tant** qu'ils descendent . . .*) and the *locution conjonctive* was born. Similarly, *pour ce que* 'because' originates in contexts like: *por ce sanz plus **qu'**il l'a besie . . . (Châtelaine de Vergi)* 'merely because he kissed her' (lit. 'for this reason merely, that he kissed her'). In the type PREPOSITION + *que* (e.g. *sans que, après que*), *que* serves merely to introduce the clause that acts as the complement of the preposition.

It is to be noted that OFr had a number of pairs of the type *sans que ~ sans ce que, après que ~ après ce que*; in ModFr, the *ce* remains only in *parce que* (< *par ce que*) and *jusqu'à ce que*.

(b) In OFr expressions of the type *à l'heure que, au jour que, totes les foiz que*, etc., *que* is not the conjunction but the relative pronoun (as in ModFr *chaque fois que* 'each time that', i.e. 'each occasion *on which*'); this was probably the original value of *que* also in some *locutions conjonctives* such as *lorsque (lors < illa hora* 'at the time [when]').

(c) To express the comparative of equality, OFr used *comme* (corresponding to English 'as' in 'as soon **as**, as long **as**'), e.g. *tant comme* 'as long as', *aussi tost comme, einsi comme*; by analogy with other *locutions conjonctives*, *comme* was replaced by *que (aussitôt que, ainsi que*, etc.), though *comme* occasionally occurs as late as the 16th century.

12.4.6. The origin of the *locutions conjonctives* is reflected in the following features:

(a) The two elements can occasionally still be separated, as in *lors même que* = 'même lorsque', *avant même que*, or such comparatively rare examples as the following:

'**bien**, dit-on, **qu'**il nous ait nui . . .' (Béranger)
'**Sans**, presque, **qu'**ils y songent' (P. Moreau)

(b) The second element *que* alone may be used to avoid repetition of a complete *locution conjonctive*:

'**Pour qu'**un enfant s'accoutume à être attentif, et **qu'**il soit bien frappé de quelque vérité sensible . . .' (Rousseau)
'**Lorsque** sa femme lui eut servi sa soupe . . . et **qu'**il se fut assis . . .' (Balzac)

163

'**Tandis qu**'il prenait congé de tout le petit cercle et **qu**'Emilie le reconduisait . . .' (P. Bourget)

12.4.7. Many *locutions conjonctives* have changed their meaning. For example:

(a) *puisque* and *du moment que*, that originally expressed a temporal relationship, have taken on a causal value (cf. English 'since'); a causal value has also been taken on by *parce que* that in OFr expressed means (*par* = 'by means of') but which by the 17th century replaced *pour ce que*, and by *attendu que*[16] amongst others; (b) *tandis que* and *alors que*, that originally had a temporal value, have taken on an adversative value: *Plaire n'est pour lui qu'un moyen de succès*; **tandis que** *pour elle c'est le succès même* (Laclos) (cf. English 'while').

---

[16] E.g. *Il prêchait le travail, attendu que le travail ennoblit l'homme* (Zola).

13 Verbs

I PRELIMINARIES

13.1. *Introduction.* It is impossible to discuss within the space available either all the uses of the various tenses in ModFr[1] or the history thereof. In this chapter we shall, by way of introduction, discuss in general terms (i) the relationship of tense and time and (ii) the relationship of time and aspect. Some of the uses of particular tenses are discussed in later chapters.

13.2. *Tense and time.* There is no constant relationship between tense and time. The 'present' tense,[2] for example, may refer to the past (the so-called 'historic present'):

'1925: premier entraînement de base à Moscou. L'homme **est** si doué qu'il **est** promu instructeur. Son ascension au sein du parti **est** lente, mais déjà sûre.
'Au Reichstag, 1928. [Il] **s'oppose** avec véhémence et systématiquement à l'éloquent Goebbels ... Après la prise du pouvoir par Hitler, il **émigre** en U.R.S.S.'[3]

or to the future:

Je pars demain.

On the other hand, the 'future' may refer to a present probability:

Il sera déjà là

and the imperfect to a hypothetical future:

S'il arrivait demain ...

[1] The reader is referred to (i) H. Sten, *Les temps du verbe fini (indicatif) en français moderne*, Copenhagen, 1952 (ii) P. Imbs, *L'emploi des temps verbaux en français moderne*, Paris, 1960 (iii) E. Benveniste, 'Les relations de temps dans le verbe français,' in *Bulletin de la Société de Linguistique de Paris*, 54 (1959), 69–82, and (iv) H. G. Schogt, *Le système verbal du français contemporain*, The Hague—Paris, 1968. For the use of tenses in MidFr, see M. Wilmet, *Le système de l'indicatif en moyen français*, Geneva, 1970, which also contains an extensive bibliography of works relating to the use of tenses in French at all periods.
[2] The 'present' tense is sometimes considered as a 'timeless' tense which relates to present time only in the absence of any indication to the contrary.
[3] *Paris-Match*, 7.3.1970.

In reality, such oppositions as PRESENT ~ FUTURE, PRESENT ~ IMPERFECT, IMPERFECT ~ PRETERITE, etc. express many values other than or in addition to that of temporality, e.g.

(a) *Il est déjà là* ~ *Il sera déjà là*—fact as opposed to probability;
(b) *Il écrivait la lettre* ~ *Il écrivit la lettre*—process as opposed to accomplished fact;
(c) *S'il est malade, il ne viendra pas* ~ *S'il était malade, il ne viendrait pas*—'real' as opposed to 'unreal' condition.[4]

13.3. *Time and aspect.* One essential point to bear in mind is that the French verbal system is structured around the expression not only of *time* but also of *aspect*. In particular, for each of past, present and future, the system expresses the opposition *completed action* ('perfective aspect') ~ *uncompleted action* ('imperfective aspect').[5] With reference to *present time*, for example, we have:

(a) imperfective: *je chante*—either 'I am singing [at the moment]' or 'I sing [habitually]';
(b) perfective: *j'ai chanté*[6] 'I have sung', i.e. 'at the present time, I am in the position of having completed the action of singing'.[7]

Similarly, with reference to *past time*:

(a) imperfective: *je chantais*   (b) perfective: *j'avais chanté*
and with reference to *future time*:

(a) imperfective: *je chanterai*   (b) perfective: *j'aurai chanté*

13.4. *Durative and punctual aspects.* With reference to *past time*, there is a further aspectual opposition, i.e. that between a 'durative' aspect (*je chantais*) and a 'punctual' aspect[8] (*je chantai*). It is to be

---

[4] *S'il est* . . . , etc. allows the possibility that the condition may be met, i.e. it expresses a 'real' condition, *s'il était* . . . , etc. assumes that the condition cannot be met, i.e. it expresses an 'unreal' condition.
[5] This is only one of a number of possible analyses of aspect in French. For others, see for example (i) H. B. Garey, 'Verbal aspect in French', in *Language*, 33 (1957), 91–110 (which also contains a summary of discussions of aspect by other scholars), and (ii) H. G. Schogt, 'L'aspect verbal en français et l'élimination du passé simple', in *Word*, 20 (1964), 1–17. See also **13.6** below.
[6] For a discussion of the origin and development of the perfective tenses, see **17.2.**
[7] The perfective value is particularly noticeable in association with a present tense expressing habitual action, e.g. *Quand j'ai déjeuné, je fais la sieste* 'When I've had lunch, I take a nap'.
[8] 'Punctual' in the sense that it expresses the action as happening at a given *point* in time, without reference to its duration.

noted that, in the spoken language, the 'present perfect', *j'ai chanté*, has taken over the functions of the preterite or 'past punctual' (*je chantai*) (see **17.3**). It is further to be noted that, since the OFr period, the preterite has been ousted by the imperfect in various contexts (**18.2.6**).

13.5. *Other aspectual features.* Other aspectual features of the verbal system, such as *venir de*, *aller* + INFINITIVE, *aller* + PRESENT PARTICIPLE, are discussed in **18.2**.

13.6. *Time, aspect and stage.* A critical appraisal of a number of studies and interpretations of aspect in French by various scholars is given by T. B. W. Reid in his article 'Verbal aspect in modern French'.[9] In this same article, he also takes up and develops a persuasive theory that he first enunciated in an earlier article, 'On the analysis of the tense-system in French',[10] viz. that we need not two categories, 'time' and 'aspect', but three, 'time,' 'aspect', and 'stage'. The term 'aspect' would relate to a category having two members—represented by *chantait ~ chanta*—i.e. to the opposition to which the terms *imperfective* and *perfective* have often been applied, though Reid would prefer to adopt the terms 'aspect of continuance' and 'aspect of attainment'. The term 'stage' would relate to a category having three members—represented for example by *a chanté ~ chante ~ va chanter*—to which Reid applies the terms 'stage of completion', 'stage of actuality' and 'stage of imminence' respectively.

[9] In *The French Language: Studies presented to Lewis Charles Harmer*, 1970, 146–171.
[10] In *Revue de Linguistique Romane*, XIX (1955), 23–38.

14 Verbs

II STEMS, INFIXES AND ENDINGS

14.1. *Introduction.*

14.1.1. The traditional classification of French verbs into three main conjugations: (i) *-er* verbs (*chanter*); (ii) *-ir* verbs of two types (*finir, dormir*); (iii) *-re* verbs (*vendre*), with a considerable number of 'irregular' verbs, is not an adequate framework for a descriptive analysis of the ModFr verbal system. A recent attempt by J. Dubois at such an analysis[1] without reference to historical considerations classifies French verbs in seven conjugations, according to the number of *bases* (stems) they have, ranging from seven (*être*) or six (*aller, faire*) to two (e.g. *finir, dormir, écrire, jeter*) or one (e.g. *chanter, ouvrir*). Dubois's classification, however, excludes (1) the preterite (past historic) and the imperfect subjunctive, which are rarely used in speech, and (2) the infinitive and the present and past participles. If account is taken of these, many verbs will be found to have one or, in some cases, two additional bases.

14.1.2. For our purposes, a different approach is called for. Some topics under discussion relate only to one particular tense, but others—certain stems and certain endings—are common to many or all tenses. In the interests of economy, therefore, it is desirable to discuss in one place each of these common elements.

14.1.3. The morphology of the French verb is commonly discussed as if there were only two elements, the stem and the ending, e.g.

	Stem	*Ending*
je chante	chant-	-e
je finis	fini-	-s
nous chantons	chant-	-ons
nous finissons	fini-	-ssons
je chantais	chant-	-ais
nous chantions	chant-	-ions
je chantasse	chant-	-asse
je chanterai	chant-	-erai

[1] J. Dubois, *Grammaire structurale du français: le verbe*, 1967.

There is, however, a case for considering that the 'ending' consists in some cases of two parts, which we shall refer to as the **infix** (of which there are sometimes two) and the **ending**, e.g.

	Stem	Infix(es)	Ending
je chantais	chant-	-ai-	-s
je chanterai	chante-[2]	-r-	-ai
je chanterais	chante-[2]	-r- + -ai-	-s
nous chantions	chant-	-i-	-ons
nous finissons	fini-	-ss-	-ons
nous finissions	fini-	-ss- + -i-	-ons

This reduces considerably the number of forms to be discussed: for example, -ions, -iez are no longer considered as distinct endings from -ons and -ez but as a combination of the infix -i- and the endings -ons, and -ez.

14.1.4. Many endings that were once audible and are still reflected in the written language have disappeared in pronunciation as a result of the loss of final consonants (**3.8.4**) and of final [ə] -e (**4.12.3**). Consequently, we shall have to discuss both (i) the origin and development of the endings still found in the written language, and (ii) the situation created by the loss or falling together of many of these in the spoken language.

14.2. *The endings.*

14.2.1. *The three persons singular.*

14.2.1.*1.* With very few exceptions, the endings of the three persons singular follow one of three patterns:

	(1)	(2)	(3)
1 sing.	-e	-s	-ai
2 sing.	-es	-s	-as
3 sing.	-e	-t	-a

14.2.1.*2.* *Type 1*: -e, -es, -e.

(a) These endings are found:

(i) in the present indicative of -er verbs: *je chante, tu chantes, il*

[2] For the future stem *chante-*, see **15.4.6.**

169

chante and a few other verbs, in particular *ouvrir/couvrir/offrir/ souffrir*: *j'ouvre, tu ouvres, il ouvre*:

(ii) in the present subjunctive of all verbs except *être* and *avoir*:

je chante, tu chantes, il chante
je vende, tu vendes, il vende   je fasse, tu fasses, il fasse.

(b) Regular phonetic development left [ə] -*e* in French either (1) as a reflex of unstressed -*a* (**4.3.2** (a)) or (2) as a supporting vowel (**4.3.3**). These two factors explain certain cases of the pattern -*e*, -*es*, -*e*; the others are due to analogical remodelling (3).

(1) -**e**, -**es**, -**e** *as reflexes of* **a**. The present subjunctive of Latin verbs except those of the first conjugation (*cantare > chanter*) ended in -*am*, -*as*, -*at*, of which the endings -*e*, -*es*, -*e* are a regular phonetic development:

vendam > vende	faciam > fasse	videam > voie
vendas > vendes	facias > fasses	videas > voies
vendat > vende	faciat > fasse	videat > voie

(2) -**e**, -**es**, -**e** *as supporting vowels*. In *couvrir, ouvrir, souffrir* and *offrir* whose present indicative endings in Latin were - (*i*)*o*, -(*i*)*s*, -(*i*)*t*, the -*e* is a supporting vowel after the consonant groups -*vr*-, -*fr*- (cf. *librum > livre*):

cooperio > (je) couvre   cooperis > (tu) couvres
     cooperit > (il) couvre

(3) *Analogical extension of* -**e**, -**es**, -**e**. The present indicative of first conjugation verbs developed into OFr as follows:

canto > (je) chant   cantas > (tu) chantes
     cantat > (il) chante

—i.e. 2 and 3 sing. had -*es*, -*e* corresponding to Latin -*as*, -*at*, but there was no ending in 1 sing. which had -*o* in Latin. However, some verbs of this conjugation had an -*e* in 1 sing. as a supporting vowel after -*bl*-, -*fl*-, -*tr*-, -*vr*-, [dʒ-]:

símulo > (je) semble   inflo > j'enfle   intro > j'entre
líbero > (je) livre   júdico > (je) juge [dʒydʒə]

During the OFr period, the present indicative of *chanter* etc. began to fall into line with the -*e*, -*es*, -*e* pattern with the re-
170

modelling of 1 sing. to (*je*) *chante, je dure* (for earlier *dur*), etc. The new forms became general in the 14th century.

The present subjunctive of the first conjugation had no -*e* in OFr, the Latin endings -*em*, -*es*, -*et* having regularly disappeared:

cantem > (je) chant   cantes > (tu) chanz   cantet > (il) chant
durem > (je) dur   dures > (tu) durs   duret > (il) durt

As in 1 sing. of the indicative, however, verbs such as *entrer*, *sembler*, *livrer*, etc. had a supporting vowel throughout:

j'entre, tu entres, il entre

and by analogy with these and with all other subjunctives in -*e* (see above), the subjunctive of *chanter* etc. was remodelled:[2a]

je chante, tu chantes, il chante   je dure, tu dures, il dure

These analogical forms were well established by the 14th century, though the original forms are occasionally found later, and (*Que*) *Dieu vous gard'* (= 'Que Dieu vous garde') is found in the 17th century and even in Voltaire.

14.2.1.3. *Type 2*: -**s**, -**s**, -**t**.
(a) These endings are found:

(i) in the present indicative of all verbs except regular -*er* verbs, *avoir* and *aller*, e.g.:

je finis, tu finis, il finit   je dors, tu dors, il dort
je romps, tu romps, il rompt je connais, tu connais, il connaît
je viens, tu viens, il vient   je dis, tu dis, il dit
  Note that the stem of most regular -*re* verbs ends in -*d* which functions as a purely orthographical substitute for -**t** in 3 sing.:

je rends, tu rends, il rend

[2a] The fact that the indicative and the subjunctive were identical in the plural in OFr (e.g. *chantons, chantez, chantent*, see **15.2.1**) may also have encouraged the tendency to eliminate the formal distinction between the two moods in the singular.

(cf. *répondre, vendre, descendre, étendre, défendre, perdre, fendre*, etc.)
In *vaincre* and *convaincre*, the -t is omitted after the -*c* of the stem:

je vaincs, tu vaincs, il vainc.

-**x** serves as a purely orthographical substitute for -**s** in *je/tu veux, je/tu peux, je/tu vaux.*

(ii) In the preterite (past historic) of all verbs except -*er* verbs:

je finis, tu finis, il finit	je parus, tu parus, il parut
je dis, tu dis, il dit	je crus, tu crus, il crut

(iii) In the imperfect indicative and conditional of all verbs:

je chantais	tu chantais	il chantait
je chanterais	tu chanterais	il chanterait

(b) In OFr, the endings -*s*, -*s*, -*t* were phonetically regular in the present indicative in verbs that ended in -*sco*, -*scis*, -*scit* in Latin,[3] viz. the -*ire* verbs that had adopted the inchoative endings -*isco* etc.,[3a] and *cognoscere, crescere, nascere*, etc.

Latin	OFr	ModFr	Latin	OFr	ModFr
*finisco	fenis	finis	cresco	crois	crois
*finiscis	fenis	finis	crescis	crois	crois
*finiscit	fenist	finit	crescit	croist	croît

Similarly, OFr *conois—conois—conoist, nais—nais—naist.*

(c) In OFr, the preconsonantal -*s*- of *fenist, conoist*, etc., regularly disappeared in pronunciation (3.5.2) and consequently, in -*ir* verbs, -*ist* > -*it*; in other verbs, however, -*s*- remained in spelling until the 18th century when it was replaced by a circumflex (*connaît, croît, naît*).

(d) In the preterite (past historic), the ending -*s* in 1 sing. was

[3] This is of course an over-simplification. Historically, the -*s* of 1 sing. represents the inchoative infix -*sc*- (*finisco > fenis*), the -*s* of 2 sing. represents both the infix and the Latin ending -*is* (*finiscis > fenis*), and the -*t* of 3 sing. represents the Latin ending -*t* (*finiscit > fenist*). Descriptively, the OFr endings may be analysed as:
(a) stem *fenis-* + endings ø, ø, -*t*;
or (b) stem *feni-* + endings -*s*, -*s*, -*st*;
or (c) stem *feni-* + (a) endings -*s*, -*s* (1 and 2 sing.), (b) infix -*s*- + ending -*t* (3 sing.).
[3a] For a fuller discussion of the inchoative endings, see 15.2.2.

regular in OFr in a number of verbs that had inherited an *s* from Latin.[3b] The ending -*s* of 2 sing. is problematic: regularly, -*isti* would have given -*ist* (see **14.2.1.4** (d)).

The following are some typical examples:

Latin	OFr	ModFr	Latin	OFr	ModFr
misi	mis	mis	dixi	dis	dis
misisti	mesis[4]	mis	dixisti	desis[4]	dis
misit	mist	mit	dixit	dist	dit
*presi[5]	pris	pris	conclusi	conclus	conclus
*presisti	presis[4]	pris	conclusisti	conclusis[4]	conclus
*presit	prist	prit	conclusit	conclust	conclut

Similarly, in 1 sing. of some other verbs:

scripsi > escris[6]   feci > [fits] > fis   conduxi > conduis[6]

(e) In other verbs, however, there was no -*s* in 1 sing. in the present indicative and/or preterite:

PRESENT

Latin	OFr	ModFr	Latin	OFr	ModFr
vendo	vent	vends	video	voi	vois
vendis	venz	vends	vides	voiz	vois
vendit	vent	vend	videt	voit	voit

Similarly, in 1 sing. of some other verbs:

dormio > OFr dor(m) > dors   dico > OFr di > dis
credo > OFr croi > crois   lego > OFr li > lis
prehendo > OFr prent > prends   venio > OFr vien (viegn) >
                                                         viens

vivo > OFr vif > vis   bibo > OFr boif > bois

[3b] As in the case of *fenis* < *finisco* (see note 3 above), the -*s* of *mis* < *misi*, *escris* < *scripsi*, etc., though not deriving from a Latin ending, may be considered as an ending in OFr.

[4] For these 2 sing. forms and their subsequent replacement by *mis*, *dis*, *pris*, *conclus*, see **15.5.7** and **8**.

[5] For ClLat *prehendi*.

[6] For the replacement of these forms by *écrivis* and *conduisis*, see **15.5.7** (e).

173

PRETERITE

Latin	OFr	ModFr	Latin	OFr	ModFr
finivi	feni	finis	parui	parui	parus
finivisti	fenis	finis	paruisti	parus	parus
finivit	feni	finit	paruit	paru	parut
vidi	vi	vis	debui	dui	dus
vidisti	vēis	vis	debuisti	dĕus	dus
vidit	vit	vit	debuit	dut	dut

(f) It is clear that, in the OFr and MidFr periods, -s came to be regarded as a characteristic ending of 1 sing. and that 1 sing. forms ending in -i or a consonant were gradually remodelled on the basis of those forms ending in -s. As late as the 16th and 17th centuries, however, there is still considerable fluctuation in usage and much debate amongst grammarians as to which forms are to be recommended; Marot, for example, uses both *je dy/escry/croy*, etc. and *je dis/escris/crois*, etc.

As a general rule, the forms in -s were well established in both tenses by the end of the 17th century, though later poets occasionally make use of forms without -s in the present tense for reasons of rhyme, e.g. *je croi* rhyming with *roi* (Musset), *je te voi* with *moi* (Hugo).[7]

(g) In early OFr, 3 sing. of the preterite of verbs like *finir*, *paraître* ended in a -t, pronounced [θ], and as everywhere else (**3.8.2** (b)) this [θ] disappeared around 1200:

Latin	Early OFr	Later OFr
finivit	fenit [-iθ]	feni
paruit	parut [-yθ]	paru

In 3 sing. of all strong preterites, however, (for the term 'strong', see **15.5.7** (c)) the ending was -t [t],[8] as also in the present indicative of many verbs, and the imperfect indicative

---

[7] One of the more absurd conventions of French versification is that words ending in a vowel in spelling may not rhyme with words ending in a consonant in spelling, even if to the ear the words form a perfect rhyme (e.g. *moi* and *vois*).

[8] If we accept the view that *finivit, paruit*, etc. became *finit, parút*, etc. in VL (see **15.5.1**), then the final [t] was at all stages unsupported (i.e. preceded by a vowel) and so became [θ] and later disappeared; the [t] of *vidit, misit, dixit*, etc. was supported by the preceding consonant when the unstressed vowel of the final syllable disappeared, and so remained in OFr as [t] (*misit > mist*, etc.), even when the supporting consonant itself disappeared (*vidit > *vid't > vit*).

and subjunctive of all verbs. -*t* therefore came to be considered as a characteristic 3 sing. ending and gradually this ending appeared in *fenit, dormit, parut*, etc., for earlier *feni, dormi, paru*, etc. The first examples of this are found in the 13th century, and by the 16th century the forms in -*i*, -*u* had been virtually eliminated.
(h) In the types of verbs we have so far been discussing, OFr had the following types of endings (℺ = 'no ending'): ·

(i) -s, -s, -t $\begin{cases} \text{Present: } \textit{fenis, fenis, fenist} \\ \text{Preterite: } \textit{dis, desis, dist} \end{cases}$

(ii) ℺, -s, -t $\begin{cases} \text{Present: } \textit{voi, vois, voit} \\ \text{Preterite: } \textit{vi, veïs, vit} \end{cases}$

(iii) ℺, -s, ℺   Preterite: *feni, fenis, feni*

(iv) -i, -s, ℺   Preterite: *parui, parus, paru*

By early ModFr, these had been reduced to one type only, viz. (1): -s, -s, -t.
(j) For the spread of the -*s*, -*s*, -*t* endings to the imperfect indicative and the conditional, see **15.3.4.3**.

14.2.1.4. *Type 3*: -ai, -as, -a.
(a) These endings are found:

(i) in the present tense of avoir: *j'ai, tu as, il a*;
(ii) in the future tense of all verbs: *chanterai, chanteras, chantera*;
(iii) in the preterite of -*er* verbs: *chantai, chantas, chanta*.

(b) The present indicative of the Latin verb *habere* 'to have' underwent certain contractions in VL, and the probable development is:

ClLat	VL	OFr
habeo	[ajo]	ai
habes	[as]	as
habet	[at]	at [aθ] > a

(c) As we shall see (**15.4.2.1**), the French future tense derives from the syntagm INFINITIVE + *habeo*, etc. The endings -*ai*, -*as*, -*a* of the future are therefore historically as well as descriptively identical with those of the present indicative of *avoir*.
(d) In the preterite, Latin 1 sing. *cantavi* > VL *cantái* (see **15.5.1**); the development of *cantái* to OFr *chantai* poses no problem. The 2 and 3 sing. forms however are perplexing:

2 sing.: ClLat *cantavísti* > VL *cantásti* (cf. Spanish *cantaste*,

175

Italian *cantasti*); this would have given in French not *chantas* but *chantast, and similarly *finivisti, paruisti* would have given **fenist,* *parust. However, the forms in *-st* do not occur in French. It may be that, even before the emergence of OFr as a written language, *-s* was regarded as a 2 sing. ending and *-st, -t* as 3 sing. endings, and so the anomalous 2 sing.-*st* of the preterite was replaced by *-s* by analogy with other tenses.

3 sing.: just as *cantavi* and *cantavisti* were reduced to *cantai* and *cantasti*, so, in 3 sing., *cantavit* was sometimes reduced to *cantāt*; examples of the ending *-āt* are attested in ClLat (e.g. *irritāt, disturbāt* in Lucretius) and this ending would satisfactorily explain *chanta* etc. in French. However, the attested examples of *-āt* are very rare and the evidence of other Romance languages suggests that the form that *cantavit* etc. generally took in VL was not *cantāt* but *cantaut—such forms are occasionally found in non-Classical sources, e.g. *exmuccaut* in one of the Pompeiian inscriptions. This *-aut* ending, however, which is the origin of Italian *cantò*, Span. *cantó*, Port. *cantou*, would have given in French a form *chantó, which does not occur. If *chanta* is not a derivative of *cantāt*, it is probably to be explained as an analogical formation: as the preterite already shared the 1 and 2 sing. endings *-ai* and *-as* with the present tense of *avoir* and all futures, 3 sing. was remodelled on the basis of (*il*) *a, chantera*, etc., to give *chanta*.

14.2.1.5. *Mixed sets.* The only tenses that do not conform to the above patterns are:

(a) the imperfect subjunctive of all verbs, which has the endings **-e, -es, -t**, i.e. a mixture of types 1 and 2 (*chantasse, chantasses, chantât; finisse, finisses, finît*, etc.); for further discussion, see **15.6.2**;
(b) the present indicative of *aller*, which has the endings **-s, -s, -a** (i.e. a mixture of types 2 and 3) and a variation in the stem: *je vais, tu vas, il va*; in a purely formal sense, *être* conforms to type 2— *je suis* (OFr *sui*), *tu es, il est*—but differs from all other verbs that follow this pattern in that the stem is not the same throughout the three persons of the singular;
(c) the present subjunctive of *avoir: aie, aies, ait*.

14.2.1.6. *The spoken language.* The [ə], represented by *-e, -es, -e*, and the consonantal endings *-s, -s, -t* having all disappeared, there are in the spoken language only two possibilities in the three persons singular of any tense or mood:

(a) All three persons are identical, having no ending, e.g.

je/tu/il   [ʃɑːt] (*chante, -es, -e*)   [vɑ̃] (*vend, -s*)
          [fini] (*finis, -t*)   [sɛ] (*sais, -t*)
          [vwa] (*vois, -t*)   [fas] (*fasse, -es, -e*)
          [ʃɑ̃tɛ] (*chantais, -t*)   [vɑ̃di] (*vendis, -t*)
          [pary] (*parus, -t*)   [fy] (*fus, -t*)

The [ə] may, however, reappear in certain phonetic circumstances, e.g. *je/tu/il* [parlə bjɛ̃] (see **4.12.4**). Final [z] *-s* and [t] reappear in liaison forms, e.g. [ʒə sɥiz eme] *je suis aimé*, [prɑ̃z ɑ̃] *prends-en*, [vwat il] *voit-il?* Further, in 3 sing. a [t] appears when the pronoun subject follows the verb, not only in such forms as [dit il] *dit-il?* [kə fɛt ɛl] *que fait-elle?* but also, by analogy with these, in *-er* verbs, e.g. [ʃɑ̃tə t il] *chante-t-il?*
(b) 1 sing. is distinguished from 2 and 3 sing. which are identical with one another; with the exception of the present tense of *être* (*je* [sɥi] ~ *tu/il* [ɛ]) and of *aller* (*je* [vɛ] ~ *tu/il* [va]), we have the opposition [e] ~ [a]:

Present indicative of *avoir*:   *j'*[e] ~ *tu/il* [a]
Future of all verbs, e.g.:   *je* [finire] ~ *tu/il* [finira]
Preterite of *-er* verbs, e.g.:   *je* [ʃɑ̃te] ~ *tu/il* [ʃɑ̃ta]

Je [sɥi], *tu* [ɛ], *il* [ɛ] become [sɥiz], [ɛz] and [ɛt] in liaison, e.g. [ʒə sɥiz œrø] *je suis heureux*, [ty ɛz eme] *tu es aimé*, [il ɛt isi] *il est ici*. In 3 sing. of other verbs, by analogy with [fɛt il] *fait-il*, [vøt ɛl] *veut-elle?* [dit ɔ̃] *dit-on*, etc., a [t] is introduced when the pronoun subject follows the verb, e.g. [vat il] *va-t-il?* [at ɔ̃] *a-t-on?* [finirat ɛl] *finira-t-elle?*
The only exception is the imperfect subjunctive (a tense that has in any case virtually disappeared from spoken usage), in which 1 and 2 sing. are distinguished from 3 sing., e.g.

je/tu [ʃɑ̃tas], [fys], etc. ~ *il* [ʃɑ̃ta], [fy], etc.

14.2.2. *The first and second persons plural.*

14.2.2.1. The 1 and 2 plur. endings are of two types:

	(1)	(2)
1 plur.	**-mes**	**-ons**
2 plur.	**-tes**	**-ez**

14.2.2.2. *Type 1*: -mes, -tes.

(a) This type is characteristic only of the preterite:

chantâmes, chantâtes; dormîmes, dormîtes; parûmes, parûtes

Exceptionally, it also occurs in the present tense of the verb *être*: *nous sommes, vous êtes*, and, in 2 plur., in *dire* and *faire*: *vous dites, vous faites*. (In OFr, *dire* and *faire* conformed to this pattern in 1 plur. also: *dimes, faimes*.)

(b) The history of these forms is obscure. In the preterite, the reduced forms of Latin *cantavimus, cantavistis, dormivimus, dormivistis*, viz. *cantamus, cantastis, dormimus, dormistis*, would by regular phonetic development have given **chantains, *chantaz, *dormins*,[9] **dormiz*, and it is far from clear why French has forms that appear to retain as -*e*- the vowel of the unstressed final syllable. The same is true of *sommes, êtes, dimes, dites, faimes, faites* for Latin *súmus, éstis, dícimus, dícitis, fácimus, fácitis*.

14.2.2.3. *Type 2*: -ons, -ez

(a) **-ons.** In addition to the 'irregular' form *somes*, OFr also had a form *sons* < Latin *súmus* 'we are'. This is the only verb in which the ending **-ons** is phonetically regular: *cantamus, debemus, partimus*, for example, would, by regular phonetic development, have given in French **chantains, *deveins* and **partins*. It is widely—though not universally—accepted that *sons* is the origin of the ending -*ons* which spread analogically to all tenses except the preterite.[10]

(b) **-ez.** In accordance with the regular development of tonic free *a* (**4.5.4.4**), Latin -*atis* > -*ez* [ets] > [e]: so, *cantatis* > *chantez*. Latin -*ētis* and -*itis*, however, would give French -*eiz* > -*oiz* (cf. *tēla* > *teile* > *toile*) and -*iz* respectively. In fact, -*eiz* < -*ētis* occurs in OFr, only rarely in the present tense (e.g. *atendeiz*) but commonly in the future tense, which, as we shall see, is formed from the infinitive + -*ētis* (for *habētis*): e.g. *portereiz, ireiz* in the *Roland*, *porroiz* (= '*pourrez*'), *feroiz* in Villehardouin; furthermore, -*iz* < -*itis* occurs in OFr in eastern dialects (e.g. *moriz, deveniz*=

---

[9] Forms such as *venins* (= 'venîmes'), *atendins* (= 'attendîmes') do in fact occur in OFr in some northern and eastern dialects.

[10] There is some supporting evidence for this in the fact that forms such as *avomes, demandomes*, which may originate in the alternative 1 plur. of *être*, viz *somes* (now *sommes*), occur in OFr in northern and north-eastern dialects and still survive in the Picard and Lorrain dialects.

'mourez, devenez'). After a palatal, -atis > -iez (**4.8.6**): peccatis > pecchiez, etc.; in the 15th and 16th centuries, this was replaced by -ez, in the same way as the infinitives pechier, aidier, etc. were replaced by pécher, aider, etc. (see **16.1.2**).

Except in the future tense, -ez < -atis had already almost entirely replaced the other 2 plur. endings in OFr, and in later OFr -ez for earlier -oiz became usual in the future tense too.

14.2.2.4. *The spoken language.* 1 and 2 plur. are the only persons that, in every tense of every verb, have a characteristic ending:

1 plur. [ɔ̃] or [m] (-ons, -mes)
2 plur. [e] or [t] (-ez, -tes)

The final consonant -s may reappear as [z] in liaison forms, e.g. [nu sɔmz arive] *nous sommes arrivés*, [alɔ̃z i] *allons-y*, [vuz avez eme] *vous avez aimé*.

14.2.3. *The third person plural.*

14.2.3.1. The 3 plur. endings are:

(a) **-ent**, when unstressed;
(b) **-ont** when stressed, i.e. in the future tense of all verbs (*chanteront, dormiront*, etc.) and, in four verbs only, in the present tense, viz, *sont, ont, font, vont*.

14.2.3.2. **-ent** represents the development of the Latin unstressed endings -ant, -ent and -unt (and, indirectly, of -iunt which was replaced by -unt in VL):

cántant > chantent   pérdunt > perdent
débent > doivent   dórmiunt > *dormunt > dorment

14.2.3.3. *Sont* is a regular phonetic development of Latin sŭnt 'they are'; *ont, font, vont* are not regular developments of the corresponding Latin forms *habent, faciunt, vadunt* but presuppose the existence in VL of forms such as *aunt (for *habunt), *faunt (for *facunt) and *vaunt. As the endings of the future tense are those of the present tense of *avoir* (**15.4.3**), the ending -ont of *chanteront* etc. needs no further explanation.

14.2.3.4. *The spoken language.*

(a) -ent has generally disappeared (e.g. [il parl] *ils parlent*), but remains as [ə], [ət] or [t] in certain circumstances, e.g. [il parlə

179

bjɛ̃] *ils parlent bien,* [ʃɑ̃tət il] *chantent-ils?,* [vjɛnt il] *viennent-ils?*
(b) [ɔ̃] *-ont* remains, being expanded to [ɔ̃t] as a liaison form, e.g.
[il sɔ̃t a pari] *ils sont à Paris* ,[u vɔ̃t ɛl] *où vont-elles?*

14.3. *The infixes.* The infixes to be discussed are **-ss-, -i-, -ai-** and
-r-. In the spoken language these are [s], [i] or [j], [ɛ] and [r].

14.3.1. *The infix* **-ss-**. This infix occurs:

(a) in the three persons plural of the present indicative, the
whole of the imperfect indicative and the present participle of
verbs of the *finir* type:

nous finissons, vous finissez   ils finissent
je finissais, etc.   finissant

(b) in all persons except 3 sing. of the imperfect subjunctive of all
verbs:

chantasse	chantasses	(chantât)		
		chantassions	chantassiez	chantassent
finisse	finisses	(finît)		
		finissions	finissiez	finissent
parusse	parusses	(parût)		
		parussions	parussiez	parussent

In (a) ,the **-ss-** derives from the Latin inchoative endings *-sco,
-scis*, etc.; see **15.2.2.**
In (b), the **-ss-** derives from the **-ss-** of the Latin pluperfect
subjunctive, *canta(v)issem, fini(vi)ssem,* etc.; see **15.6.3.**

14.3.2. *The infix* **-i-**.

14.3.2.1. The infix **-i-** occurs in 1 and 2 plur. of all verbs in the
following tenses:

(a) Present subjunctive (*nous chantions, vous chantiez,* etc.) [11]
(b) imperfect indicative (*nous chantions, vous chantiez,* etc.)
(c) conditional (*nous chanterions, vous chanteriez,* etc.)
(d) imperfect subjunctive (*nous chantassions, vous chantassiez,* etc.)

14.3.2.2.
(a) The usual present subjunctive endings in OFr were the
ubiquitous *-ons, -ez: chantons, vendons, vendez,* etc. After a palatal,

[11] N.B. the spelling *-y-* in *nous soyons, vous soyez, nous ayons, vous ayez.*

however, the Latin endings -*amus*, -*atis* (characteristic of the sub-junctive of all except first conjugation verbs) regularly became -*iens* and -*iez* (cf. *canem* > *chien*, **4.14.6.3**, and *carum* > *chier*, **4.8.6**):

dicamus > dïiens	faciamus > faciens	habeamus > aiiens
dicatis > dïiez	faciatis > faciez	habeatis > aiiez

(b) The origin of the endings of the imperfect indicative is somewhat obscure, but it seems probable that Latin -*ebamus*, -*ebatis* were reduced in VL to *-*eamus*, *-*eatis*, which developed into French as [jamus], [jatis] (cf. *vinea* > [vinja], **4.3.2** (b)), i.e. as palatal + -*amus*, -*atis* (cf. (a) above):

debebamus > devïiens   debebatis > devïiez

For reasons that are not clear, the endings -*ïiens*, -*ïiez* were at first disyllabic [i-jĕns, i-jets], but in late OFr they became mono-syllabic [jĕns, jets].

(c) The endings of the conditional were the same as those of the imperfect indicative (**15.4.2.2**).

(d) The imperfect subjunctive derives from the Latin pluperfect subjunctive whose endings were -*emus*, -*etis*. The 1 plur. ending in OFr was regularly either -*ons* or -*iens*, neither of which is a phonetic development of -*emus*; in 2 plur., the phonetically regular -*eiz*/-*oiz* < -*etis* coexisted with the analogical endings -*ez* and -*iez*:

Latin	OFr
canta(vi)ssemus	chantissons, -iens
canta(vi)ssetis	chantisseiz, -ez, -iez
Latin	OFr
fini(vi)ssemus	finissons, -iens
fini(vi)ssetis	finisseiz, -ez, -iez

14.3.2.3. In the 13th century, the new ending -*ions*—arising from a contamination of -*ons* and -*iens*—appeared in all four tenses, and in MidFr -*ions*, -*iez* became fully established in the imperfect indicative, the conditional and the imperfect subjunctive. In the present subjunctive, -*iez* first began to replace -*ez* in MidFr; however, -*ons* and -*ez* both survived for some considerable time and it was not until the late 16th century that—as a result of the generalization of -*ions*, -*iez* in the subjunctive and the spread of -*ez* to those verbs that originally had -*iez* in the indicative (*pechiez*, *aidiez*, etc., see **14.2.2.3** (b))—the modern opposition

181

INDICATIVE *-ons*, *-ez* ~ SUBJUNCTIVE *-ions*, *-iez* was finally established.

The infix **-i-**, which had its origins in a purely phonetic feature, viz. the development of tonic free *a* after a palatal (pal. + *-amus* > *iens*, pal. + *-atis* > *-iez*) has therefore taken on a morphological function and become a characteristic marker of the present and imperfect subjunctive, the imperfect indicative and the conditional.

14.3.2.4. In the spoken language, the infix *-i-* occurs:

(a) as [i] after a consonant cluster having [l] or [r] as the second element: [sifliɔ̃] *sifflions*, [uvriɔ̃] *ouvrions*, [ɑ̃triɔ̃] *entrions*, [raklie] *racliez*, [vɑ̃drie] *vendriez*:

(b) as [j] elsewhere: [ʃɑ̃tjɔ̃] *chantions*, [finirjɔ̃] *finirions*, [vɑ̃dje] *vendiez*, [finisje] *finissiez*.

14.3.3. *The infix* **-ai-**. For the origin and development of the **-ai-** infix in the imperfect indicative and the conditional, see **15.3.4.**

14.3.4. *The infix* **-r-**. For the origin of the characteristic **-r-** infix of the future and conditional, see **15.4.4.**

14.4. *The stem (excluding the past participle).*

14.4.1. The following examples illustrate the variety of stems that can occur within the forms of one and the same verb:

mets [mɛ] **mettent, mis**
doit, doivent, devons, dut
voit [vwa], **voyons** [vwaj-] **verrai, vit**
veut, veulent, voulons, voudrai, veuille
prends [prɑ̃], **prennent, prenons, prendrai** [prɑ̃d-], **pris**
peut, peuvent, pouvons, pourrons, puisse, put

These variations in stem arise in part from variations already existing in Latin and in part from later modifications brought about by phonetic changes and analogical remodellings.

The only verbs having the same stem in all parts are those of the *finir, punir* type, which invariably have a stem in *-i*, e.g. *fini-, puni-*.

14.4.2. *Present and perfect stems in Latin.*

14.4.2.1. For our present purposes it can be said that Latin verbs had two stems, a present stem and a perfect stem, and that in many verbs the perfect stem can be further analysed as:

PRESENT STEM + INFIX (*-av-*, *-u-*, *-v-*) (see below)

Of the fifteen inflected tenses of the Latin verb, indicative and subjunctive, active and passive,[12] only five have come down into French:

(a) from the present stem: present indicative and subjunctive, imperfect indicative;
(b) from the perfect stem: perfect indicative (which has become the preterite), pluperfect subjunctive (which has become the imperfect subjunctive).[13]

The following table gives for a few typical verbs the 3 sing. forms of those Latin tenses that have survived:

	amare	*debēre*	*dormire*	*mittĕre*
Pres. Indic.	amat	debet	dormit	mittit
Pres. Subjunct.	amet	debeat	dormiat	mittat
Imperf. Indic.	amabat	debebat	dormiebat	mittebat
Perfect Indic.	amavit	debuit	dormivit	misit
Pluperf. Subj.	amavisset	debuisset	dormivisset	misisset

14.4.2.2. In verbs of the *amare* and *dormire* types and in some verbs of the *debēre* type (e.g. *parēre*, having the perfect *paruit*), the distinction between the two Latin stems is, according to the type of analysis we adopt, reflected in ModFr by the existence, in the preterite, of a particular thematic vowel: e.g. (*nous*) *aimâmes, dormîmes, parûmes.*

---

[12] There were also five other passive tenses formed by means of the perfect participle and various tenses of the verb 'to be', e.g. *amatus est* 'he has been loved'.

[13] In very early OFr a few examples of forms deriving from the Latin pluperfect indicative survive with the value of a simple past tense, e.g. *voluerat* 'he had wished' > *voldret* 'he wished', *fecerat* 'he had made' > *firet* 'he made'.

14.4.2.3. The different reflexes of the Latin present and perfect stems are also clearly seen in such verbs as the following:

Present Stem	Perfect Stem		
	Latin	*OFr*	*ModFr*
mittit > met	mīsit	mist	mit
vĭdet > voit	vīdit		vit
facit > fait	fĕcit[14]	fist	fit
prehendit > prend	*prēsit[14]	prist	prit

Preterites of these types are discussed more fully in **15.5.7**.

14.4.3. *Strong and weak stems*

14.4.3.1. The main stress in a Latin or French verb form falls either on the stem or on the ending. When the stress falls on the stem, this stem is said to be **strong**. When the stress falls on the ending, the stem is said to be **weak**. In nearly all French verbs, the stress pattern is as follows, the stressed element being indicated by small capitals:

Strong (stressed) stem

Present indicative and subjunctive *1, 2, 3 sing., 3 plur.*: je CHANTe, tu CHANTes, il CHANTe, ils CHANTent

Weak stem (stressed ending)

Present indicative and subjunctive—*1 plur.*: nous chantONS, chantIONS *2 plur.*: vous chantEZ, chantIEZ

Imperfect indicative (throughout)—je chantAIS, tu chantAIS, il chantAIT, nous chantIONS, vous chantIEZ, ils chantAIENT

Present participle—chantANT

The future and conditional on the one hand and the preterite

---

[14] **Prēsit* for ClLat *prehendit*. *Fēcit* and *prēsit* would normally have given **foist* and **proist* (tonic free *ē* > *oi*). However, in 1 sing. the presence of a long final *-i* (*fēcī*, **prēsī*) influenced the development of the preceding *ē* (*fis*, *pris*) and, by analogy, this vowel was adopted in other persons of the verb as well.

184

and imperfect subjunctive on the other have, in many though not all verbs, their own special stems and so are left out of account here (see **15.4.5** and **15.5**), as are also the infinitive (**16.1**) and the past participle (**17.1**).

14.4.3.*2*. We have seen (**4.2** to **4.6**) that Latin vowels often developed differently according to whether or not they bore the main stress. In many verbs, this has resulted in different developments of the same Latin present stem, e.g.

Latin stem	Weak	Strong	
		(Tonic free [e] > [oi])	
dēb-	devons	doivent	doit
recĭp-	recevons	reçoivent	reçoit
bĭb-	bevons > buvons	boivent	boit
vĭd-	vëons > voyons	voient	voit
crēd-	crëons > croyons	croient	croit
		(Tonic free [ɔ] > [ø, œ])	
pŏt-	pöons > pouvons	pueent > peuvent	peut
vŏl-	vo(u)lons	veulent	veut
mŏr-	mo(u)rons	meurent	meurt

In *voir* and *croire* the original weak stems *ve-*, *cre-* have been replaced by the strong stems *voy-*, *croy-* (=*voi-*, *croi-*). This was presumably the result of a reaction by speakers of the language against the tendency for [ə] to disappear when in hiatus (**4.12.2**): had not the weak stem been reinforced in this or some other way, the forms in question would have been reduced to *vons, *crons, etc. The reasons for the remodelling of *buv-* and *pouv-* are uncertain.

The reasons for the existence of two strong stems in some verbs (*doiv-* ~ *doi-*, *veul-* ~ *veu-*, etc.) are discussed below.

14.4.3.*3*. *Strong stems of the type* **doiv-** ~ **doi-**. We have seen (**3.6** (b)) that consonant clusters were frequently simplified by the elimination of one or other member of the cluster. So, where a verb had a -*v*- in its stem (from Latin intervocalic -*p*-, -*b*- or -*v*-) which became -*f* when final (cf. *viva* > *vive* ~ *vivum* > *vif*), this disappeared before -*s*, -*t* of 2 and 3 sing., e.g. *vivis* > *vifs > (tu) *vis, vivit* > *vift > (il) *vit* (cf. OFr *le chief* ~ *les chiés*, etc., **6.2.2.4**(b)) :

Weak	Strong
vivons	**vivent**, je **vif**,[15] tu **vis**, il **vit**
bevons > **buv**ons	**boivent**, je **boif**,[15] tu **bois**, il **boit**
recevons	**reçoivent**, je **reçoif**,[15] tu **reçois**, il **reçoit**
devons	**doivent**, je **doi**,[16] tu **dois**, il **doit**

14.4.3.4. *Strong stems of the type* **veul-** ~ **veu-**. The difference between the two strong stems of *vouloir* and *valoir* results from the fact that *l* remained when intervocalic but vocalized to [w], combining with the preceding vowel to form a diphthong, when preconsonantal (**3.5.6**) :

Weak	Strong	
voulons	**veul**ent	**veut**
valons	**val**ent	**vaut** [vawt] > [vo]

14.4.3.5. *Strong stems of the type* **vienn-** [vjɛn] ~ **vien-**[vjɛ̃]. We have seen (**4.14.4**) that, when final or preconsonantal, a nasal consonant disappeared after nasalizing the previous vowel and that the vowel remains nasalized (e.g. *ventum* > *vent* [vɑ̃]) but that, when it was intervocalic, the nasal consonant has remained and the preceding vowel, that at one stage was nasalized, has since denasalized. This has resulted in the creation of different verb stems in different phonetic circumstances :

Weak	Strong	
venons	**vienn**ent [vjɛn]	**vien**t [vjɛ̃]
tenons	**tienn**ent	**tien**t
plaignons	**plaign**ent [plɛɲ]	**plain**t [plɛ̃]
joignons	**joign**ent [ʒwaɲ]	**join**t [ʒwɛ̃]

14.4.3.6. In ModFr, the only -*er* verbs having a distinction between weak and strong stems are those having the alternation [ə] ~ [ɛ] or ∅ ~ [ɛ],[17] i.e. verbs like *jeter* and *acheter* :

jetons [ʒətɔ̃] ~ jette [ʒɛt]   achetons [aʃtɔ̃] ~ achète [aʃɛt]

A similar alternation exists in the present subjunctive.

[15] These 1 sing. forms were later replaced by *je vis, bois, reçois*, when the -*s* spread to those verbs that previously had the ∅ -s -t pattern (**14.2.1.3** (e) and (f)).

[16] The form *doi* (instead of *doif) suggests that in VL *debeo* > [dejo], cf *habeo* > [ajo] > *ai*.

[17] It could be argued that there is also apophony in verbs like *tuer, jouer* and *lier*, e.g. (*je*) *tue* [ty] ~ (*nous*) *tuons* [tɥɔ̃], (*je*) *joue* [ʒu] ~ (*nous*) *jouons* [ʒwɔ̃], (*je*) *lie* [li] ~ (*nous*) *lions* [ljɔ̃]; this however is a case of regular allophonic variation—see Chapter 5, note 3.

In OFr however, as a result of the divergent development of the same stem in tonic and non-tonic syllables, very many -*er* verbs had two stems. Some of the more common of these 'apophonous' verbs, as they are known, are the following, of which we give the full present indicative and subjunctive of one (*pleurer*) and the 3 sing. and 1 plur. forms of the present indicative of the others:

Infinitive: *Latin* plorare, *OFr* plorer
Indicative: pleur   pleures   pleure   plorons   plorez   pleurent
Subjunctive: pleur   pleurs   pleurt   plorons   plorez   pleurent

(N.B. The imperfect indicative, infinitive and present participle had the weak stem.)

LATIN	OLD FRENCH		
Infinitive	*Infinitive*	*3 sing.*	*1 plur.*
amare	amer	aime	amons
lavare	laver	leve	lavons
sperare	esperer	espoire	esperons
prŏbare	prover	prueve	provons
*trŏpare	trover	trueve	trovons
*paraulare[18]	parler	parole	parlons
*disjejunare	disner	desjune	disnons
prĕcare	proiier	prie	proions
nĕcare	noiier	nie	noions
nĕgare	noiier	nie	noions

These alternations have now all been eliminated by the generalization of one or other stem:

(a) The strong stem has been generalized in *il pleure/nous pleurons, il aime/nous aimons, il prie/nous prions, il nie/nous nions*, etc.
(b) The weak stem has been generalized in *il lave/nous lavons, il espère/nous espérons, il prouve/nous prouvons, il trouve/nous trouvons, il parle/nous parlons, il noie/nous noyons*, etc.; note that, although the strong stems of *il espoire, il preuve* and *il parole*, etc., have disappeared, the corresponding nouns are still *l'espoir* (which is derived from the OFr verb), *la preuve* (<*próba*) and *la parole* (<*paráula* < *parabola*).
(c) Both the weak and the strong stems of *desjune ~ disnons* have

---

[18] *Pàrabolàre* > *pàrab'làre* > *pàraulàre* > *parler*.

been generalized to give two different verbs: *il déjeune/nous déjeunons ~ il dîne/nous dînons.*

14.4.4. *The subjunctive stem.*

14.4.4.1. A few verbs have a stem that is reserved solely for the present subjunctive and, occasionally, the imperative and present participle, e.g.

avoir: nous ayons, ayez, ayant   *savoir*: je sache, sachez, sachant
vouloir: je veuille, veuillez *pouvoir*: je puisse *faire*: je fasse
valoir: je vaille   *aller*: j'aille

The existence of a special subjunctive stem in French is a direct result of the fact that, in those verbs in which the endings -*am* etc. were preceded by -*e*- or -*i*-, this regularly became a yod in VL (**4.3.2** (b)) and consequently palatalized the preceding consonant (**3.9.4**) and in some cases also affected the development of the preceding vowel. The Latin and OFr forms of, for example, *valēre (valoir)* are:

| valeam [valjam] | valeas | valeat |
| valeamus | valeatis | valeant |

| vaille [vaλə] | vailles | vaille |
| vailliens | vailliez | vaillent |

Similarly:

*volēre (vouloir): Latin voleam, etc.
 OFr vueille, vueilles, vueille, voilliens, voilliez, vueillent

facere (faire): Latin faciam, etc.
 OFr face [fatsə] faces face faciens faciez facent

*sapēre (savoir): Latin sapiam, etc.
 OFr sache saches sache sachiens sachiez sachent

venire (venir): Latin veniam, etc.
 OFr viegne [vjɛɲə] viegnes viegne vegniens vegniez viegnent

tenēre (tenir): Latin teneam, etc.;
 OFr tiegne, etc.

188

*potēre (*pouvoir*): VL *poteam (possiam?), etc.
OFr puisse   puisses   puisse   puissiens   puissiez   puissent

These verbs illustrate the main analogical developments that have taken place between OFr and ModFr:

(a) In *venir* and *tenir* the subjunctive stem has been completely replaced by the indicative stems: *je vienne, nous venions, ils viennent*, by analogy with *il vient, nous venons, ils viennent*, etc.; likewise, *je tienne, nous tenions*, etc.
(b) In some verbs the subjunctive stem has been abandoned in 1 and 2 plur. but retained for the other persons: ModFr *nous valions, vous valiez, nous voulions, vous vouliez* (but *je vaille, je veuille*, etc.).

ModFr *je sache, nous sachions, je fasse, nous fassions, je puisse, nous puissions*, etc., retain the OFr stem throughout the tense.

It is unnecessary here to go into details of the phonetic history of other verbs. We shall merely quote some representative OFr forms and comment on later developments:

aller: in OFr, there was a variety of subjunctive forms (*il aille, aut, alge, voise*); of these *aille* has remained except in 1 and 2 plur., where *ailliens, ailliez* have disappeared before *allions, alliez*.
devoir: the OFr subjunctive forms *il doie, il doient*, etc., have been replaced by *il doive, ils doivent*, etc., modelled on the indicative form *ils doivent*.
avoir and *être*: for the subjunctive forms *il ait, il soit*, etc., see **15.2.4.2**.
It is noteworthy that only some of the most frequently used verbs have retained a distinct subjunctive stem. Verbs that have lost the subjunctive stem completely include (in addition to *venir, tenir*, see above), *mourir* (OFr subjunctive *je muire*, etc.) and *plaire* (OFr subjunctive *je place*, etc.). The subjunctive of these verbs has been remodelled on the strong stem of the indicative (ModFr *je meure, je plaise*).

14.4.4.2. For imperatives and present participles remodelled on the basis of the subjunctive stem, see **15.7.4** and **16.2.3** respectively.

189

14.4.4.*3*. For 1 sing. present indicative forms having the same stem as the subjunctive, see **15.2.4.*1*.**

14.4.5. *The future stem.* For the development of the characteristic future stems of some verbs (e.g. *verrai, viendrai, aurai*), see **15.4.5.**

15 Verbs

III THE SIMPLE TENSES

15.1. *Introduction.* **Throughout this chapter the following points should be borne in mind:**

(a) The gradual establishment of a threefold set of singular endings, (i) *-e, -es, -e* (ii) *-s, -s, -t,* (iii) *-ai, -as, -a,* is discussed in **14.2.1.**

(b) The 1 and 2 plur. endings *-ons* and *-ez* had been widely generalized in proto-French and were further generalized in OFr and MidFr (see **14.2.2.3**).

(c) Analogical innovations that have come about between early OFr and ModFr are indicated in bold type.

15.2. *The present indicative and subjunctive.* These derive from the corresponding tenses in Latin.

15.2.1. -er *verbs.*

PRESENT INDICATIVE			PRESENT SUBJUNCTIVE		
Latin	*OFr*	*ModFr*	*Latin*	*OFr*	*ModFr*
cánto	chant	chante	cántem	chant	chante
cántas	chantes	chantes	cántes	chanz	chantes
cántat	chante	chante	cántet	chant	chante
cantámus	chantons	chantons	cantémus	chantons	chantions
cantátis	chantez	chantez	cantétis	chantez	chantiez
cántant	chantent	chantent	cántent	chantent	chantent

(a) For the generalization of the **-e, -es, -e** endings, see **14.2.1.2**.

(b) Note that 1 and 2 plur. were the same in the subjunctive as in the indicative in OFr; for the *-i-* infix of the ModFr subjunctive, see **14.3.2**.

(c) OFr apophonous verbs had an alternation of strong and weak stems in both indicative and subjunctive, e.g.

> *Indic.* pleur pleures pleure plorons plorez pleurent
> *Subjunct.* pleur pleurs pleurt plorons plorez pleurent

For a discussion of the reduction of apophony, see **14.4.3.6**.

15.2.2. -ir *verbs.* Many Latin verbs had, as well as the simple form, an 'inchoative' form incorporating the infix *-sc-* which indicated the beginning of the action denoted by the simple verb: e.g. *pallēre* 'to be pale' ~ *pallescĕre* 'to turn pale', *gemĕre* 'to groan' ~ *gemiscĕre* 'to begin to groan'. In the course of time, these inchoative verbs lost their original value and became, semantically, the equivalent of the simple verb. Consequently, the original inchoative forms served merely as morphological alternatives to the simple forms. In French this has affected particularly *-ir* verbs, in which the endings *-isco* etc. had spread to very many verbs that originally had had no inchoative forms. The reflex of *-isc-* in OFr is *-iss-*, or, when final or before a consonant, *-is*. In verbs like *finir*, the reflexes are found in the present indicative and subjunctive, the imperfect indicative and the present participle. Some *-ir* verbs, however, such as *servir* and *dormir*, have not adopted the infix. We therefore have two types of *-ir* verbs in French:

INDICATIVE

Latin		*OFr*	*ModFr*
finio	*finisco	fenis	finis
finis	*finiscis	fenis	finis
finit	*finiscit	fenist	finit
finimus	*finiscimus	fenissons	finissons
finitis	*finiscitis	fenissez	finissez
finiunt	*finiscunt	fenissent	finissent

servio > *servo		serf	sers
servis		sers	sers
servit		sert	sert
servimus		servons	servons
servitis		servez	servez
serviunt > *servunt		servent	servent

SUBJUNCTIVE

Latin		*OFr*	*ModFr*
finiam	*finiscam	fenisse	finisse
finias	*finiscas	fenisses	finisses
finiat	*finiscat	fenisse	finisse
finiamus	*finiscamus	fenissiens	finissions
finiatis	*finiscatis	fenissiez[1]	finissiez
finiant	*finiscant	fenissent	finissent ·

[1] *-iez* is the regular development of *-atis* after [k] (see **4.8.6**); however, by analogy with other verbs, forms such as *fenissez* also occur in OFr.

serviam	*servam	serve	serve
servias	*servas	serves	serves
serviat	*servat	serve	serve
serviamus	*servamus	servons	servions
serviatis	*servatis	servez	serviez
serviant	*servant	servent	servent

In OFr and MidFr, some verbs fluctuated between the *finir* type and the *servir* type, and a certain amount of inconsistency persists in the case of derivatives of *sortir* and *partir*. For example, *ressortir* 'to go out again' is conjugated *il ressort, nous ressortons*, etc., but *ressortir* 'to come under someone's jurisdiction' is conjugated *il ressortit, nous ressortissons*, etc.; *repartir* 'to set out again' is conjugated *il repart, nous repartons*, etc., but *répartir* 'to distribute' is conjugated *il répartit, nous répartissons*, etc.

15.2.3. *Regular -re verbs* (**vendre** *type*)

	INDICATIVE			SUBJUNCTIVE	
Latin	*OFr*	*ModFr*	*Latin*	*OFr*	*ModFr*
vendo	vent	vend**s**	vendam	vende	vende
vendis	venz	vends	vendas	vendes	vendes
vendit	vent	vend	vendat	vende	vende
vendimus	vendons	vendons	vendamus	vendons	vendions
venditis	vendez	vendez	vendatis	vendez	vendiez
vendunt	vendent	vendent	vendant	vendent	vendent

In the indicative, the ending **-s** has been introduced in 1 sing., and *d* functions as an orthographical variant for *t* in 3 sing. (*vend-il?* is, however, still [vãtil] in pronunciation).

15.2.4. *Irregular verbs*

15.2.4.1. *Present indicative*
Être: as in very many other languages, including English, the verb 'to be' is completely irregular:

Latin: sum, es, est, sumus, estis, sunt
OFr: sui, es, est, somes, estes, sont
ModFr: suis, es, est, sommes, êtes, sont

We have discussed above (**14.2.2.2**) the problem presented by *somes, estes*, which clearly derive from the Latin forms but are not regular phonetic developments thereof. OFr *sui* had been partially remodelled on the basis of other 1 sing. forms in -*i*, in particular perhaps *ai*; it has since, like other 1 sing. forms in -*i*, taken an analogical -*s*.

Avoir: the 1 and 2 plur. forms *avons* and *avez* derive regularly (apart from the usual change of ending) from Latin *habemus* and *habetis*; the other forms and corresponding forms in other Romance languages lead us to conclude that, in VL, contracted forms were in use:

habeo > [ájo] > ai   habes > [as] > as
habet > [at] > a   habent > [áunt] > ont

Aller: The strong forms, *vais, vas, va, vont*, derive from the present tense of the verb *vadĕre* 'to go or walk', apparently via contracted spoken forms (e.g. *vadunt* > [váunt] > *vont*); the origin of the *al*-forms (OFr *aler, alons, alez*, now spelt *aller*, etc.) is obscure.

Faire and *dire*:

Latin: facio, facis, facit, fácimus, fácitis, faciunt
OFr: faz, fais, fait, faimes, faites, font
ModFr: **fais**, fais, fait, **faisons** [fəzɔ̃], faites, font

Latin: dico, dicis, dicit, dícimus, dícitis, dicunt
OFr: di, dis, dit, dimes, dites, dient
ModFr: **dis**, dis, dit, **disons**, dites, **dis**ent

Faz has been remodelled on the basis of 2 and 3 sing. (see below), *di* by the addition of the usual analogical -*s* (**14.2.1.**3 (e) and (f)). Though *faimes* and *dimes* have been replaced by forms based on the weak stem, *fais*- [fəz] and *dis*-, *faites* and *dites* remain—but in compounds of *dire* we have the analogical forms *vous contredisez, interdisez, médisez, prédisez*. The weak stems *fais*- and *dis*- originate in the imperfect tense: *faciebam, dicebam*, etc., > OFr *fesoie* (>*faisais*), *disoie*, etc., as a result of the palatalization of -*c*-before a front vowel, cf. *placere* > *plaisir*, etc. (**3.9.3**).

Other verbs: The endings of other irregular verbs now follow the pattern -*s*, -*s*, -*t*, -*ons*, -*ez*, -*ent*. The stems frequently have a three-fold pattern, two strong (one in the singular and one in 3 plur.) and one weak (1 and 2 plur.). The principal reasons for the existence of these different stems are discussed in **14.4**. Some 1 sing. forms in OFr had a further stem, identical to that of the subjunctive, brought about as a result of palatalization:

194

facio > faz [fats]   *voleo [vɔljo] > vueil
valeo > vail [vaλ]   *poteo (?) > puis
venio > viegn [vjẽɲ]   *morio > muir

(Cf. the OFr subjunctives *face* [fatsɔ], *vueille, vaille, puisse, viegne, muire*.)

These 1 sing. forms have now given way to forms modelled on 2 and 3 sing., *je fais, vaux, veux, peux, viens, meurs*, though *puis* also remains, principally as an interrogative form (*puis-je?*).

The principles having been discussed above (**14.4**), we shall here merely list a number of typical OFr and ModFr forms, showing in bold type the stems or endings that have been analogically remodelled between OFr and ModFr—other differences (e.g. *tu vueus > veux*) are the result of phonetic and orthographical changes:

Vouloir:

| OFr | vueil | vueus | vueut | volons | volez | vuelent |
| *ModFr* | **veux** | veux | veut | **voulons** | voulez | veulent |

Pouvoir:

| OFr | puis | pues | puet | pöons | pöez | pueent |
| *ModFr* | **peux** | peux | peut | pouvons[2] | pouvez[2] | peuvent |

Savoir:

| OFr | sai | ses | set | savons | savez | sevent |
| *ModFr* | **sais** | sais | sait | savons | savez | **sav**ent |

Devoir:[2a]

| OFr | doi | dois | doit | devons | devez | doivent |
| *ModFr* | **dois** | dois | doit | devons | devez | doivent |

Voir:

| OFr | voi | vois | voit | vēons | vēez | voient |
| *ModFr* | **vois** | vois | voit | **voy**ons | **voy**ez | voient |

Venir:[3]

| OFr | viegn | viens | vient | venons | venez | viennent |
| *ModFr* | **viens** | viens | vient | venons | venez | viennent |

Écrire:

| OFr | escrif | escris | escrit | escrivons | escrivez | escrivent |
| *ModFr* | **écris** | écris | écrit | écrivons | écrivez | écrivent |

---

[2] Opinions differ as to whether the -*v*- *of pouvons, pouvez* is a phonetic or an analogical development.

[2a] Like *devoir* are *recevoir, concevoir, percevoir, apercevoir.*

[3] Like *venir* is *tenir.*

Croire:

OFr	croi	crois	croit	crēons	crēez	croient
ModFr	crois	crois	croit	**croy**ons	**croy**ez	croient

Mourir:

OFr	muir	muers	muert	morons	morez	muerent
ModFr	**meurs**	meurs	meurt	mourons	mourez	meurent

Prendre:

OFr	prent	prenz	prent	prendons	prendez	prendent
ModFr	prends	prends	prend	**pren**ons[4]	**pren**ez[4]	**prenn**ent[4]

15.2.4.2. *Present subjunctive.* With the exception of *être* and *avoir*, all irregular verbs have in 1, 2, 3 sing. and 3 plur. the endings **-e, -es, -e, -ent,** deriving regularly from the Latin subjunctive endings *-am, -as, -at, -ant*; for the 1 and 2 plur. endings **-ions** and **-iez** see **14.3.2.**

In OFr, the subjunctive of *être*, which derived from 'regularized' VL forms **siam, *sias,* etc. (for ClLat *sim, sis*, etc.), and that of *avoir*, which derived from contracted forms **aiam,* etc. (for ClLat *habeam*, etc.) formed two parallel series:

soie, soies, soit, soiiens, soiiez, soient
aie, aies, ait, aiiens, aiiez, aient

At this stage, *soit* and *ait* are already irregular, as the regular phonetic developments of **siat* and **aiat* would have been **soie* and **aie*. Though *aie* and *aies* have since developed regularly, the modern *je sois* and *tu sois* are problematic: these could either result from the loss of the *e* [ə] in hiatus with the preceding vowel and the addition of the usual analogical *-s* in 1 sing., or else have been formed on the analogy of *soit*.

We have discussed above (**14.4.4**) the existence in some other verbs of a special subjunctive stem and the fact that yet other verbs that had such a stem in OFr have since lost it.

15.3. *The imperfect indicative*

15.3.1. The forms of the imperfect indicative in Latin can be illustrated by the verbs *cantare* 'to sing', *debēre* 'to owe', *vendĕre* 'to sell' and *finire* 'to finish':

---

[4] The OFr forms derive from Latin forms with a stem in *prehend-* (*prehendunt*, etc.). The modern forms *prenons, prenez, prennent*, are probably formed on the basis of *tenons, tenez, tiennent*.

cantábam	cantábas	cantábat		
		cantabámus	cantabátis	cantábant
debébam	debébas	debébat		
		debebámus	debebátis	debébant
vendébam	vendébas	vendébat		
		vendebámus	vendebátis	vendébant
finiébam	finiébas	finiébat		
		finiebámus	finiebátis	finiébant

15.3.2. In some Romance languages, e.g. Occitan and Spanish, the first conjugation has retained endings derived from *-abam* etc., whereas the other conjugations have a different set whose origin is probably *-ebam*, e.g. in Spanish:

cantaba	cantabas	cantaba		
		cantábamos	cantabais	cantaban
vendía	vendías	vendía		
		vendíamos	vendíais	vendían

Similarly in OFr, the first conjugation (*chanter*) was distinguished—except in 1 and 2 plur.—from other conjugations. In the following tables, we give two forms for the first conjugation, (a) those of western dialects, (b) those of eastern dialects:[5]

chanter:
(a) chantoue chantoues chantout   chantouent
                          chantïiens chantïiez
(b) chanteve chanteves chanteve   chantevent

vendre:
vendoie vendoies vendoit vendïiens vendïiez vendoient

fenir: fenissoie, etc.   *devoir*: devoie, etc.

Already in OFr *-oie* etc. were beginning to be adopted in the first conjugation also and eventually *chantoie* etc. triumphed completely over *chantoue/chanteve*, etc.

---

[5] The *-eve* endings represent a regular development of *-abam*, etc. (cf. *faba* > *fève*, etc., **4.5.4.4**); *-oue* etc. probably also derive from *-abam* etc., though the earlier stages in their development are not fully clear.

15.3.3. *The stem.* As the stress in the imperfect indicative is in-variably on the ending, it is the weak stem that is found in this tense, as in 1 and 2 plur. of the present indicative and subjunctive, e.g.

nous devons, voulons, venons
nous devions, voulions, venions
je devais, voulais, venais

There has been remodelling on the basis of the strong stem in *je vëoie, crëoie > je voyais, croyais*, and in those apophonous *-er* verbs in which the strong stem has been generalized (**14.4.3.***6*), e.g. *j'amoie, je plouroie > j'aimais, je pleurais.*

15.3.4. *The infix* **-ai-** *and the endings.*

15.3.4.*1.* The 1 and 2 plur. endings are discussed in **14.3.2.***2* (b). and **14.3.2.***3.* Here we shall be concerned only with the other persons. What is said about the imperfect indicative also applies to the conditional.

The original first conjugation endings having completely dis-appeared (**15.3.2**), we shall here discuss only the forms that are now used uniformly with all verbs.

15.3.4.*2.* There can be little doubt that OFr *-oie* etc. derive from the Latin endings *-ēbam*, etc. However, the intermediate stages are not clear: *-ēbam* etc., by regular phonetic change, would have given in early OFr **-eive*, etc., which in later OFr would have become **-oive*, etc. In fact, there is no trace in the OFr forms of a [v] representing the Latin *b* and it is therefore to be supposed that, for reasons that are not clear, *-ēbam, -ēbas* were replaced in VL by **-eam,* **-eas,* etc. (which could also be the source of the *-ía* forms of Spanish, etc.).[6]

The successive stages that are actually attested are:

Latin	Early OFr	Later OFr	MidFr	17th c.	ModFr
-ebam	-eie	-oie	-oi	-ois	-ais
-ebas	-eies	-oies	-ois	-ois	-ais
-ebat	-eiet > -eit	-oit	-oit	-oit	-ait
-ebant	-eient	-oient	-oient	-oient	-aient

[6] One widely accepted view is that the endings *-ēbam* etc. were first reduced to *-eam* etc. in verbs having a stem ending in *-b-*, e.g. *habebam, debebam*; according to this theory, the second of two *b*'s in close proximity disappeared and the resulting endings *-eam* etc. later spread analogically to other verbs.

198

15.3.4.*3*. For reasons that are not clear, *-eiet* became *-eit* in very early OFr. Later, by regular phonetic development (cf. *teile* > *toile*, **4.5.4.*3*),** *ei* in all the endings became *oi*. In MidFr, either by analogy with *-oit* or as a result of the loss of unstressed *e* in hiatus with a preceding vowel, *-oie* and *-oies* became *-oi* and *-ois* respectively. The adoption of *-s* as the characteristic 1 sing. ending in the present and the preterite (**14.2.1.*3*)** also affected the imperfect and conditional: forms such as *serois* first occur in the 14th century and become fully established in the 16th century.

We saw in **4.10** that by the end of the OFr period [ɔj] had come to be pronounced [wɛ], though the spelling *oi* remained. [wɛ] later developed in two ways: in most words it became [wa] (*toile*, etc.) but in a few words it became [ɛ] (e.g. *croie* > *craie*). This latter development triumphed in the imperfect indicative, and there are indications that the pronunciation [ɛ] for *-ois*, *-oit* and *-oient* was frequent even in Court circles in the 16th and 17th centuries; the spelling *-ais*, *-ait*, *-aient*, though recommended in the 18th century by Voltaire and others, was not sanctioned by the Académie Française until 1835.

15.3.4.*4*. *The spoken language.* With reference to the written language, we have analysed *-ais* etc. as infix *-ai-* + ending. With reference to the spoken language, since *-s*, *-t* and *-ent* have disappeared, [ɛ] (= *-ais*, *-ait*, *-aient*) can legitimately be considered as an ending which in liaison has the extended forms [ɛz] and [ɛt], e.g. [ʒ etɛz œrø] *j'étais heureux*, [dizɛt il] *disaient-ils*.

15.4. *The future and conditional tenses.*

15.4.1. The Latin future tense was formed on the basis of the present stem. There were two sets of endings, one used with *-are* and *-ĕre* verbs, and the other with *-ire* and *-ĕre* verbs, e.g. from *amare* 'to love' and *mittĕre* 'to send':

amabo	amabis	amabit	amabimus	amabitis	amabunt
mittam	mittes	mittet	mittemus	mittetis	mittent

Likewise, *habēre* 'to have' has *habebo*, *habebis*, etc., and *finire* 'to finish' has *finiam, finies*, etc.

15.4.2. *The new future and conditional tenses.*

15.4.2.*1*. *The future.* The Latin future forms have disappeared in the Romance languages and have been replaced by various periphrastic constructions using reflexes of one of the verbs *venire* 'to come', *volĕre 'to wish', debĕre 'to have to' or habēre 'to have'. 'I shall sing', for example, is *jeu vegnel a cantar* (literally 'je viens à chanter') in Romansh, *voi cînta* (lit. 'je veux chanter') in Rumanian and *deppo kantare* (lit. 'je dois chanter') in Sardinian. The most widely used auxiliary of the future tense, however, is *habēre*.

The future tense in French (e.g. *je chanterai*), Occitan (*cantarai*), Italian (*canterò*), Spanish (*cantaré*) and Portuguese (*cantarei*) goes back to a Latin construction, INFINITIVE + PRESENT INDICATIVE of *habere* 'to have'—so the forms just quoted derive from *cantare habeo* or, more precisely, from a VL contraction of this that was probably *cantar-ajo*. The semantic development is clear and some of its stages have parallels in English:

(i) In *I have a letter to post*, the verb *have* retains its possessive value, but an idea of obligation may be implied ('I have a letter which is to be posted').

(ii) In *I have a letter to write*, which has an identical surface structure to the previous one, the verb *have* has lost its possessive value (I do not possess the letter, which is not yet written) and the idea of obligation that is merely implicit in *I have a letter to post*, is now dominant.

(iii) Within the construction expressing obligation there is an implication that the action will in fact be performed, i.e. an implication of futurity; in the Romance languages, though not in English, this implication has come to the fore and ousted the implication of obligation; examples of this occur in late Latin, e.g. *Tempestas illa **tollere habet** totam paleam de area* 'That tempest will carry away all the straw from the threshing-floor' (St. Augustine, writing c. A.D. 416).

In the Romance languages, the word order INFINITIVE + *habeo* has become fixed and the reflexes of *habeo* etc. have become reduced to the level of mere endings. In Portuguese the two parts are still to some extent separable, in that object pronouns can come in between them: *dir-lhe-ás* 'tu lui diras', *falar-me-á* 'il me parlera'; similar examples occur in Old Spanish (e.g. *dezir vos lo he* 'je vous le dirai') and Old Occitan (*servir l'ai* 'je le servirai', *pregar vos ai* 'je vous prierai').

15.4.2.2. *The conditional.* The origin of the conditional is identical with that of the future except that the imperfect tense of *habere* was used:

cantare habebam > OFr chanteroie > (je) chanterais.

200

15.4.3. *The endings.* The endings of the future tense are identical, in origin (**15.4.2.***1*) and form, with the present indicative of *avoir* (except that 1 and 2 plur. have the reduced forms *-ons* and *-ez* instead of *avons, avez*):

chanter**ai** chanter**as** chanter**a** chanter**ons** chanter**ez** chanter**ont**

The endings of the conditional, deriving as they do from the imperfect indicative of the verb *habēre*, are identical with the endings of the imperfect indicative (**15.3.4**).

15.4.4. *The infix* **-r-**. The infix **-r-** that regularly precedes the endings of the future and the conditional is a reflex of the **-r-** of the Latin infinitive, e.g. *cantare + habeo > chanterai, mittere + habes > mettras, valere + habebat > vaudrait* (for further examples, see **15.4.5.***3*).

15.4.5. *The stem.*

15.4.5.*1.* Though the stem of the future and the conditional— which for convenience we shall refer to as the future stem—is, historically, the stem of the infinitive, the identity between the infinitive and the future stems has been obscured in some verbs as a result of phonetic and analogical change.

15.4.5.*2.* Latin infinitives ended in *-are, -ēre, -īre* (each of which had the stress on the penultimate vowel) or *-ĕre* (in which the stress was on the antepenultimate vowel), e.g.

cantáre, debére, puníre, míttĕre

The fact that the syntagm INFINITIVE + *habeo* etc. was treated as one word meant that the infinitive lost its main stress:[7]

càntáre + hábeo > càntar-ájo   vèníre + hábeo > vènir-ájo
dèbére + hábeo > dèber-ájo   míttere + hábeo > mìtter-ájo

Consequently, whether the main stress originally fell on the ending of the infinitive or on the stem, all verbs in this syntagm had the same stress pattern.

[7] A similar shift of accent when two originally independent words fuse into a single word is frequently found in English—compare, for example, *pénce* [pens] with *síxpence* [sikspəns] or *bódy* [bɔdi] with *nóbody* [nowbədi].

15.4.5.3. In conformity with the fate of unstressed vowels generally (**4.3**), the regular development was that -*a*- remained as *e* [ə] and *e* and *i* disappeared:

càntar-ájo > chanterai   mòrir-ájo > mourrai
dèber-ájo > devrai   mìtter-ájo > mettrai

Later, [ə] < *a* disappeared in pronunciation in many verbs:

prierai [prire]   chanterai [ʃɑ̃tre]

but *porterai* [pɔrtəre], *parlerai* [parləre], etc. (see **4.12.4**).

As a consequence of the loss of the unstressed *e* or *i*, a glide consonant [d] (**3.7**), developed in such verbs as the following:

*voler-ajo > voldrai > voudrai   valer-ajo > valdrai > vaudrai
venir-ajo > vendrai > viendrai (**15.4.5.4** (b)).

A *t* or *d* that was intervocalic or occurred between a vowel and *r* became [ð] and then disappeared (cf. *patrem* > *pedre* < *père*, **3.4.3** (a)):

*poter-ajo > poḍrai > pourrai   vĭder-ajo > veḍrai > verrai
creder-ajo > creḍrai > crerrai > croirai (**15.4.5.4** (b))
(N.B. ḍ = [ð]).

15.4.5.4. From the time before the emergence of French as a written language, analogical processes had been at work bringing about the remodelling of the future stem. Such remodelling has taken place on the basis (a) of the infinitive, (b) of the strong stem of the verb:

(a) *Remodelling on the basis of the infinitive*: whereas *venir-ajo* and *morir-ajo* gave quite regularly *vendrai* and *mourrai*, the future tense of *finir*, for example, is *finirai* (or, in OFr, *fenirai*) not **findrai*; likewise, the future of *punir, partir, servir, dormir*, and other verbs is invariably, from earliest OFr onwards, *punirai, partirai, servirai, dormirai*, etc.

(b) *Remodelling on the basis of the strong stem*: OFr *bevrai, crerrai, vendrai* (*venir*), *tendrai* (*tenir*) have been replaced by new forms based on the strong stem (*boi-, croi-, vien-, tien-*): *boirai, croirai,*[8]

---

[8] *Boirai, croirai* could equally well be based on the infinitives *boire* (itself a re-modelled form replacing earlier *boivre*) and *croire*.

viendrai, tiendrai. Verrai (voir) has resisted remodelling, though this has occurred in some of the compounds of *voir*, e.g. *prévoirai, pourvoirai.*

In the case of apophonous -*er* verbs (**14.4.3.**6), the future took the weak stem in OFr (*amerai, plorerai,* etc.) but was remodelled in common with all other parts in those verbs in which the strong stem was generalized: *aimerai, pleurerai,* etc. In those -*er* verbs that retain apophony (*je jette, nous jetons,* etc.), the strong stem has been adopted in the future: *jetterai, achèterai,* etc.

15.4.5.5. A few verbs call for particular comment:

être in OFr had three sets of future forms, two of them deriving in the usual way from the infinitive **essĕre* (for ClLat *esse*) + *habeo,* etc.: *estrai, serai;* of these, *estrai*—which has since disappeared—is a regular phonetic development, the -*t*- having developed (as in the infinitive *estre < *essĕre*) as a glide consonant between -*s*- and -*r*- when the *ĕ* disappeared, but the explanation of the irregular development *serai* (which has its parallels in other Romance languages, e.g. Italian *sarò,* Spanish *seré*) is uncertain; the third form—which went out of use during the OFr period—derives from the Latin future: *ier < ĕro, iers < ĕris, iert < ĕrit, iermes < ĕrimus, ierenț < ĕrunt* (no examples of 2 plur. are known).

avoir, savoir: the regular developments of **haber-ajo* and **saper-ajo* were *avrai* and *savrai,* which are the usual OFr forms; the explanation of modern *aurai, saurai* is unclear.

aller: the stem of *irai* derives from Latin *ire* 'to go', a verb that has otherwise left no trace in French.[8a]

faire: ferai (like Italian *farò*) appears to derive not directly from Latin *facĕre* but from a reduced form **fare.*

envoyer: the irregular form *enverrai* was created on the model of *verrai (voir).*

15.4.6. In conclusion we can say that the structure of the future tense is:

STEM + INFIX -*r*- + ENDING.

[8a] *Ire* remains in its entirety in no Romance language. It is best preserved in Spanish and Portuguese. Spanish for example has, in addition to the future and conditional *iré, iría,* etc., the infinitive *ir,* the present and past participles *yendo, ido,* the 2 plur. imperative *id* and the imperfect indicative *iba,* etc., while Portuguese has parallel forms to all these and in addition 1 and 2 plur. of the present indicative *imos, ides.*

Very many verbs have a special future stem, and these include not only the more obvious 'irregular' verbs such as *être, avoir, voir, faire,* etc., but also:

(a) regular -*er* verbs which in this tense have in the written language an extended stem in -*e* (***chanterai, porterai***) which may or may not correspond to an extended stem in [ə] in the spoken language ([pɔrtəre] *porterai* but [ʃɑ̃tre] *chanterai*);
(b) -*ir* verbs of the *dormir* type (***dormirai*** as opposed to ***dormons, dormais,*** etc.).[9]

15.4.7. For the construction *aller*+INFINITIVE that is frequently but not entirely appropriately referred to as a *futur proche*, see **18.2.5.**

15.4.8. *Devoir*+INFINITIVE. We shall not here discuss the use of *devoir*+INFINITIVE where there is an idea of obligation, e.g. *Je dois y aller demain* 'I am to go there tomorrow'. The construction is, however, important in connection with the future in that, just as the type **cantar-ajo* that at one stage expressed obligation came to express futurity (**15.4.2.***1*), so the syntagm *devoir*+INFINITIVE has come to supplement the future tense in those functions from which the type *chanterai* is excluded, in particular:

(a) where the construction imposes the use of the subjunctive but it is necessary to maintain the PRESENT ∼ FUTURE opposition that the subjunctive cannot express, e.g. *je ne crois pas qu'il doive jouer* (='will play') *ce morceau aujourd'hui,*[10] *quoique je doive le rencontrer*;

(b) to form a future infinitive:[11]

'Il avance d'un bon vent et qui a toutes les apparences de **devoir durer**' (La Bruyère)
'Les raisonnables pronostics d'Hollington ne semblèrent pas **devoir se réaliser**' (Gervais)

---

[9] As mentioned above (**14.4.1**), verbs of the *finir* type invariably have a stem in *fini-* (*finirons* therefore has the same stem as *finissons, finissais,* etc.).
[10] Quoted by M. Cohen, *Le subjonctif en français contemporain*, 2nd edn., Paris, 1965, 36.
[11] See Sandfeld, III, 20, and P. Imbs, *L'emploi des temps verbaux en français moderne*, Paris, 1960, 58.

15.5. *The preterite or past historic.*

15.5.1. The ModFr preterite (otherwise known as the past historic, the *passé simple* or the *passé défini*) derives from the Latin perfect tense. It is conjugated in one of three ways (*venir* and *tenir* and their compounds being the only exceptions, see **15.5.9**) :

(I) chantai, chantas, chanta, chantâmes, chantâtes, chantèrent
(II) dormis, dormis, dormit, dormîmes, dormîtes, dormirent
(III) parus, parus, parut, parûmes, parûtes, parurent

Earlier stages of these verbs are:

ClLat	*VL*	*OFr*
cantávi	cantái	chantai
cantavísti	cantásti	chantas
cantávit	cantáut	chanta
cantávimus	cantámus	chantames
cantavístis	cantástis	chantastes
cantavérunt	cantárunt	chanterent

ClLat	*VL*	*OFr*
dormívi	dormí	dormi
dormivísti	dormísti	dormis
dormívit	dormít	dormi
dormívimus	dormímus	dormimes
dormivístis	dormístis	dormistes
dormivérunt	dormírunt	dormirent

ClLat	párui	paruísti	páruit	parúimus	paruístis	paruérunt
VL	parúi	parústi	parút	parúmus	parústis	parúrunt
OFr	parui	parus	paru	parumes	parustes	parurent

The main differences between ClLat and VL are the loss of *-v-* (in types I and II) and various shifts of stress so that in VL the main stress fell on the same syllable throughout the tense.

15.5.2. *The endings.* More often than not, the endings of the preterite have been subject either before or since the OFr period to various types of analogical remodelling. These have been discussed above and here we merely list them:

(a) In 1 sing. of types II and III, the ending *-s* was characteristic only of a minority of verbs in the preterite in OFr and has since been generalized (**14.2.1.3** (d) to (f)).

205

(b) By regular phonetic development, the *-sti* endings of 2 sing. would have given **chantast*, **dormist*, **parust*, etc. (**14.2.1.4** (d)).

(c) In 3 sing. of type I, the ending *-a* is probably analogical (**14.2.1.4** (d)).

(d) In 3 sing. of types II and III, the ending *-t* was characteristic only of a few 'strong' preterites (see **15.5.7** (c)) in OFr, and has since spread analogically to all verbs (**14.2.1.3** (g)).

(e) The explanation of the 1 and 2 plur. endings *-mes* and *-tes* is uncertain (**14.2.2.2**).[12]

15.5.3. *The infix* **-r-**. The *-r-* of Latin *cantaverunt*, *dormiverunt*, *paruerunt*, etc., remains in 3 plur. of all types of French preterite as an infix between the stem and the usual unstressed 3 plur. ending *-ent*.

15.5.4. *The stem.* In ModFr, types II and III have a characteristic vowel, *-i-* or *-u-*, throughout all the persons of the verb. The stages by which this position has been reached are discussed below (**15.5.7** and **8**). For the moment, we shall merely draw attention to the fact that the result of various phonetic and analogical processes has been to create in very many verbs a special preterite stem (which is also that of the imperfect subjunctive, **15.6.4**): this may be either

(a) the ordinary weak stem of the verb + the vowel *-i-* or *-u-*, e.g. *dormi-*,[13] *écrivi-*, *voulu-*, *valu-*, *couru-*; or

(b) a much reduced form, e.g. *fi-* (*faire*), *vi-* (*voir*), *mi-* (*mettre*), *cru-* (*croire*), *bu-* (*boire*), *reçu-* (*recevoir*), *pu-* (*pouvoir*), *su-* (*savoir*); or

(c) a stem having little or nothing in common with that of other tenses, e.g. *naqui-* (*naître*), *fu-* (*être*), *eu-* (*avoir*), *vécu-* (*vivre*).

In type I, the aberrant 3 plur. stem *chantè-* has withstood pressures to remodel it on the basis of the *chanta-* stem; however, forms such as *commandarent*, *tombarent*, *couparent*, *donnarent*, were widely

---

[12] Between OFr and ModFr the *-s-* of 2 plur. *-astes*, *-istes*, *-ustes* has regularly disappeared, giving ModFr *-âtes*, *-îtes*, *-ûtes*; in 1 plur. (< *-avimus*, etc.) there was no corresponding *-s-* etymologically, but one was sometimes introduced in spelling in OFr (*chantasmes*, *finismes*, *parusmes*, etc.) by analogy with the 2 plur. forms—this too was later replaced by a circumflex accent (*-âmes*, *-îmes*, *-ûmes*). Note that although the spelling *â* generally represents the pronunciation [ɑ] in ModFr, the endings *-âmes* and *-âtes* are pronounced [am], [at].

[13] In *-ir* verbs of the *finir* type, the stem is identical with that of all other parts of the verb, i.e. *fini-* etc.

used in the 16th century and were recommended by some grammarians of the time.[14]

15.5.5. We can now discuss more fully the origins of each of the three main types of ModFr preterite.

15.5.6. *Type I*: **chantai**, *etc.* This type derives directly from the corresponding type in OFr. Note that, just as -*are* and -*atum* gave -*ier* and -*ié* after a palatal, so *-*arunt* gave -*ierent* in OFr in similar circumstances (*jugierent, laissierent*, etc.); this has now been replaced by -*èrent* as a result of the same phonetic and analogical processes that resulted in the disappearance of -*ier* and -*ié* and the generalization of -*er* and -*é* (**16.1.2** and **17.1.2** (a)).

15.5.7. *Type II*: **finis, fis**, *etc.* The verbs now composing this type have various origins in OFr:

(a) The *dormir* type, which includes all regular -*ir* verbs (e.g. *finir*).
(b) The VL and OFr forms for regular -*re* verbs (e.g. *vendre*) were:

VL vendědi vendedísti vendědit vendedímus vendedístis
                                                venděderunt
OFr vendi vendis vendié vendimes vendistes vendiérent

The origin of these forms is to be found in the ClLat perfect of the verb *dare* 'to give': *dedi, dedisti*, etc.[15] In VL this type of formation spread to many other verbs whose stem ended in -*d*-, e.g. *vendere, perdere, credere, respondere*, etc. In OFr a few other verbs were also assimilated to this type (e.g. *rompre: il rompié, naître: il nasquié*). However, this type differed from the *dormir* type only in

---

[14] On the other hand, there is evidence that in some eastern dialects there was a tendency to remodel 3 plur. of the preterite on the basis of the 3 persons singular. In the present tense of *avoir* (*ai, as, a, ont*) and in the future tense of all verbs (e.g. *serai, seras, sera, seront*) the endings -*ai*, -*as*, -*a* of the singular are associated with the 3 plur. ending -*ont*: consequently, if -*ont* is regarded as forming part of the same set of endings as -*ai*, -*as*, -*a* one is not surprised that, beside *aidai, aidas, aida*, etc., 3 plur. preterite forms such as *aidont, entront, laissont* are found in some MidFr dialects.

[15] -*dēdit, -dēderunt* give -*dié, -diérunt* (as in *vendié, vendiérent*) as a result of regular phonetic development (cf. *pědem > pié* [now written *pied*]). The development of the endings of the other persons of the verb from VL to OFr is not fully regular (see Ewert § 343, Pope § 1006).

3 sing. and 3 plur. and the verbs in question were later fully
absorbed into the *dormir* type with the creation of new, analogical
3rd person forms, e.g. *vendi, vendirent*.

(c) The types of OFr preterites we have so far discussed are
known as 'weak' preterites since the stress falls not on the stem
(which is therefore 'weak') but on the ending. In many OFr
verbs, however, the stress falls on the stem in 1 and 3 sing. and 3
plur. of the preterite, i.e. these parts are 'strong'; preterites of this
type are generally referred to as 'strong preterites'. Of these we
shall deal in some detail with one in particular, the verb *voir*,
whose preterite went through the following stages (OFr strong
forms are given in small capitals):

VL	Early OFr	Later OFr	ModFr
vídi	VI	VI	vis
vidísti	veḍis	vĕis [vəis] [16]	vis
vídit	VIT	VIT	vit
vidímus	veḍimes	vĕimes [vəiməs]	vîmes
vidístis	veḍistes	vĕístes [vəistəs]	vîtes
víderunt	VIḌRENT	VIRENT	virent

N.B. ḍ = [ð] (English *th* in *then*).
(Apart from the usual analogical -*s* in 1 sing., the ModFr forms
come directly from the OFr ones.)

(d) The OFr preterites of *mettre, prendre, dire* and *faire* are:

MIS	mesis	MIST	mesimes	mesistes	MISDRENT
PRIS	presis	PRIST	presimes	presistes	PRISDRENT
DIS	desis	DIST	desimes	desistes	DISTRENT
FIS	fesis	FIST	fesimes	fesistes	FIRENT

Though these do go back to the Latin perfects *misi*, *presi (for
ClLat *prehendi*), *dixi, feci*, a good deal of analogical remodelling
had already taken place before the OFr period. Such changes
made for much more regularity in the forms of the preterite than
would otherwise have been the case (the normal phonetic development would have given in the singular of *faire*, for example, *fiz
[fits], *foisis, *foist); note that in 1 sing., these verbs inherited an

---

[16] Intervocalic [ð] disappeared, as always in OFr, leaving the [ə] of the first
syllable of the weak forms in hiatus with the following vowel, e.g. [vəis], in
which circumstances it regularly disappeared in MidFr (cf. *maturum > maḍur >
mĕur > mûr*). The OFr weak forms therefore give regularly ModFr *vis, vîmes,
vîtes*. Likewise, *viḍrent* regularly > *virent*.

-*s* from Latin (*misi* > *je mis*, etc.). Analogical changes that took place during the OFr and MidFr periods finally brought these verbs into line with the *dormir, vendre* and *voir* types:

(i) Unlike the intervocalic [ð] of *vedis*, etc., intervocalic -*s*- [z] does *not* normally disappear in French, so, if no remodelling had taken place, the weak forms *mesis*, etc., would have remained in ModFr. However, in the 12th and 13th centuries, new forms *mëis, mëimes, mëistes, prëis, dëis, fëis*, etc., based on the corresponding forms of *voir*, came into use and eventually replaced the older forms completely, giving ModFr *mis, mîmes, mîtes*, etc.

(ii) New 3 plur. forms, *mirent, prirent, dirent*, built on the analogy of *virent, firent, dormirent, vendirent*, etc., finally replaced earlier *misdrent, distrent*, etc. (For the reasons for the variation in the OFr 3 plur. forms, see Pope §§ 370, 1018.)

(e) Other types of OFr strong preterites are represented by *conduire, joindre* and *écrire*, whose OFr forms, derived from Latin *conduxi, junxi, scripsi*, etc., are:

CONDUIS	conduisis	CONDUIST	conduisimes	conduisistes
				CONDUISTRENT
JOINS	joinsis	JOINST	joinsimes	joinsistes
				JOINSTRENT
ESCRIS	escresis	ESCRIST	escresimes	escresistes
				ESCRISTRENT

These have now been replaced by new sets of forms of the *dormir* type, based on the weak stem of other parts of the verb (e.g. *nous conduisons, nous conduisions, conduisant, nous joignons, nous écrivons*, etc.):

conduisis[17]	conduisis	conduisit	conduisîmes	conduisîtes
				conduisirent
joignis[18]	joignis	joignit	joignîmes	joignîtes
				joignirent
écrivis	écrivis	écrivit	écrivîmes	écrivîtes
				écrivirent

[17] Like *conduire* are all verbs in -*uire*, e.g. *construire, cuire, détruire, luire* (OFr *luisir*), *nuire* (OFr *nuisir*).
[18] Like *joindre* are *atteindre* (OFr *j'atteins*, ModFr *j'atteignis*), *craindre* (OFr *criembre*: *je crens, tu crensis*, ModFr *je craignis*), *éteindre, peindre, plaindre* (OFr *je plains*, ModFr *je plaignis*), etc.

209

Such forms as these are first found as early as the 13th century, but the older forms are still occasionally found as late as the 16th century.

The ModFr *-is* type of preterite is therefore the result of at least five different processes:

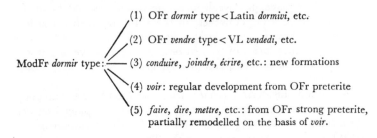

ModFr *dormir* type:

(1) OFr *dormir* type < Latin *dormivi*, etc.

(2) OFr *vendre* type < VL *vendedi*, etc.

(3) *conduire*, *joindre*, *écrire*, etc.: new formations

(4) *voir*: regular development from OFr preterite

(5) *faire*, *dire*, *mettre*, etc.: from OFr strong preterite, partially remodelled on the basis of *voir*.

15.5.8. *Type III*: **parus, dus**, *etc.* Type III also now includes verbs of different origins:

(a) The *paraître* type discussed above; other verbs in this group are *mourir*, *courir* and *valoir*.

(b) In OFr *résoudre* had a strong preterite *resols*, *resolsis* and *vouloir* had *four* preterites, two strong (*je vols*, *tu volsis*; *je voil*, *tu volis*, *il volt*) and two weak (*je volsis*; *je volis*); by the 16th century, these had been completely supplanted by new weak preterites based on the past participles *résolu* and *voulu*: *je résolus*, *je voulus*; the OFr preterite of *vivre* (*je vesqui*, *il vesquié*, etc.) has also been replaced by a new form based on the past participle, *vécu*: *je vécus*.

(c) *Conclure* and *exclure* originally had strong preterites of the type *je conclus*, *tu conclusis*, *il conclust*, *nous conclusimes*, etc.; this type was later replaced by a new type, *je conclus*, *tu conclus*, *il conclut*, *nous conclûmes*, etc., perhaps under the influence of the past participles *conclus* and *exclus* (which have themselves now been replaced by *conclu* and *exclu*).

(d) *Devoir* was one of a group of verbs having an OFr strong preterite in *-u-* (derived, with a complicated phonetic development, from Latin *debui*, etc.):

DÚI dĕús DÚT dĕúmes dĕústes DÚRENT

With the introduction of a new 1 sing. form in *-s* and the phonetically regular elimination of the *e* [ə] of the weak forms in

210

hiatus with another vowel, the preterite of *devoir* fell into line with that of *paraître*:

ModFr je dus, tu dus, il dut, nous dûmes, vous dûtes, ils durent

Other verbs having an OFr preterite like that of *devoir*, derived in each case—after a complicated phonetic development and various analogical remodellings—from VL and not from ClLat perfects, are *boire* (*je búi, tu bëus, il but*, < **bibui*, etc.), *connaître* (*conúi, conëus*, < **cognovui*, etc.), *croire* (*crúi, crëús*, < **credui*, etc.), *lire* (*lúi, lëús*, < **legui*, etc.) and *recevoir* (*reçúi, recëús*, < **recipui*, etc.) whose modern forms are *je bus, connus, crus, lus, reçus*, etc. (The ClLat perfects of these verbs were *bibi, credidi, cognovi, legi, recepi.*) (e) The preterite of *savoir* (< VL **sapui*, etc.) illustrates another kind of *-u-* preterite:

OFr SÓI SËÚS SÓT SËÚMES SËÚSTES SÓRENT

With the loss of *e* [ə] in hiatus, the weak forms gave regularly the modern forms. The strong forms, which did not have the root vowel [y] in OFr, were replaced by analogical ones created on the model (i) of the weak forms and (ii) of verbs that had [y] throughout the preterite (the *devoir* and *paraître* types):

ModFr je sus, tu sus, il sut, nous sûmes, vous sûtes, ils surent.

Other verbs of this type are *avoir* (OFr *j'ói, tu ëús, il ot* < *habui*, etc.), ModFr *j'eus* [y] and *pouvoir* (OFr *pói, pëús, pot* < *potui*, etc.; ModFr *je pus*). Here again, the processes by which the OFr forms developed from the VL ones are extremely complicated. (f) The verb *être* was the only verb that was strong (i.e. had the accent on the stem) in *all* parts of the preterite in OFr. Apart from the usual remodelling of 1 sing. and the introduction of a *-t* in 3 sing. (cf. *dormir* and *paraître*), the OFr forms developed regularly into the ModFr ones:

ClLat	*VL*	*OFr*	*ModFr*
fúi	fúi	FÚI	fus
fuísti	fúisti	FUS	fus
fúit	fúit	FU	fut
fúimus	fúimus	FUMES	fûmes
fuístis	fúistis	FUSTES	fûtes
fuérunt	fúerunt	FURENT	furent

The origins of the modern -*us* type of preterite are therefore as follows:

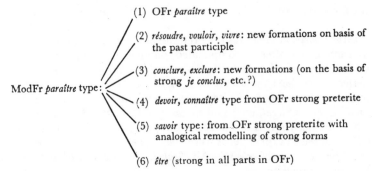

ModFr *paraître* type:

(1) OFr *paraître* type

(2) *résoudre, vouloir, vivre*: new formations on basis of the past participle

(3) *conclure, exclure*: new formations (on the basis of strong *je conclus*, etc.?)

(4) *devoir, connaître* type from OFr strong preterite

(5) *savoir* type: from OFr strong preterite with analogical remodelling of strong forms

(6) *être* (strong in all parts in OFr)

15.5.9. Venir *and* **tenir** *and their compounds.* In OFr these verbs had strong preterites, as follows:

VIN	venis	VINT	venimes	venistes	VINDRENT
TIN	tenis	TINT	tenimes	tenistes	TINDRENT

The weak forms (2 sing., 1 and 2 plur.) have been remodelled on the basis of the strong forms, and so we now have *vins, vins, vint, vînmes, vîntes, vinrent* (replacing *vindrent*), etc.

15.5.10. *Conclusion.* Here, as when studying many other aspects of French morphology, we observe that many of the ModFr forms are new creations and that the links between the system as a whole and that of Latin are comparatively slight. Already in VL the stem and/or endings of many verbs had been remodelled, and in the course of the development of the tense from VL to OFr much more remodelling took place; the details of these changes are often obscure, but the result was greater uniformity both within the conjugation of one verb and amongst the forms of different verbs. The remodelling continued throughout the OFr and MidFr periods, with the result that, whereas OFr had four types of weak preterite (*chanter, dormir, vendre, paraître*) and a wide range of strong preterites (for example, the common verbs *voir, mettre, dire, faire, devoir, avoir, être* and *venir* were all conjugated differently from one another), the modern language has (with the sole exception of *venir* and *tenir* and their compounds) only three types of preterite.[19]

[19] For the loss of the preterite in speech, see **17.3**. For the use of the preterite instead of the pluperfect in OFr, see Ch. 17 note 8.

15.6. *The imperfect subjunctive.*

15.6.1. The two French tenses deriving from Latin tenses based on the perfect stem are the preterite and the imperfect subjunctive. The imperfect subjunctive derives from the Latin pluperfect subjunctive, and the relationship between the two is still apparent in such verbs as *chanter* and *dormir*:

Latin [20]

cantassem	cantasses	cantasset		
	cantassémus	cantassétis	cantassent	
dormissem	dormisses	dormisset		
	dormissémus	dormissétis	dormissent	

OFr

chantasse	chantasses	chantast		
	chantissons	chantissez	chantassent	
dormisse	dormisses	dormist		
	dormissons	dormissez	dormissent	

ModFr

chantasse	chantasses	chantât		
	chantassions	chantassiez	chantassent	
dormisse	dormisses	dormît		
	dormissions	dormissiez	dormissent	

Similarly, *paruissem* etc. > *parusse* etc.

15.6.2. *The endings.*

(a) The imperfect subjunctive is the only ModFr tense whose endings in the three persons singular do not conform to one of the types (1) *-e, -es, -e*, (2) *-s, -s, -t*, (3) *-ai, -as, -a* (**14.2.1**).

(b) The preservation in OFr (and, in spelling, in ModFr) of the final *-e* of 1 and 2 sing. is irregular: normal phonetic change would have resulted in **chantas* from both *cantassem* and *cantasses*, and **dormis* from both *dormissem* and *dormisses*; the fact that such forms would have coincided with those of 2 sing. of the preterite (*tu chantas, dormis*) may have been a factor in preserving the final *-e*.

---

[20] The usual ClLat forms had the *-vi-* infix that is also found in the perfect, i.e. *cantavissem, dormivisset,* etc., but the reduced forms that we quote do occasionally occur in ClLat.

(c) In 1 and 2 plur., the endings *-ons, -iens, -ez, -iez, -eiz* all occur in OFr; for the generalization of *-ions, -iez* see **14.3.2.**

15.6.3. *The infix.* The infix *-ss-* is a direct continuer of the *-ss-* of the Latin pluperfect subjunctive; in 3 sing., in which it became preconsonantal with the loss of the unstressed vowel of the final syllable, it remained into OFr as *-s-* and then disappeared:

cantasset > chantast > chantât [ʃɑ̃ta]

15.6.4. *The stem.* We have seen that, in the preterite, many verbs had two different stems, a weak one and a strong one. The stem of the imperfect subjunctive in OFr corresponds to that of the weak stem of the preterite, e.g.

PRETERITE		IMPERFECT
Weak	*Strong*	SUBJUNCTIVE
vĕis	vit	vĕisse
desis	dist	desisse
escresis	escrist	escresisse
dĕus	dut	dĕusse
sĕus	sot	sĕusse
venis	vint	venisse

In those verbs in which the original weak stem has been eliminated in the preterite by analogical remodelling, a similar remodelling has taken place in the imperfect subjunctive, e.g.

PRETERITE		IMPERFECT SUBJUNCTIVE	
OFr	*ModFr*	*OFr*	*ModFr*
mesis	mis	mesisse	misse
venis	vins	venisse	vinsse
joinsis	joignis	joinsisse	joignisse
escresis	écrivis	escresisse	écrivisse
vesquis	vécus	vesquisse	vécusse
volsis	voulus	volsisse	voulusse
conclusis	conclus	conclusisse	conclusse

15.6.5. With the exception of *venir, tenir* and their compounds that have special forms analogous to those of the preterite (*vinsse, tinsse*, etc.), all imperfect subjunctive forms in ModFr conform (except in 3 sing.) to the pattern:

STEM *in* **-a-**, **-i-** *or* **-u-** + INFIX **ss** + PERSONAL ENDING

The spread of -*a*- throughout all forms of the first conjugation dates only from MidFr. In OFr, 1 and 2 plur. were *chantissons*, *chantissez*, etc.—the origin of the -*i*- is unknown—and such forms are recommended by some grammarians as late as the early 17th century.

15.6.6. *The loss of the imperfect subjunctive.* The imperfect subjunctive has completely gone out of use in unaffected spoken usage, and even in the literary language is generally avoided except in 3 sing. and, occasionally, 3 plur. There is evidence that the tense was disappearing in eastern dialects in the early 17th century, and by the end of the 18th century it seems to have been lost in Parisian spoken usage. The reasons for the disappearance of the imperfect subjunctive are uncertain: possible contributory factors are the comparative infrequency of its occurrence and the loss of the preterite (**17.3**), with which the imperfect subjunctive had close morphological ties (**15.6.1** and **15.6.4**). The suggestion frequently made that the tense disappeared because the endings -*assions*, -*assiez*, etc. sounded 'harsh' or 'ridiculous' is untenable: 'C'est parce qu'il est mort qu'*aimassions* est ridicule; il n'est pas mort parce qu'il est ridicule.'[21]

The imperfect subjunctive is now regularly replaced by the present subjunctive:

'Il fallait qu'un jour le général de Gaulle **revienne** à la tête de l'état' (M. Debré)
'Il ne croyait d'ailleurs pas qu'elle en **vienne** à l'accuser' (R. Vailland)
'Il s'appliquait à ménager la suite afin que je **trouve** à Paris un jeu sans fâcheuses hypothèques' (de Gaulle)[22]

15.7. *The imperative.*

15.7.1. With the exception of four verbs (see **15.7.4**), the imperative in modern French can be characterized as follows:

(a) In 2 sing. it is identical with the present indicative except in -*er* verbs (and those verbs similarly conjugated, e.g. *ouvrir*) in which it lacks the final -*s* of the indicative (*finis! réponds! viens! dis!* but *parle! ouvre!* beside *tu parles, tu ouvres*).
(b) In 2 plur. it is identical with the present indicative (*finissez! répondez! venez! dites! parlez!*).

[21] Bruneau and Brunot, § 536, p. 385.
[22] These examples are taken from M. Cohen *op. cit.*

15.7.2. *Latin.* In Latin the imperative had its own characteristic forms throughout, e.g.

PRES. INDIC.		IMPERATIVE	
2 sing.	*2 plur.*	*2 sing.*	*2 plur.*
cantas	cantatis	canta	cantate
dormis	dormitis	dormi	dormite
vendis	venditis	vende	vendite
dicis	dicitis	dic	dicite

15.7.3. *2 sing. and 2 plur. forms in French.* In OFr the original imperative forms had already been replaced by those of the indicative in 2 plur. (*chantez!* etc., which cannot come from *cantate* which has no final *-s*), but in 2 sing. the original imperatives remained, e.g. *voi!* [23] *di! vien! tien! met!* These have since been replaced by the present indicative forms in *-s*, except in the verb *aller* (*va!* beside *tu vas!*), in regular *-er* verbs (*chante!* etc.) and in verbs of the *ouvrir* type (*ouvre!*); even here forms in *-s* occur before the adverbial pronouns *y* and *en*: *Vas-y! Penses-y! Donnes-en à ton frère!*

15.7.4. *Imperatives based on the subjunctive stem.* The imperative of the verbs *être, avoir, savoir* and *vouloir* is derived from the subjunctive, though the forms are no longer all identical with those of the subjunctive:

Subjunctive		*Imperative*	
sois	soyez	sois	soyez
aies	ayez	aie	ayez
saches	sachiez	sache	sachez
veuilles	vouliez	veuille	veuillez

Note in particular:

(a) the lack of the infix *-i-* in the 2 plur. imperative of *savoir* and *vouloir*: this is a result of the normal phonetic absorption of yod in a preceding [ʃ] or [λ] (**4.8.6**); the subjunctive *sachiez* illustrates the triumph of the needs of morphological regularity (*-iez* being the characteristic 2 plur. subjunctive ending) over regularity of phonetic change;
(b) that the original 2 plur. subjunctive of *vouloir*, viz. *voilliez*, has been replaced by a new form based on the stem *voul-*.

15.7.5. *1 plur. forms.* Except in the four verbs discussed in **15.7.4**, the 1 plur. imperative is identical with the present indicative: *chantons! finissons! vendons! faisons!* etc., but *soyons! ayons! sachons! veuillons!*

[23] *Voi* remains in *voici < voi ci!* 'behold here' and *voilà < voi là!*

16 Verbs

IV THE INFINITIVE AND THE PRESENT PARTICIPLE

16.1. *The infinitive.*

16.1.1. In ModFr, every infinitive is of one of four types, ending in *-er*, *-ir*, *-oir* and *-re* respectively.

16.1.2. *-er* < Latin *-are* (tonic free *a* > [e]) :

portare > porter   durare > durer

As tonic free *a* after a palatal became *ie* (**4.8.6**), some OFr verbs had infinitives in *-ier*. In the following examples, the source of the palatalizing process is printed in bold type:

peccare > pechier   tractare > traitier
dignare > deignier   jud(i)care > jugier
adj(u)tare > aidier   *consiliare > conseillier
vig(i)lare > veillier   laxare[laksare] > laissier

As a result of later phonetic change and analogical remodelling, these *-ier* infinitives have been eliminated:

(a) Phonetic change: by about the 16th century, a yod following [ʃ], [ʒ], [ʎ] or [ɲ] had been absorbed into the preceding consonant (**4.8.6**):

pechier > pécher   veillier > veiller
deignier > daigner   jugier > juger

(b) The few remaining *-ier* infinitives were analogically remodelled on the basis of all other first conjugation infinitives:

aidier > aider   traitier > traiter   laissier > laisser

The infinitive of apophonous verbs (**14.4.3.**6) had the weak stem which, in certain verbs, was later remodelled on the basis of the strong stem in common with other parts of the verb:

Latin	OFr	ModFr	Latin	OFr	ModFr
amare	amer	aimer	precare	proiier	prier
plorare	plorer	pleurer	negare	noiier	nier

217

16.1.3. -*ir* < Latin -*īre*:

finire > finir	punire > punir	venire > venir
dormire > dormir	servire > servir	*morire > mourir

16.1.4. -*oir* < Latin -*ēre* (tonic free *ē* > *oi*):[1]

habēre > avoir	*volēre > vouloir	debēre > devoir
vidēre > OFr vĕoir > voir	*sapēre > savoir	

16.1.5. -*re* < Latin -*ĕre* (unstressed penultimate vowels disappear):

perdĕre > perdre	vendĕre > vendre	cognoscĕre > connaître
mĭttere > mettre	facĕre > faire	jungĕre > joindre
credĕre > croire	dicĕre > dire	*essĕre > être

In some verbs, the infinitive has been remodelled since OFr, e.g.

(a) Latin *bĭbĕre* and *scrībĕre* regularly gave OFr *boivre, escrivre*, which have been remodelled to *boire, écrire*.

(b) *recipĕre, percipĕre*, etc. > OFr *reçoivre, perçoivre*, which, on the basis of the weak stem (*nous recevons*, etc.) have been remodelled to *recevoir, percevoir*.

(c) After a palatal, -*ēre* had become not -*oir* but -*ir* (**4.8.6**):

placēre > plaisir	nocēre > nuisir
tacēre > taisir	lucēre > luisir

Such verbs as these did not conform to either of the usual -*ir* conjugations (the *finir* and *dormir* types) but had much in common with verbs like *faire* and *conduire*; consequently, the infinitives were remodelled to *plaire, nuire, luire* and *taire* (though *plaisir* remains as a noun).

(d) OFr *courre* < *currĕre* and *querre* < *quaerĕre* were replaced by the analogical forms *courir* and *quérir* (with its compounds *acquérir, conquérir*, etc.); *courre* however remains as a technical term of hunting, e.g. *la chasse à courre* 'stag-hunting', *courre le cerf* 'to go stag-hunting', *laisser courre les chiens* 'to slip the hounds'.

[1] A number of verbs had changed their conjugation in VL, e.g. *respondĕre, ridēre* were replaced by *respondĕre, ridĕre*, and conversely *sapĕre, pluĕre* were replaced by *sapēre, *plovēre. This was not a change affecting merely the infinitive but a case of the verb as a whole changing conjugation.

218

16.2. *The present participle.*

16.2.1. Corresponding to the English present participle—the form in -*ing*, e.g. *singing, writing*—Latin verbs had two forms, the present participle and the gerund. The syntax of these two forms can be summarized as follows:

(a) The present participle can vary in gender, case and number and indicates an action contemporaneous with that of the verb:

> *Haec dixit **moriens*** 'He said this as he was dying' (*moriens* is masc. sing. nom., to agree with the subject of the verb),
> *Haec dixerunt **morientes*** 'They said this as they were dying' (*morientes* is masc. plur. nom.),
> *Audivi te **dicentem*** 'I heard you saying' (*dicentem* is acc. sing., agreeing with *te*).

(b) The gerund is a noun used in such constructions as the following (amongst others):

> *Ad bene **vivendum** breve tempus satis est longum* 'For living well, a short time is quite long enough',
> *Ars **scribendi*** 'the art of writing',
> ***Fugiendo** vincimus* 'we conquer by taking flight'.

16.2.2. The forms of the accusative case (omitting the neuter forms of the participle) of the present participle and gerund of some typical verbs are as follows:

INFINITIVE	PARTICIPLE masc. and fem. sing.	masc. and fem. plur.	GERUND
portāre	portantem	portantes	portandum
debēre	debentem	debentes	debendum
finīre	finientem	finientes	finiendum
vivěre	viventem	viventes	vivendum

With the loss of the unstressed final vowel and the consequent unvoicing of *d* to *t* when it became final (**3.8.3**), both *portantem* and *portandum* gave *portant* in OFr.[2] Analogy took the levelling

[2] This illustrates how phonetic change can have a far-reaching effect on grammatical structure: two formally and syntactically distinct features of Latin have become identical. Though some grammars still speak both of the present participle and of the gerund when discussing modern French syntax, this is a carry-over from Latin syntax—what they should be discussing is the syntax of the 'form in -*ant*' (whatever one may choose to call it).

process even further when the *-ant* ending of the first conjugation spread to *all* verbs. This had already happened before the emergence of French as a written language and so OFr has the forms *devant, finissant, dormant, vivant,* etc.

16.2.3. Where a verb has more than one stem, that of the present participle is typically the weak one, e.g. *venant, disant, écrivant, voulant, faisant,* etc. Where the original weak stem has been replaced by the original strong stem in the present and imperfect tenses (**14.4.3.***3*), this has also happened in the present participle, e.g.

> OFr vĕant, vĕons, vĕoie > voyant, voyons, voyais
> crĕant, crĕons, crĕoie > croyant, croyons, croyais

and various first conjugation apophonous verbs (**14.4.3.***6*), e.g. *amant > aimant, plorant > pleurant.* The form *amant,* however, remains as a noun.

A few verbs had in OFr an alternative form of the present participle modelled on what we have called (**14.4.4**) the 'subjunctive stem':

Infinitive	1 sing. pres. subjunct.	Participles
avoir	aie	avant, ayant
savoir	sache	savant, sachant
pöoir (> pouvoir)	puisse	pöant, puissant
vo(u)loir	vueille	vo(u)lant, vueillant
valoir	vaille	valant, vaillant

Ayant, sachant, pouvant (< *pöant*), *voulant, valant* remain as participles, and *savant, puissant* and *vaillant* as adjectives—a reflex of *vueillant* also remains in the adjectives *bienveillant* and *malveillant. Avant,* which is rare even in OFr, has not survived.

17 Verbs

V THE PAST PARTICIPLE AND THE COMPOUND TENSES

17.1. *The past participle.*

17.1.1. In Latin, there were three basic types of past participle:

(a) *weak* participles having the stress on the ending:

cantátum   complétum   finítum   minútum

(b) *strong* participles having the stress on the stem and the ending *-ĭtum*:

hábĭtum   crédĭtum   pérdĭtum   véndĭtum

(c) *strong* participles having the stress on the stem and the ending *-sum* or *-tum*:

mórsum	míssum	cláusum	cúrsum
díctum	rúptum	scríptum	fáctum

In VL, there was a good deal of remodelling of past participles, a process that has continued in all the Romance languages.

17.1.2. *Weak participles.* Of the four varieties of weak participles, two, namely *-ātum* and *-ītum*, which occurred in a great number of verbs, have generally speaking remained in the Romance languages, while the other two, which were relatively uncommon, have had very different fortunes: *-ētum* has disappeared everywhere but *-ūtum* has enjoyed great success and spread to many verbs that had a strong participle in VL (see (c) below).

(a) *-atum*, corresponding to infinitives in *-are*, has, with the regular development of tonic free *a* to [e] (**4.5.4.4**), given *-é* in French:

portatum > porté   cantatum > chanté

Just as *-are* gave *-ier* in OFr after a palatal, *-atum* in like circumstances give *-ié*:

pechié   laissié   jugié   mangié   conseillié   aidié   traitié
deignié   veillié

221

These have since been levelled out to *péché, jugé, aidé, laissé, conseillé*, etc., as a result of the same phonetic or analogical changes that brought about the replacement of *-ier* by *-er* (**16.1.2**).

The past participle of OFr apophonous verbs (**14.4.3.***6*) had the weak stem which has since given way to the strong stem in certain verbs, e.g.

amé > aimé   proiié > prié
ploré > pleuré   noiié > nié

(b) *-itum*, corresponding to infinitives in *-ire*, has regularly given French *-i*:

finitum > fini   dormitum > dormi

The strong participle of some *-ire* verbs was replaced in VL by a more 'regular' participle in *-itum*, e.g. *sensum* (past participle of *sentire*) and *sepultum* (past participle of *sepelire*) by **sentītum > senti* and *sepelītum > (en)seveli*.

(c) In ClLat, the ending *-utum* occurred only in those few verbs whose infinitive and perfect tense ended in *-uĕre* and *-ui* etc. respectively, e.g.

consuĕre 'to stitch'   consui   consutum > Fr. cousu

It seems likely that, by analogy with verbs such as these, *-utum* type participles spread in VL to other verbs that had a perfect tense in *-ui*, including the VL 'regular' verbs **potēre* and **volēre* (which replaced the highly 'irregular' ClLat verbs *posse* and *velle*), **sapēre* (which replaced ClLat *sápĕre*), *bĭbēre* (that had no past participle in ClLat), *habēre* and *debēre*:

LATIN PERFECT	LATIN PARTICIPLE		FRENCH PARTICIPLE	
	ClLat	*VL*	*OFr*	*ModFr*
habui	hábitum	*habutum	ēu	eu
debui	débitum	*debutum	dēu	dû
*bibui[1]	—	*bibutum	bēu	bu
potui	—	*potutum	pēu	pu
volui	—	*volutum	volu	voulu
*sapui	—	*saputum	sēu	su

The supposition that the *-utum* ending existed in VL rests on

[1] The ClLat perfect was *bibi*.

the fact that the past participle of these verbs in many Romance languages can be explained as deriving from forms in -*utum*:

Latin	Provençal	Engadinese Romansh	Italian	Rumanian
*habutum	agu	gnü	avuto	avut
*debutum	degu	dovü	dovuto	—
*bibutum	begu	bavü	bevuto	băut
*potutum	pouscu	pudü	potuto	putut
*volutum	vougu	vuglü	voluto	vrut
*saputum	sachu	savü	saputo	—

Later, -*utum* or its reflexes spread to many other verbs that had no -*ui* in Latin. It is in most cases impossible to determine whether this took place in VL or later and independently in the various Romance languages. For example, the existence of French *perdu*, Provençal *perdu*, Catalan *perdut*, Old Spanish *perdudo*, Italian *perduto*, Rumanian *pierdut*, suggests that in VL the verb *perdĕre* (perfect *perdidi*) had the participle **perdutum* for ClLat *pérditum*. On the other hand, the evidence of the various Romance languages probably justifies us in doubting whether a form like **rumputum*, for example (for *ruptum*, the participle of *rumpĕre* 'to break'), that is given in many manuals, ever in fact existed in VL: not only did OFr have *rot* < *ruptum*, beside *rompu*, but many other Romance languages also have reflexes of *ruptum*—Provençal *rout*, Italian *rotto*, Spanish *roto*, Romansh *rut*, Rumanian *rupt*. It is true that Catalan and some Occitan dialects have *romput*, but it seems more reasonable to suppose that *rompu* and *romput* are new creations arising analogically in each of the languages in which they occur rather than reflexes of a hypothetical VL **rumputum*.

In view of what has just been said, we shall not quote hypothetical Latin origins for the following examples of French participles in -*u*, i.e. in effect we shall not attempt to determine whether the analogy that brought them into being occurred in VL or in French:

ClLat	OFr		ModFr
creditum	crēu		cru
venditum		vendu	
responsum	respondu		répondu
visum	vēu [2]		vu
cursum		couru	
lectum	lēu [3]		lu

[2] In earlier OFr *vedu* [vəðy].   [3] OFr also had *lit* < *lectum*.

223

ventum		venu
receptum	receu	reçu
morsum	mors, mordu	mordu
victum		vécu
cognitum	connēu	connu
tentum/tensum		tendu
pensum		pendu

Many other analogical participles that came into existence in OFr and MidFr—e.g. *nascu* (from *naître*), *ouvru, mouru, prendu, partu, sentu*—have not survived.

17.1.3. *Strong participles.*

17.1.3.1. As we have seen in **17.1.2**, many of the Latin strong participles have been replaced by French weak particles in *-u*. However, a few Latin strong participles in *-sum* and *-tum* remain, e.g.

clausum > clos	scriptum > écrit	conductum > conduit
prehensum > pris [4]	dictum > dit [4]	coopertum > couvert
missum > mis [4]	factum > fait	coctum > cuit
junctum > joint		

Others have lost their final *-s* or *-t* since the OFr period, probably by analogy with the numerous other participles in *-i* and *-u*, e.g.

Latin	OFr	ModFr
risum	ris	ri
conclusum	conclus	conclu
exclusum	exclus	exclu
suffĕctum	suffit	suffi

17.1.3.2. Although many Latin strong past participles have been replaced by analogical forms, numerous relics of the earlier forms remain in French as nouns. *Perditum, venditum, debitum,* have, for example, given way to *perdu, vendu, dû,* but the neuter plural forms *perdita, vendita, debita,* meaning 'things lost, things sold, things owed' remain in ModFr as *la perte* 'loss', *la vente* 'sale', *la dette*

---

[4] By regular phonetic change, *prehensum* (> VL [preso]), *dĭctum* and *missum* would have given **prois, *doit* and **mes*. The vowel of *pris, dit, mis* is probably due to the influence of the preterite *je pris, dis, mis*.

224

'debt'; *rupta*, the fem. sing. of *ruptum* (replaced by *rompu*), has given *la route*—this is a reduction of *via rupta*, referring to a new road broken through terrain where there was no road before. Some other examples are:

Latin participle	Relic	ModFr participle
morsum	(le) mors 'bit'	mordu
cursum	cours	couru
tortum	tort	tordu
responsa	réponse	répondu
recepta	recette	reçu
electa	élite	élu
missum	mets [5]	
missa	messe [6]	mis

17.2. *New tenses using the past participle.*

17.2.1. We saw in **15.4.2.*1*** how a gradual shift in the meaning of the syntagm *habere* + INFINITIVE led to the creation of a new future tense. As a result of a somewhat similar shift, the verbal system of all the Romance languages acquired various tenses constructed by means of a given tense of *habere* and the past participle, e.g. French *j'ai chanté, j'avais chanté*.

17.2.2. *Compound tenses taking the verb* **avoir.** These tenses have their origin in Latin constructions employing *habere* and the past participle in which *habere* retained its full meaning of 'to have'. A sentence like, for example, *habeo scriptam epistolam* (literally: 'I have' + 'written' + 'the letter') meant 'I have the letter which has been written': there is not necessarily any implication that I wrote the letter myself. Frequently, however, there was such an implication, as in the following: *in ea provincia pecunias magnas **collocatas habent*** (Cicero) 'they have huge sums invested in that province', *venenum quod ... **praeparatum habebat*** (Livy) 'the poison that he was keeping already prepared': clearly, it is but a step to the meaning 'they have invested huge sums ...' and 'the poison that he had prepared'. Gradually, the idea that the subject of the verb had himself performed the action in question, an idea that at first was merely implicit in the construction, became dominant and in post-classical writers we find examples in

---

[5] Earlier spelled *mes*; the meaning was presumably 'that which is *put* before one [to eat]'.
[6] From the formula *Ite missa est* that occurs in the Roman Catholic mass.

which the construction *habere*+PAST PARTICIPLE must be considered as the equivalent of French *j'ai chanté*, etc.: e.g. St. Augustine (354–430) writes *metuo enim ne ibi vos* **habeam fatigatos** 'for I fear I may have wearied you' and in the writings of the 6th-century bishop Gregory of Tours, there are numerous examples, e.g. *episcopum* **invitatum habes** 'you have invited the bishop'. So far had the construction progressed by Gregory's time that he could use it even when the verb had no direct object, as in **promissum habeo** ... *nihil sine eius consilio agere* 'I have promised to do nothing without taking his advice'.

17.2.3. *Compound tenses taking the verb* **être**. A somewhat similar development gave rise to forms such as *je suis venu* 'I have come' (an earlier meaning of the construction probably having been 'I am [one who has] come'), *j'étais venu* 'I had come', etc.

17.2.4. A whole series of compound tenses can be formed by means of the various simple tenses of the verb 'to have' and the past participle, e.g.

French	Italian	Spanish
j'ai chanté	ho cantato	he cantado
j'avais chanté	avevo cantato	había cantado
j'eus chanté	ebbi cantato	hube cantado
j'aurai chanté	avrò cantato	habré cantado
j'aurais chanté	avrei cantato	habría cantado
que j'aie chanté	abbia cantato	haya cantado
que j'eusse chanté	avessi cantato	hubiese cantado

Similarly, with *être*: *je suis venu, j'étais venu, je fus venu, je serai venu,* etc.

17.3. *The opposition* PRETERITE ~ PERFECT. As we have seen (**13.3**), the primary function of the compound tenses in the verbal system of literary French is to express the perfective aspect, as opposed to the imperfective aspect expressed by the simple tenses.

The distinction between the preterite (*je chantai*, etc.) and the perfect (*j'ai chanté*, etc.) is the following:

(a) The preterite situates the action squarely in the past, without any implication as to its relationship with the present, e.g.

Victor Hugo mourut en 1885.
Jean lui écrivit à Noël.

It is the normal tense for narrating action in the past, e.g.

'Xavier Frontenac **jeta** un regard timide sur sa belle-sœur . . . et il **comprit** qu'elle était irritée. Il **chercha** à se rappeler ce qu'il avait dit, pendant le dîner: et ses propos lui **semblèrent** dénués de toute malice. Xavier **soupira, passa** sur son crâne une main fluette' (Mauriac)

(b) The perfect is truly a *present* perfect and envisages the past action as in some way linked to the present, through, for example, having present consequences or being of present interest or having occurred in a given period of time that has not yet completely elapsed, e.g.

La Tour Eiffel a été édifiée en 1889 [and is still there]
Jean m'a écrit deux fois cette semaine

The distinction between the two is well illustrated by the following example:

'Nous nous **adressâmes** la parole quelques jours plus tard, un dimanche matin, en des circonstances dont **j'ai** bien **gardé** la mémoire' (Lacretelle).

In the spoken language, however, the preterite has disappeared and its functions have been taken over by the perfect, e.g.:

Victor Hugo est mort en 1885
Jean lui a écrit à Noël

and, in a narrative style that is deliberately modelled on spoken usage:

'Tout mon être **s'est tendu** et **j'ai crispé** ma main sur le revolver. La gâchette **a cédé, j'ai touché** le ventre poli de la crosse et c'est là . . . que tout **a commencé. J'ai secoué** la sueur et le soleil. **J'ai compris** que j'avais détruit l'équilibre du jour . . .' (Camus).

The loss of the opposition PRETERITE ∼ (PRESENT) PERFECT means that modern spoken French no longer specifically expresses *either* of these two values. As long as the opposition existed, the perfect was a 'marked' form expressing the relationship of the past event to the present; having taken over the functions of the preterite, it can no longer be considered as *specifically* fulfilling its own earlier function.

It is far from certain when or why the preterite went out of use in the spoken language. Already in late OFr there are occasional examples in which the perfect seems to be used instead of the preterite, but on the other hand the preterite has still not completely disappeared in some western patois. Many manuals suggest that the somewhat complicated morphology of the preterite was the prime reason for or at least an important contributory factor in its disappearance.[7] This argument is unconvincing: the present indicative after all still retains a much greater variety of forms than the preterite ever had. The fact that 16th- and 17th-century writers are sometimes uncertain of the conjugation of the tense (*prévit* or *prévut*? *vesquit* or *vescut*? *interdit* or *interdisit*? etc.) is probably an indication that they were unfamiliar with the forms for the reason that the tense was no longer in common use.

17.4. *The opposition* PLUPERFECT ~ PAST ANTERIOR. The perfective aspect in the past is normally expressed in French by the pluperfect (type *j'avais chanté*). However, in certain constructions the past anterior (type *j'eus chanté*) is used, in particular:

(a) after conjunctions expressing immediate anteriority such as *dès que, aussitôt que* and sometimes *quand*:

> 'Dès qu'elles **eurent entendu** leur mère, elles éteignirent' (Mauriac)
> 'Quand il les **eut reconnus**, il leva les bras en l'air' (Sartre)

Similarly with *à peine . . . que . . .* :

> 'A peine la jument **eut-elle senti** sur ses flancs ces jambes craintives, qu'elle partit au galop' (Mauriac)

(b) instead of the preterite and in association with adverbial

---

[7] For a different explanation, see H. G. Schogt, 'L'aspect verbal en français et l'élimination du passé simple,' in *Word*, 20 (1964), 1–17.

E. Benveniste, 'Les relations de temps dans le verbe français,' in *Bulletin de la Société de Linguistique de Paris*, 54 (1959), 69–82, argues persuasively that French tenses are organized in two distinct systems, one for *le récit historique* (i.e. the objective narration of past events) and one for *le discours* (i.e. any linguistic activity, oral or written and including correspondence, didactic works, etc., in which the speaker or writer addresses himself to someone else with a view to influencing him). The system of tenses in the *récit historique* is restricted to the aorist (or preterite), the imperfect and the pluperfect, while *discours* admits all tenses except the aorist.

expressions like *en un instant, vite, tôt,* to express the speed with which an action came about:

'Ils **eurent rejoint** la chasse en un instant' (Mérimée)
'Cependant il **eut** bien vite **deviné** que . . .' (Hugo)
'En quelques semaines, le notaire **eut achevé** de régler la situation de Marie Bonifas' (Lacretelle)

In OFr the past anterior was widely used where the pluperfect is now required,[8] e.g.:

'Li cuens Guillelmes reperoit de berser D'une forest ou **ot** [='eut'] grant piece **esté. Pris ot** dos cers . . .'[9] (*Charroi de Nîmes*)
'Les trois enfanz que il **ot engendrez** jeuent et rient . . .'[10] (*ibid.*)

By the 14th century, the modern usage was well on the way to being established. In modern spoken French, the past anterior has been replaced by the *passé surcomposé* (**17.5.**).

17.5. *The double-compound tenses.* The compound tenses of *avoir* and *être* in turn can be combined with a past participle to form various DOUBLE-COMPOUND tenses (*temps surcomposés*),[11] e.g.

j'ai eu fini, j'ai été venu (*passé surcomposé*)
j'avais eu fini, j'avais été venu (*plusqueparfait surcomposé*).[12]

---

[8] The use of tenses was generally much looser in OFr than in ModFr, and the preterite is often found where a pluperfect is now required, e.g. *Dis blanches mules fist amener Marsilies, Que li **tramist** li reis de Suatalie* (*Roland*) 'M. sent for ten white mules that the king of S. *had sent* him', *distrent lor message ensi com-manderent li baron* (Villehardouin) 'They delivered their message as the barons *had commanded*'; similar examples occur occasionally as late as the 15th century (see W. Rothwell, 'Quelques aspects du manque de relief temporel en moyen français', in *Revue des Langues Romanes*, 78 [1969], 285–91).

[9] 'Count William was returning from hunting, from a forest where he had long been. He had taken two stags.'

[10] 'The three children he had begotten play and laugh.'

[11] For a full treatment of these tenses, see J. Cornu, *Les formes surcomposées en français*, Bern, 1953, a work I have drawn on freely in writing this section; see also H. Nilsson-Ehle, 'Remarques sur les formes surcomposées en français,' in *Studia Neophilologica*, 26 (1953–54), 157–67.

[12] Other *temps surcomposés* also exist, e.g. *Chacun **aurait eu** vite **fait** de retrouver son bien* (Bazin)—but Cornu points out that most of them only rarely occur and that the instances of, for example, the *futur antérieur surcomposé* cited by various grammarians (e.g. *dès que j'aurai eu lu ce livre*) are invented for the purpose and that authentic ones are hard to come by.

Although occasional examples are attested from late OFr onwards, some grammars still do not recognize the double-compound tenses and Cornu reports that he knew people who denied such forms even existed . . . until he showed them examples from letters written by themselves, examples that the authors then sought to explain away as 'slips'.[13]

Given that the perfect has completely taken over the functions of the preterite in spoken French, it is not surprising that the *passé surcomposé* (formed on the basis of the perfect of *avoir* or *être*) has taken the place of the *passé antérieur* (formed on the basis of the preterite of the auxiliary), e.g.

Dès que **j'eus lu** sa lettre, je lui répondis
Dès que **j'ai eu lu** sa lettre, je lui ai répondu.

Cornu's examples include the following:

'Sitôt que **j'ai eu acquis** quelques notions générales touchant la physique . . .' (Descartes)
'Je l'ai démêlé après que Monsieur **a été parti**' (Marivaux)
'Quand . . . ma tante m'**a eu dit** cette nouvelle, la joie m'a coupé la parole' (Balzac)

It is possible but not certain that the *passé surcomposé* had its origin in this construction. However this may be, the double-compound tenses have long since taken on other functions in which they cannot be considered as substitutes for the *passé antérieur*. For example, we find the *plusqueparfait surcomposé* in a subordinate corresponding to the pluperfect in the main clause (as the *passé surcomposé* corresponds to the perfect in the examples quoted above), e.g.

'Quand **il avait eu rassemblé** les plus effrontés de chaque métier, il leur avait dit "régnons ensemble"' (Stendhal)

Various double-compound tenses also occur in main clauses with an adverbial expression of time or manner (particularly *vite*), (cf. **17.4** (b)), e.g.

'En un quart d'heure **j'ai eu fait** le tour de la partie habitée de ce désert' (Dumas)
'Ce petit vin . . . **a eu** vite **grisé** tous ces buveurs de bière' (Daudet)

[13] Cornu, *op. cit.*, 9.

' **J'avais eu** vite **fait** de le reconnaître' (P. Benoît)
'**Ils avaient eu** vite **tourné** le câble autour des bittes' (R. Vercel)

The particular value of the double-compound tense in such examples as these is to stress that the action has (or had) been completely carried through: Cornu for example[14] paraphrases *il a eu déjeuné en un quart d'heure* by 'au bout d'un quart d'heure son déjeuner était déjà achevé' whereas *il a déjeuné en un quart d'heure* is paraphrased 'son déjeuner n'a duré qu'un quart d'heure'; likewise, the quotation from Vercel reproduced above means 'il leur avait fallu peu de temps pour achever de fixer les câbles autour des bittes', whereas if the pluperfect *ils avaient vite tourné . . .* were used, the meaning would be 'ils s'étaient hâtés de fixer les câbles autour des bittes'.

17.6. *The agreement of the past participle with* **avoir**.

17.6.1. In modern literary French usage, the past participle of a compound tense formed with *avoir* 'agrees' with (i.e. takes the same gender and number as) the direct object when this precedes the verb, but not otherwise:

La maison **que** j'ai **vue**	Je l'ai **vue**
Les livres **que** j'ai **achetés**	Je **les** ai **achetés**

but:

J'ai **vu** la maison	J'ai **acheté** les livres

17.6.2. The reason why the participle takes the same gender and number as the direct object is to be found in the Latin origins of the construction. In *habeo scriptam epistolam* 'I have a letter [which has been] written', the participle has an adjectival value and so takes the same gender and number as the noun it relates to— compare *habeo epistolam longam* 'I have a long letter' or French *j'ai les yeux ouverts* 'I have my eyes open' (which is not the same as *j'ai ouvert les yeux* 'I have opened my eyes'). When the original value of the construction was lost and it took on the function of a compound tense, two conflicting tendencies operated:

(a) On the one hand, there was the tendency to maintain the tradition of making the participle agree with the noun—as, for example, in the 13th century *Queste del Saint Graal: j'ai faites les granz proeces dont toz li mondes parole* 'j'ai fait les grandes prouesses

[14] *Op. cit.*, 50.

dont tout le monde parle', *quant . . . il li avoit dites les paroles'*
'quand il lui avait dit les paroles'.

(b) On the other hand, insofar as the participle came to be considered as primarily forming part of a tense of the verb, its earlier
role as an adjectival form relating to the direct object was lost
sight of and as early as the 6th century we find (in the Latin translation of a Greek medical work by Oribasius) the following example in which the participle does not agree: *haec omnia **probatum** habemus* 'we have tried all these things', in which the direct
object, *haec omnia*, is neuter plural and the participle *probatum*
is neuter (or masculine) singular; in some Romance languages
this tendency has completely triumphed and the participle remains invariable, e.g. Spanish *los he **visto***, Rumanian *i-am
văzut*, but French *je les ai **vus***.

17.6.3. In OFr, usage fluctuated. The participle sometimes
agreed and sometimes not, whether or not the direct object preceded the verb, e.g.

Agreement:
'Cels que vos avez **nomez**' (*ceux que vous avez nommés*)
'Il les ad **prises**' (*il les a prises*)
'Li emperere ad **prise** sa herberge' (ModFr *a pris*)

No agreement:
'Cez paroles que vous avez ci **dit**' (ModFr *dites*)
'Sempres les unt **purtét** (ModFr *tout de suite ils les ont portés . . .*)
'Jo ai **veüt** les Sarrazins' (*j'ai vu*)

(The first of the above six examples is from the *Charroi de Nîmes*,
the others from the *Roland*.)

This fluctuation continued throughout the OFr and MidFr
periods, but in the 16th and 17th centuries, grammarians at-
tempted to lay down hard-and-fast rules. The first to do so was
the poet Marot who, basing his argument partly on the usage of
Italian, proclaimed (in verse!) that the first of two terms governed
the second, i.e., in the case in point, that a preceding object required the following past participle to agree with it. However,
this 'rule' was frequently ignored by other 16th-century writers,
e.g.[15]

'Toutes les choses que tu m'as **conté**' (Palissy)
'Les loix qu'elle a **donné** et **publié** depuis tant de siècles' (Du
Vair)

[15] For many more examples, see F. Brunot, *Histoire . . .* , II, 470.

Examples are also still found in the 16th century of an agreement with a *following* direct object—e.g. *Les grands ... ont* **remplis** *leurs esprits de haines mutuelles* (d'Aubigné).

In the 17th century, though agreement with a following direct object was now rare,[16] there was much debate about the circumstances in which the participle should agree with a *preceding* direct object. Vaugelas, for example, recommended that there should be no agreement with a preceding direct object *if the subject followed the verb*, e.g. *La peine que m'a donné cette affaire*, and others would make the participle invariable if *any* element followed, i.e. one would write *La lettre que j'ai reçue* but *La lettre que j'ai reçu ce matin*. There are indeed numerous examples in 17th-century writers of a lack of agreement not only in such circumstances, e.g.[17]

'les applaudissements qu'on leur a **donné** dans la province' (Guez de Balzac)
'les premières paroles que Dieu a **dit** à l'homme depuis sa chute' (Pascal)

but even before a pause, e.g.

'Laisser désunis ceux que le ciel a **joint**' (Corneille)
'Tous les maux que j'ai **eu**' (La Rochefoucauld)

The modern rule was finally established in the literary language in the 18th century. It is, however, an artificial rule that is widely ignored in speech and—even if only by inadvertence—occasionally in the written language as well: André Thérive, for example, says with reference to phrases like *Cette lettre, c'est ma femme qui l'a ouverte* and *la jeune fille qu'il avait séduite* that 'l'immense majorité des Français prononce bel et bien *ouvert* après *lettre*, et *séduit* après *jeune fille*. Et n'écrirait *ouverte, séduite* qu'avec un rude effort'.[18]

17.6.4. The modern rule that the past participle constructed with *avoir* agrees with the preceding direct object is not as simple as

---

[16] Corneille can still write, for reasons of rhyme:

> Et c'est enfin à lui que mes vœux ont **donnée**
> **Cette virginité** que l'on a condamnée.

[17] For further examples, see A. Haase, § 92.
[18] A. Thérive, *Clinique du langage*, 1956, 256. For other examples of lack of agreement of the past participle where strict grammar requires it, see Grevisse, § 783.

may appear at first sight. We shall not here go into all the real or apparent exceptions[19] but shall discuss only those cases in which the participle is followed by an infinitive:

(a) *fait* + an infinitive is invariable in ModFr—*je les ai fait partir*, etc.—but as late as the 16th century, it could agree with a preceding or following direct object, e.g. in the *Ménéstrel de Reims* (13th cent.) [il] *avoit ja faite faire la couronne*; modern authors sometimes slip up, e.g. .... *l'histoire dont la sauvagerie allemande les a faits devenir les héros* (E. Henriot).

(b) The agreement of other participles followed by an infinitive depends in ModFr on whether or not the direct object is 'logically' that of the participle or of the infinitive—e.g. *la jeune fille que j'ai entendue chanter* (I heard the girl), but *la chanson que j'ai entendu chanter* (*que* is the object of *chanter*—I heard someone singing the song); similarly *les livres que j'ai essayé de lire* (*que* is the object of *lire*, not of *essayer*). However, as late as the 17th century one finds examples such as *les bons sentiments que l'on a tâchés de vous inspirer* (Racine).

(c) There is hesitation regarding the agreement of *eu* followed by an infinitive, e.g.

'la première lettre ... que j'aie eue à écrire' (Rolland)
'les combats qu'il a eu à soutenir' (Proust)

17.7. *The agreement of the past participle with être.* Generally speaking, the past participle constructed with *être* agreed with the subject in OFr and MidFr in all circumstances. Examples of non-agreement are, however, found from early times, but, except for the special case of pronominal verbs, agreement has become an invariable rule of modern French grammar.[20] The rule regarding pronominal verbs in ModFr is that the participle agrees with the preceding direct object: *elle s'est lavée, ils se sont regardés; les lettres qu'ils se sont envoyées*, but *elle s'est fait mal* (*se* = 'to herself'), *ils se sont téléphoné* (*se* = 'to one another').

One difficulty arises with the 'pure pronominal verbs' in which it may not be at all clear from the general sense whether or not the reflexive pronoun functions as a direct object. In practice, it functions as such with nearly all these verbs, e.g. *elle s'est aperçue*

[19] For a full discussion of the circumstances in which the participle does or does not agree, see Grevisse, §§ 781–95.
[20] The participles of *venir* and *aller* followed by an infinitive frequently failed to agree in 17th-century French, e.g. *elle étoit venu prendre l'air* (Racine), *elle même est allé quérir ...* (Malherbe).

que . . . , ils se sont **écriés**, *elle s'est* **abstenue** *de le dire, elles se sont* **efforcées** *de rire*; an important exception is *se rire de*, so we have the curious situation in which one writes *elle s'est* **ri** *de lui* but *elle s'est* **moquée** *de lui* and *elle s'est* **jouée** *de lui*.

As late as the 17th century one finds frequent examples in which the participle of a pronominal verb agrees with the subject:[21]

'Ils se sont **donnés** l'un et l'autre une promesse de mariage' (Molière)
'Nous nous sommes **rendus** tant de preuves d'amour' (Corneille)

The modern rule is therefore a fairly recent innovation, and the following examples (quoted by L. C. Harmer, p. 25) provide ample illustration of the difficulty that writers have in observing it:

'La fantaisie et l'imagination de l'auteur se sont **données** libre cours' (G. Pillement)
'Madeleine ne s'était pas **rendue** compte de son départ' (J. J. Bernard)
'Elle s'était **aperçu** qu'il triait son courrier' (C. Bertin)

[21] For other examples, see Haase, § 93.

18 Verbs

VI VOICE, ASPECT AND MOOD

18.1. *The passive voice.*

18.1.1. *Synthetic and analytic forms.* Latin verbs had a special passive conjugation, e.g. *amor* 'I am loved', *amamini* 'you are loved', *scribetur* 'it will be written', *audiebamur* 'we were being heard'. These 'synthetic' forms have completely disappeared in the Romance languages and, generally speaking, have been replaced by 'analytic' constructions formed on the basis of the verb 'to be' and the past participle, French *je suis aimé, ce sera écrit, nous étions entendus.*[1]

18.1.2. *Miscellaneous French constructions.* French disposes of various other constructions that, in certain contexts, serve as the equivalent of the passive, in particular:

(a) a pronominal construction, as in *cela ne se fait pas, votre inquiétude se comprend, ce livre se vend à cinquante francs*; this construction is not possible if the agent is indicated (e.g. *votre inquiétude est comprise par tout le monde*, not . . . **se comprend par . . .*);

(b) *se faire* + INFINITIVE, e.g. *il s'est fait écraser/arrêter/piquer* 'he got run over/arrested/stung'.

18.1.3. *Type:* **se voir offrir quelque chose.** In English, a sentence such as *The son offers a book to his father* has two passive transformations, one in which the original direct object becomes the subject, *A book is offered to the father by his son*, and one in which the original indirect object becomes the subject, *The father is offered a book by his son.*

Likewise, in addition to the passive construction having the original direct object as its subject (*Le livre est offert au père*), ModFr has developed a second passive construction having the original indirect object as its subject: *Le père se voit offrir un livre* 'the father is offered a book'. Though this construction is ignored by most grammars, it is first recorded in the 17th century[2] and it is now in

---

[1] Latin used constructions of this type to express perfective aspect, e.g. *amatus sum (eram)* 'I have (had) been loved'.

In Romansh the verb 'to come' is used to form the passive, e.g. *ils luvrers vegnan pagai* 'the workers are paid'; this can also occur in Italian as an alternative to the use of 'to be', e.g. *il ladro venne arrestato* 'the thief was arrested'.

[2] E.g. in Racine's *Bérénice*:

> Bérénice, seigneur, ne vaut point tant d'alarmes
> Ni que par votre amour l'univers malheureux . . .
> **Se voie** en un moment **enlever** ses délices.

common use, particularly but not exclusively in journalistic style, e.g.[3]

'Il **se voyait offrir** un engagement inattendu' (*Le Monde*)
'Chaque conducteur étranger d'un véhicule entrant en France **se verra délivrer** une carte de carburant' (Ministerial statement, 1951)
'Le peuple Lombard **s'est** donc **vu refuser** le succès final' (C. Cuénot de Maupassant)

It is likely that the semantic value of *voir* is no longer felt in this construction and that the verb has become fully grammaticalized as an auxiliary of the passive. This is certainly true when it is used (i) with verbs of saying,[4] e.g.

'Le commissaire Dides **se voit reprocher** de ne pas avoir rendu compte de ses activités (*Le Monde*)
'M. Boulganine **se serait vu suggérer** de prendre sa retraite' (*Midi Libre*)
'[il] **s'est vu demander** ... par un jeune homme fort poli s'il était ...' (Daninos)
or (ii) with an inanimate subject or one who is dead:

'Il est vrai que le premier [procédé] ... **se voit attribuer** un champ beaucoup plus vaste que le second' (R. de Dardel)
'André Bloc, qui fut jusqu'à sa mort, en 1966, l'un des animateurs de l'architecture en France ... **se voit rendre** un hommage tardif au Musée des Arts Décoratifs' (*Brèves Nouvelles de France*, 1969)

18.2. *Aspects.*

18.2.1. We have discussed above the perfective ~ imperfective opposition in the French verbal system (**13.3.**).

18.2.2. *The durative aspect.* There is in ModFr no fully grammaticalized construction equivalent to the English construction 'I am

---

[3] For further examples, see H. Stimm, 'Eine Ausdrucksform passivischer Idee im Neufranzösischen', in *Syntactica und Stilistica: Festschrift für Ernst Gamillscheg*, Tübingen, 1957, 581–610, and J. Chocheyras, 'Un nouvel outil grammatical en français moderne: le verbe *voir*', in *Le français moderne*, XXXVI (1968), 219–25.
[4] It is noteworthy that, with verbs of saying, *entendre* is frequently used instead of *voir*, e.g. *Mon déguisement ne m'expose-t-il pas à **m'entendre dire** de jolies choses?* (Marivaux), *Celui-ci prit l'appareil et ... **s'entendit annoncer** que M. W. Churchill arriverait dans l'après-midi* (de Gaulle).

singing', though the language can, where necessary, express a durative aspect by means of such periphrases as *être en train de* or—less frequently—*être à*,[5] e.g.

Il est en train de chanter
Elle est à s'habiller
'J'étais donc à bavarder avec lui' (J.-R. Bloch)

OFr made quite considerable use of a construction *être* or *aller* + *-ant* to express the imperfective aspect, e.g. in the *Roland*:

'Karles l'entent ki est as porz passant'[6]
'Pur qu'alez arestant?'[7]

The construction with *aller* is still common in the 16th and 17th centuries, and *être* + *-ant* also occurs occasionally:

'Les plaisirs nous vont décevant (Malherbe)
'Dans la prison qui vous va renfermant' (Voiture)
'Il faut donc concevoir que vous êtes éternellement créant tout ce qu'il vous plait de créer (Fénelon)

Nowadays, *aller* + *-ant* (introduced or not by *en*) may still be used —but only in a literary style—when there is an idea of progression, i.e. when *aller* retains something of its semantic value, at least in a figurative sense:

'... le murmure des voix qui allait s'affaiblissant' (A. Dumas *père*)
Les difficultés vont augmentant
La rivière va en serpentant
La somme va en diminuant

18.2.3. *The use of* **venir** *and* **aller**: *introductory note.* By means of the verbs *venir* and *aller*, originally expressing 'motion towards' and 'motion away from', French has developed the possibility of indicating that past and future events are envisaged as in direct relationship with the present.[8]

---

[5] For these and other constructions discussed in this chapter, see G. Gougenheim, *Étude sur les périphrases verbales de la langue française*, Paris, 1929.
[6] 'Charles, who is going through the passes, hears it.'
[7] 'Why are you stopping?'
[8] See L. Flydal, **Aller** *et* **venir de** *suivis de l'infinitif comme expressions de rapports temporels*, Oslo, 1943.

18.2.4. *venir de*. This construction—the use of which is almost entirely restricted to the present and imperfect indicative[9]— presents the action as having occurred immediately before the moment at which the narration is taking place (*Je viens de le voir*) or before the time to which the narrative relates (*Il venait de partir au moment où j'ai reçu ta lettre*).

Examples of the construction occur as early as the 13th century, but it is not certain at what stage *venir* lost its original semantic value (i.e. when *je viens de le voir* ceased to mean 'I am coming from seeing him') and fully assumed the role of an aspectual auxiliary verb.

18.2.5. *aller* + INFINITIVE. This construction is frequently termed the *futur proche* or *futur prochain*, a misleading term since the value of the construction is not to indicate that the action referred to will take place in the near future but to express a link between the present and the future:[10] the future action is envisaged as, for example, having been already decided on or as a consequence or continuation of the present situation, e.g.

'Madame va vous voir tout de suite' (Simenon)
'Que va-t-on lui faire?' (Simenon)
Si tu ne fais pas attention, tu vas tomber.

Consequently, the construction can be used even with reference to a remote future:

'Cela va être commode pendant ces cinquante ans qui nous restent à vivre' (Anouilh)
'Et ça va durer dix-sept ans comme ça' (Labiche)

The construction may also be used with the imperfect indicative (*Il m'a dit qu'il allait partir*) but not, generally speaking, with other tenses or with the subjunctive.[11]

---

[9] Here is an example with the infinitive: *A . . . doit venir de se laver les cheveux* (Robbe-Grillet). Imbs, *L'emploi des temps verbaux en français moderne*, 116, quotes the following example of the future tense: *. . . . les quotidiens que vous viendrez d'acheter au moment où le cycliste les aura livrés* (Butor). For examples with other tenses, see Le Bidois, *Syntaxe . . , II, 698.*
[10] The future action may indeed be more often than not one that is to take place in the near future, but this is a fact of external reality and not something that is specified *linguistically.*
[11] The syntagm *devoir* + INFINITIVE (15.4.8) can, in such circumstances, stand in for *aller* + INFINITIVE as well as for the future tense (*je ne crois pas qu'il doive venir*).

This use of *aller*+INFINITIVE is first found, sporadically, in the 14th century, and by the 17th century is frequent.

Just as the syntagm INFINITIVE+*habere*, having previously had other values, finally took on the role of expressing future time (**15.4.2.1**), so, in popular French, the syntagm *aller*+INFINITIVE sometimes loses its aspectual value and serves as the equivalent of the future tense, e.g. *Quand elle **va rentrer**, nous allons la jeter dehors* (Maupassant).

18.2.6. *The opposition* PRETERITE ∼ IMPERFECT. The aspectual distinction between the preterite and the imperfect indicative is the following:

(a) The preterite (or the perfect, insofar as it has taken over the functions of the preterite in speech (**17.3**)) expresses the 'punctual' aspect, i.e. the event reported by the verb is regarded as having occurred at a given point in time, without reference to its duration.[12]

(b) The imperfect expresses (i) the 'durative' aspect, i.e. attention is drawn to the fact that an action or state lasted for a period of time, e.g. *Il **écrivait** au moment où le téléphone sonna; elle **avait** les cheveux blonds*, and (ii) the 'iterative' aspect, i.e. attention is drawn to the fact that an action took place repeatedly, e.g. *Je lui **écrivais** chaque jour*.

Latin usage was similar to that of ModFr. In OFr, however, the preterite was frequently used where ModFr would use the 'durative' imperfect, especially in descriptions, e.g. in the *Roland*:

'Bels **fut** e forz' (=*il était beau et fort*)
'La u cist **furent** des altres i **out** bien' (=*Là où ceux-ci étaient, il y en avait bien des autres*)

This construction is less frequent in later OFr than in the *chansons de geste*, but it is occasionally found as late as the 16th century, e.g. *Il **eut** la taille belle et le visage beau* (Desportes). This use of the preterite does not mean that the preterite expressed the durative aspect, but rather that the durative aspect was not always expressed where now it is: this is perhaps to be considered as a feature of style rather than of grammar.

In contemporary French, increasing use is made of the im-

[12] This is true even if the event lasted for a considerable time, e.g. *Victor Hugo vécut 83 ans*—his life is regarded as *one event*.

perfect in certain contexts in which the preterite (or perfect) might be expected, e.g.

'Il **décidait** soudain de se lever, **posait** le verre encombrant sur une console, **tirait** quelques bouffées de cigare et **arpentait** la moquette (Simenon)

This construction occurs particularly where there is a precise indication of time or date:

'A sept heures, il **poussait** la porte du *Vieux-Pressoir* et il fut presque déçu de ne pas voir Fernande perchée sur son tabouret' (Simenon)[13]
'Il y a six ans, l'armée française **débarquait** sur les côtes de Provence' (*France-Illustration*)

This again is a question of style rather than grammar. The imperfect has not assumed the 'punctual' aspect of the preterite: the effectiveness of the construction arises from the fact that the imperfect expresses the 'durative' aspect—i.e. the action is presented as unfolding before our eyes—and this use merits the name of *imparfait pittoresque* that it has been given.[14]

18.3. *Indicative and subjunctive.*

18.3.1. It is not possible to give here anything approaching a comprehensive survey of the history of the use of the indicative and subjunctive moods in French. Quite apart from considerations of space, we are faced with the problem that there is no generally accepted interpretation of the role of the subjunctive in ModFr: opinions vary widely as to whether, for example, the subjunctive has one, two or several fundamental 'values' or as to whether, in a sentence like *Je veux qu'il* **vienne**, in which the speaker has no option but to use the subjunctive, it has any value at all. A further problem is that a great deal of work still remains to be done on the history of the subjunctive in French.[15] What follows is therefore no more than an attempt to provide some kind

[13] Note the use of the preterite *fut* in the second clause.
[14] See H. Sten, *Les temps du verbe fini (indicatif) en français moderne*, 99 and 130, and P. Imbs, *op. cit.*, 92.
[15] G. Moignet's *Essai sur le mode subjonctif en latin postclassique et en ancien français*, Paris and Algiers, 2 vols., 1959, while being in many respects an invaluable work, rests on a theoretical foundation that, rightly or wrongly, is widely considered—at any rate by non-French scholars—to be unacceptable.

of framework for dealing with a mass of somewhat intractable data. It is by no means the only possible framework, it would not be accepted by all specialists in the field, and it is necessarily in some respects oversimplified.

18.3.2. *The opposition* INDICATIVE ~ SUBJUNCTIVE. If we consider the indicative and subjunctive as two moods that can be in opposition to one another, there are in ModFr four main categories of construction to be discussed:

(a) only the indicative is possible, e.g.

> Il **vient**
> Je crois qu'il **vient**

(b) Only the subjunctive is possible, e.g.

> Je veux qu'il **vienne**
> Afin qu'il **vienne**

(c) The opposition INDICATIVE ~ SUBJUNCTIVE expresses a clear distinction in meaning, e.g.[16]

> (i) Dieu vous **bénit** 'God blesses you' ~ Dieu vous **bénisse** '(may) God bless you'
> (ii) Je suppose qu'il **est** là 'I take it he's there' ~ Je suppose qu'il **soit** là 'I postulate, for the purposes of argument, that he's there'
> (iii) Je cherche une maison qui **a** des volets verts (i.e. a particular house that I know to exist) ~ Je cherche une maison qui **ait** des volets verts (i.e. that is the kind of house I am looking for, though I do not know whether such a house exists)
> (iv) Je parle fort de façon que l'on m'**entend** de loin (. . . with the result that I am heard . . .) ~ Je parle fort de façon que l'on m'**entende** de loin (. . . so that I may be heard . . .)
> (v) Dites-lui qu'il **part** demain 'Tell him [=inform him of the fact that] he is leaving tomorrow' ~ Dites-lui qu'il **parte** demain 'Tell him to leave tomorrow'

(d) The opposition INDICATIVE ~ SUBJUNCTIVE is largely one of style, involving little if any difference of meaning, e.g.

[16] On the opposition indicative~subjunctive, see Gougenheim, *Système* . . . , 191–203, from which some of our examples are taken.

D'où vient que vous **êtes** ~ **soyez** en avance?[17]
Il faudra trouver un endroit où nous **pourrons** ~ **puissions** nous asseoir[18]
Après que vous **êtes** ~ **soyez** parti[19]

It is clear that, in (c) at least, the subjunctive has a 'value' (whatever that value may be), since the meaning of sentences having a subjunctive is demonstrably different from that of otherwise identical sentences having the indicative. It is, however, at least debatable whether the subjunctive has any value in (b), where it is imposed by the structure of the sentence, having no expressive value of its own and being therefore in a sense redundant, and (d) where—at least in some cases—it is no more than a substitute for the indicative (or vice versa).[20]

18.3.3. *The classification of uses of the subjunctive: introduction.* There are almost as many patterns for classifying the uses of the subjunctive in ModFr as there are specialists who have written on the problem. One of the most convincing is that of P. Imbs in his book *Le subjonctif en français moderne.*[21] In the following paragraphs we shall adopt Imbs's main categories, with some rearrangement and much simplification, adding some historical details.

Imbs argues that the French subjunctive always occurs in correlation with some other element which is either an affective or expressive intonation, or a combination of intonation and the general sense of the main clause of the sentence, or a verb, verbal noun or conjunction (e.g. *vouloir, j'ai peur que, afin que*).

18.3.4. *The subjunctive in correlation with expressive intonation.* In ModFr, this occurs as a living feature of syntax only in clauses

[17] Example commented on in Le Bidois, *Syntaxe . . .* , II §1269, where it is suggested that *êtes* merely draws attention to the fact and enquires about the reason for it, whereas *soyez* in addition implies astonishment or disapproval on the part of the speaker. It might, however, be argued that this is reading too much into what is perhaps merely a formal distinction.

[18] *Pourrons* is more popular, *puissions* more literary, in tone.

[19] Generally accepted literary usage insists on the indicative after *après que*; in recent decades, however, the use of the subjunctive—though frowned upon by purists—has spread markedly.

[20] Harmer quotes (205–223) a number of examples in which the only valid way to account for an alternation between the indicative and the subjunctive seems to be 'to attribute it to a desire . . . for a variation in form', e.g. *Mettons que ce **sont** des rêves. Mettons que la jeune Parque **soit** un rêve* (Thibaudet); *Il semblait qu'elle n'**eût** jamais été jeune, qu'elle ne **pouvait** pas l'avoir été* (Gide).

[21] Strasbourg, 1953; many of our examples are drawn from this. See also M. Cohen, *Le subjonctif en français contemporain*, 2nd edn., Paris, 1965, and H. Nordahl, *Les systèmes du subjonctif corrélatif*, Bergen-Oslo, 1969, 271 pp.

introduced by *que* and expressing, for example, the speaker's will, e.g.

'Qu'il s'éloigne, qu'il parte' (Racine)
'Que je ne te revoie jamais!' (Mirbeau)

or his wish or resigned acceptance:

'Que demain soit doux comme hier!' (Hugo)
'Qu'ils meurent, s'il le faut!' (Leconte de Lisle)

In OFr, and occasionally as late as the 17th century, the subjunctive occurred in sentences of this type without the introductory *que*:

'Deus li otreit seinte beneïsun!' (Roland) *God grant him holy blessing*
'Mais tu aies honte touz diz' (13th-century text) *Que tu aies toujours honte*

'Je sois exterminé, si je ne tiens parole' (Molière)
'Son sang soit sur nous et sur nos enfans' (Bossuet)

This now exists only in a number of fixed expressions, i.e. it forms part of what has been called *la syntaxe figée*, e.g.

Dieu vous bénisse!   Le diable l'emporte!
Grand bien vous fasse!   Vive la France!
A Dieu ne plaise!   Advienne que pourra

18.3.5. *The subjunctive in correlation both with expressive intonation and with the sense of a preceding or following clause.*

(a) In a main clause accompanied by a clause introduced by *si*, the imperfect subjunctive is the equivalent of the compound conditional tense:

'S'il eût osé, il eût prié son nouveau patron de . . .' (Romains)

This is a literary archaism: the normal ModFr construction is *S'il avait osé, il aurait prié* . . .

For a fuller discussion of moods and tenses in hypothetical clauses, see **18.3.7.**

(b) When the subjunctive is in a subordinate clause, the correlation expresses purpose if the main clause (which is usually in the imperative) precedes:

'Ôte-toi de là, que je m'y mette',

or eventuality if the main clause follows:

' Qu'il se fasse attendre encore un quart d'heure, et je m'en vais ' (Musset)

Such constructions as:

'Un dictionnaire, si complet soit-il, ne nous donnera jamais . . .' (Brunot)
'Dût mon amour-propre en souffrir, je préférerais m'humilier devant elle' (Theuriet)

in which there is no introductory *que*, represent relics of an older state of affairs illustrated by the following examples:

'**Voelent** u nun, si guerpissent le camp'[22] (*Roland*)
'Venu li est en son corage, ou **tort** a joie ou **tort** a rage, qu'a l'ancïen parler ira'[23] (13th-century text)

18.3.6. *The subjunctive in correlation with a preceding word or group of words.* The preceding correlative element may be a group NOUN + RELATIVE PRONOUN, a VERB or VERBAL NOUN + *que*, or a conjunction (*bien que*, etc.). However, the indicative can also occur with any of these elements[24] and it is the semantic value of the correlative element that determines which mood is used. The value of the subjunctive is to make explicit a certain modality that has already been suggested by the correlative element—e.g. in *Je doute qu'il vienne*, the idea of 'doubt' is carried by the verb and not by the subjunctive.

The subjunctive is used:

(a) in correlation with an antecedent expressing some shade of will, desire, intention, purpose, etc., e.g.

[22] 'Want to or not, they leave the field.'
[23] 'The idea occurs to her that, whether it turns to joy or anger, she will go and speak to the old one.'
[24] E.g. *l'homme que j'ai vu*; *j'espère qu'il viendra*; *puisque vous êtes là*.

'O Jupiter, montrez-moi quelque asile, S'écria-t-il, qui me puisse sauver!'[25] (La Fontaine)

Je veux qu'il vienne

Je suis heureux que vous soyez venu

'Je me tais pour que vous parliez' (Romains)

'Je ferai en sorte que l'héritage de votre fille ne soit pas diminué' (P. Hervieu)

Verbs of saying fall into this category when they express the speaker's wish:

Il lui a dit qu'il parte

Nowadays, the distinction between indicative and subjunctive in these circumstances has become almost totally grammaticalized, i.e. imposed by the nature of the correlative element, allowing little freedom to the speaker to express different shades of meaning according to the mood he chooses: for example, in modern literary usage, the indicative is required after *espérer* but the subjunctive after *vouloir, souhaiter, regretter, c'est dommage, être heureux, avoir peur*, etc. However, in OFr the indicative was usual after expressions relating to the emotions where the reference was to a state of fact:

'Quel dulur que li Franceis nel sevent' (*Roland*)[26]

'C'est domage que estes por mei ocis' (*Énéas*)[27]

and examples occur as late as the 17th century:

'L'ambassadeur . . . regrettoit que tout cela ne se faisoit en la présence du prince . . .' (Malherbe)

'J'ai peur que cette grande furie ne durera pas' (Malherbe)

'Je m'étonne que vous me dites cela' (Voiture)

(b) in correlation with an antecedent expressing possibility, supposition or eventuality, e.g.

'Le chien est le seul animal dont la fidélité soit à l'épreuve' (Buffon)

[25] Here, the construction NOUN + RELATIVE PRONOUN + SUBJUNCTIVE expresses the wished for result.

[26] 'What sorrow that the French do not know it' (*sevent* = 'savent').

[27] 'What a misfortune that you are killed because of me.'

'S'il y a quelque chose qui me puisse faire corriger de mes
négligences . . .' (Boileau)
'Elle s'attendait à ce qu'il vînt à Paris' (Maurois)
Il est possible que je le fasse

Supposons qu'il en soit ainsi Jusqu'à ce qu'il parte
Pourvu que vous veniez Avant que je ne parte

Here again, the use of the subjunctive is in many cases grammaticalized. A choice of mood is however possible in, for example,
relative clauses after a superlative or *seul, unique, premier, dernier,*
etc.; the indicative expresses an objective statement of fact:

C'est le livre le plus cher qu'il a jamais acheté
C'est l'unique poste que vous pouvez remplir

while the subjunctive is used if there is a suggestion of subjective
impression (supposition, possibility, eventuality, etc.):

C'est le livre le plus cher qu'il ait jamais acheté
C'est l'unique poste que vous puissiez remplir.

Until the 18th century, there was also a variation of mood after
jusqu'à ce que, which took the indicative with reference to what is or
is considered to be a state of objective fact,[28] e.g.

'Jusqu'à ce qu'enfin il en viendra un auquel nous ne pourrons
arriver' (Bossuet)
'Il resta dans l'île jusqu'à ce qu'un officier de confiance l'alla
prendre à l'île Sainte-Marguerite' (Voltaire)

whereas the subjunctive, as now, indicated eventuality:

J'attendrai jusqu'à ce qu'il vienne.

(c) in correlation with an antecedent expressing indetermination
or generality:

Quoi que vous disiez
D'où qu'il vienne
Il semble que vous ayez raison[29]
Qu'il pleuve ou non
In this construction, the subjunctive has always been used.

[28] There are occasional examples in ModFr; see Grevisse, § 1018, c), *Remarque.*
[29] The indetermination relates to 'le degré de certitude exprimé par le verbe
antécédent (*il semble*)' (Imbs, 43).

(d) in correlation with an idea of negation or doubt:
Je ne connais personne qui puisse le faire
Je doute que ce soit possible
Je ne crois pas qu'il soit là
Sans que je le sache
Bien que (quoique) vous soyez intelligent, vous ne réussirez pas à
le faire[30]

Here again, the use of one or other mood has been grammaticalized in many circumstances in which there was formerly the
possibility of choice. For example, though either mood is possible
after *penser*, *croire*, etc. in the negative or interrogative:

Je ne crois pas qu'il pleut[31]
Je ne crois pas qu'il pleuve[32]

no such alternation is possible in the affirmative:

Je crois qu'il pleut

which is used even if there is an element of doubt ('I *think* it's
raining, but I'm not certain'); as late as the 17th century, however, the subjunctive could be used if the sentence was to convey a
degree of doubt or a mistaken belief:

'Quidet li reis que el se seit pasmee'[33] (*Roland*)
'La plus belle des deux, je crois que ce soit l'autre' (Corneille)
'On pensait que ce fussent des bohèmes' (Sévigné)

and in OFr, this was true even after verbs of saying:

'Chascuns kil veit dist qu'il seit morz'[34] (12th-century text)

On the other hand, the use of the subjunctive is now grammaticalized in the literary language after *bien que, quoique*, etc.,
whereas as late as the 17th century they could be constructed

[30] The idea of negation is conveyed by concessive conjunctions (meaning
'although') insofar as they imply that a given fact does not lead to the result
one might expect.
[31] i.e. 'I'm pretty certain it isn't raining'.
[32] i.e. 'I don't *think* it's raining, but I'm not sure'.
[33] 'The king thinks she has fainted' (*quidet*, from *cuidier* 'to think').
[34] 'Everyone who sees him says he is dead.'

with the indicative if they were considered as referring to a state of fact:[35]

'Je ne demande que cette seule chose, quoique j'ai besoin de beaucoup d'autres' (Guez de Balzac)
'... bien qu'en matière de langage il suffit que plusieurs des meilleurs juges de la langue rejettent une façon de parler' (Vaugelas)

18.3.7. *Indicative and subjunctive in hypothetical constructions.* ModFr no longer—except as an archaism—uses the subjunctive in hypothetical clauses expressing unreal situations.[36] We must distinguish between two types:

(a) *Hypothetical constructions relating to the present or the future* (Type: 'If he were here [but he is not], he would do it')
    The ModFr construction (Type: *s'il était ici, il le ferait*) was used in OFr, e.g.

'Se tu voleies Mahomet aorer ..., je te donreie onor et richeté'[37] (*Couronnement de Louis*, 12th cent.)

A construction using the imperfect subjunctive also existed in OFr but died out in MidFr:

'Se j'osasse parler, je demandasse'[38] (*Couronnement de Louis*)

(b) *Hypothetical clauses relating to the past* (Type: 'if he had been here [but he was not], he would have done it')

OFr used the imperfect subjunctive in both clauses:

'Sempres caïst, se Deus ne li aidast'[39] (*Roland*)
'... que se Dieux ne amast ceste ost, qu'ele ne peust mie tenir ensemble'[40] (Villehardouin)

---

[35] The indicative is found in contemporary popular French and occasionally, probably through inattention, in the written language: ... *bien qu'ils criaient qu'elles n'avaient rien fait* (Romains); ... *bien que le débat commencera ce matin* (*L'Humanité*); ... *quoiqu'il n'a pas réussi à montrer....* (A. Culioli).
[36] Our brief discussion of this topic is based on R.-L. Wagner, *Les phrases hypothétiques commençant par si*, Paris, 1939.
[37] 'If you were willing to worship Mahomet, I would give you honour and riches'.
[38] 'If I dared speak, I would ask ...'
[39] 'He would have fallen immediately if God had not helped him'.
[40] 'That if God had not loved that army, it would not have been able to hold together'.

However, there was competition from the pluperfect subjunctive, which ousted the imperfect subjunctive completely by the end of the MidFr period:

'Or eüssiés fait que cortois, se ça l'eussiés amené'[41] (13th cent.)
'S'ils n'eussent esté armez, il les eust tuez' (16th cent.)

Though this construction remains till today as an archaism:

'S'il eût continué, cela eût mal tourné' (Renan)

it has been virtually ousted by the construction PLUPERFECT INDICATIVE + COMPOUND CONDITIONAL:

Si je l'avais vu, je lui aurais parlé

a construction that is first attested—though rarely—in late OFr and MidFr, e.g.

'se il avoit volut, auroit pris Adenulphe son frere' (*Ystoire de li Normant*, 13th cent.)

Mixed constructions of many types are also very frequent in OFr and MidFr, e.g.

'Et s'il volsist, il l'eust mis a pié' (*Couronnement de Louis*)
'S'il eust regné puis la creation du monde il apparust plus vieux' (15th cent.)
'De sorte que si . . . il eust conjoinct à l'honnesteté la vaillance de sa personne en guerre . . . il auroit mérité d'estre mis . . . plus hault' (Amyot)

18.3.8. *The use of* **voir** *to avoid the subjunctive.* The following examples illustrate a construction in which the verb *voir* has largely lost its semantic value and has taken on the role of a grammatical device for avoiding the use of a subordinate clause containing a verb in the subjunctive:[42]

Le Japon s'attend à voir Moscou proposer un 'plan Rapacki' pour l'Extrême-Orient (='. . . s'attend à ce que Moscou propose . . .')

---

[41] 'You would have acted nobly if you had brought him here'.
[42] This construction is also possible with verbs taking the indicative such as *espérer*, e.g. *on espère voir s'implanter dans le voisinage d'autres équipements divers* (= '. . . que s'implanteront . . .').

'On ne s'étonnera pas de nous voir inaugurer [cette] collection
par . . .' (L. Halphen) (= '. . . que nous inaugurions . . .')
'On eût voulu nous voir y envoyer . . . des agents' (de Gaulle)
(= '. . . que nous y envoyions . . .')

This construction occurs at least as early as the 17th century:

'Je conserve le sang qu'elle veut voir périr' (Corneille)

19 Negation

19.1. Non *and* **ne.** The most widely used adverb of negation in Latin was *non* (e.g. *non venio* 'I am not coming') which, in stressed positions, came down into French as *non* and, in unstressed positions, as *ne*.[1]

In ModFr, the principal syntactical distinction between the two forms is that *ne* is used only with verbs (*je ne saurais le dire; il ne chante pas; pour ne pas exagérer; ne le voyant pas*) and *non* is used elsewhere (*non-fumeur; non loin de Paris; Mais Rome veut un maître, et non une maîtresse* (Racine); *vous venez ou non?*) As late as the 17th century, however, *non* could be used with verbs as an emphatic negative: *Non ferai!* 'I will not!'.

19.2. *The origin of the particles* **pas, mie** *and* **point.** From a very early period, the negation with *ne* is reinforced by the use of particles such as *pas, mie* and *point* (as in ModF *je ne chante pas*). *Point* (<*punctum*) presents special problems that we shall return to later.

Pas comes from Latin *passum* 'a step' and so was perhaps first used with verbs of motion (*je ne marche pas* perhaps meant 'I don't walk a single step') and *mie* comes from *mica* 'a crumb', but by the time these words are first attested as negative particles at the beginning of the 12th century, they had already completely lost their original meanings and are used indifferently with any verb: e.g. *Altrement ne m'amerat il mie* 'otherwise he will not love me', *blet n'i poet pas creistre* 'wheat cannot grow there' (both in the *Roland*).

Examples of *non pas, non mie, non point* are also first found in OFr.

At first, *pas* and *mie* were probably used for emphasis—they were perhaps the equivalent of the modern *pas du tout* or *nullement*—but it is extremely doubtful whether they retained this value even in the earliest texts in which they occur.

The principal distinction between *pas* and *mie* was dialectal, *pas* being characteristic of the centre (including Paris) and west of the French-speaking area, and *mie* of the north and east, though in many texts both forms occur. However, when literary French came to be equated with Parisian French, *mie* gradually

---

[1] In OFr there was also a fuller unstressed form, *nen*, that occurred only before vowels, e.g. *ki Deu nen aimet* 'qui n'aime pas Dieu' (*Roland*).

disappeared from the literary language and is only rarely found after the middle of the 15th century.[2]

19.3. *Syntactical and stylistic distinctions between* **pas** *and* **point**. In OFr there is a clear distinction in usage between *pas* and *point*. *Pas* in OFr is used exclusively as an adverb: e.g. in *Il ne l'aime pas*, the particle *pas* is just as much an adverb as *nullement* in *Il ne l'aime nullement*. *Point*, on the other hand, functions as a noun, as the direct object of the verb: e.g. in *Je n'ai point de vin, je n'en ai point*, the particle *point* stands in the same relation to the verb as does the noun *une bouteille* in *J'ai une bouteille de vin, j'en ai une bouteille*. In OFr, *pas* is never found in this latter construction, i.e. with partitive expressions; the type *Je n'ai pas de vin* is not therefore characteristic of OFr and is found only rarely before the 17th century; it is not until the early 19th century that, in literary usage at any rate, it becomes more frequent than the type *Je n'ai point de vin*. (Indeed, the OFr distinction between *pas* and *point* is still observed in some provincial patois).

Point is found, though infrequently, as the equivalent of *pas* in OFr (e.g. *Belin ne crienst point sa menace* 'Belin did not fear his threat' in the 12th-century text, *Brut*). Later, however, this adverbial use of *point* enjoyed great favour for a while and from the 15th to the 17th centuries *point* is even preferred to *pas* by some writers. This was perhaps a mainly literary fashion that did not correspond to ordinary spoken usage. Its popularity has since declined steadily. *Pas* is now the only negative particle used in unaffected Parisian speech and, indeed, by most contemporary writers.

The notorious 'rule' that *point* is a 'stronger' negative than *pas* was formulated by Vaugelas who, in his *Remarques* (1647), stated that '*point* nie bien plus fortement que *pas*'. But this phrase has been taken out of context and repeated unthinkingly up to the present day by successive grammarians who have taken no account of the fact that Vaugelas also said that it was very difficult to give rules for distinguishing between *pas* and *point*. A careful study of the actual usage of 17th-century writers does not bear out the view that *point* was stronger than *pas*. A recent grammar says, with reference to the classical period, that 'il semble bien que la répartition des deux adverbes s'opère, pour chaque écrivain, suivant une tendance qui s'explique par des raisons de

[2] For a discussion of the history of the negative particles from OFr to the present day, see my article 'The negative particles *pas*, *mie* and *point* in French' in *Archivum Linguisticum*, XIV (1962), 14–34.

goût, par l'âge, par une origine parisienne ou régionale'.[3] The distinction in contemporary usage is purely stylistic, in that *point* serves to give a highly literary and even faintly archaic flavour to the passage in which it is used.

Hereafter, we take no further account of *point*.

19.4. Ne/ne ... pas/pas. Gradually, the use of a particle, *pas* or *point*, became the norm in negative constructions of the type we have so far been discussing. By the end of the OFr period, negation is expressed by *ne* + PARTICLE rather than by *ne* alone in about 25% or 30% of the cases where the particle must or may be used today. The use of particles increased during the MidFr period and by the 17th century they were used practically everywhere where they occur today.

Though nowadays the particle is, generally speaking, an essential part of the negative construction, *ne* alone is still sufficient in certain constructions,[4] most of which are characteristic specifically of literary as opposed to spoken usage, e.g. *Que ne le prenez-vous?* ('Why ...?'), *Qui ne court après la fortune? si je ne me trompe*; *il ne cesse de parler*; *je n'ose le dire*; *il ne sait ce qu'il veut*. There are also relics of *ne* without a particle in various proverbs and expressions, e.g. *il n'est pire eau que l'eau qui dort, n'importe, à Dieu ne plaise*.

On the other hand, *pas* has become so well established as part of a negative construction that, although it originally had no negative value (*pas* < *passum* 'a step'), it has in familiar speech taken on the functions of the other element in the negative construction, *ne*, which can consequently be eliminated (all the more easily since *pas* can take a degree of stress, which *ne* cannot); constructions such as *Je suis pas venu, tu veux pas venir? j'ai pas dit ça* are used in conversational French.

The distinction between *ne/ne ... pas/pas* (alone) is therefore principally one of levels of language: the norm in the literary language is *ne ... pas*, though *ne* alone survives in certain constructions, but in conversational French it is possible and, in popular speech, usual to use *pas* alone; the use of *pas* alone has not yet, however, penetrated into normal literary usage.

19.5. Non/non pas/pas. Where the negation does not bear on the verb, the possible forms are *non/non pas/pas*. Here it is necessary to distinguish between a number of different constructions; the

[3] R.-L. Wagner and J. Pinchon, 390.
[4] For a fuller discussion of negative constructions using *ne* alone, see, for example, Grevisse, §876, Wagner and Pinchon, §§ 476–77.

following formulation is based on the very clear analysis given by Wagner and Pinchon in their *Grammaire du français classique et moderne* (401–402):

1. Two elements are presented as being in opposition:

   (a) The first element is negatived—**non/non pas**:
   Il était **non** fatigué, mais malade
   Il était **non pas** fatigué, mais malade

   (b) The second element is negatived—**non/non pas/pas**:
   Il était fatigué, **non** malade
   Il était fatigué, **non pas** malade
   Il était fatigué, **pas** malade

2. Two elements are presented as being alternatives:

   (a) The second element is expressed—the negative form is usually **pas**:
   Fatigué ou **pas** fatigué, il faut qu'il vienne

   (b) The second element is not expressed—**non/pas**:
   Fatigué ou **non**, il faut qu'il vienne
   Fatigué ou **pas**, il faut qu'il vienne

3. One element only: **non/pas**:

   though as a general rule either form is possible, in practice usage has in many particular cases decided in favour of *pas*—e.g. before certain adverbs (*pas encore, pas plus tard qu'hier*, but *pas loin de Paris* or *non loin de Paris*).

We therefore have the following pattern:

1a	non	non pas	—
1b	non	non pas	pas
2a	—	—	pas
2b	non	—	pas
3	non	—	pas

In particular we note:

(a) that *non pas* is used only to express opposition;
(b) that *pas* may be used in all constructions except to negative the first of two elements in opposition.

It should also be noted:

(i) that, where there is a choice between *non* and *pas*, the former

255

is characteristic of a more formal, the latter of a more familiar style;

(ii) that, as an alternative to *non*, *pas* is not only accepted in literary usage but in certain constructions is the usual form, whereas the use of *pas* instead of *ne* or *ne . . . pas* is not yet a feature of normal literary French.

19.6. Personne, rien, jamais, *etc.*

Such words as *personne* (<*persona* 'person'), *rien* (<*rem* 'thing'),[5] *jamais*[6] (<*iam* 'now, already' +*magis* 'more'), *plus* (<*plus* 'more') and *aucun* (<**alicunus* < *aliquis* 'someone' +*unus* 'one') originally had a positive value but, through long use in association with *ne* in negative constructions, have themselves taken on a negative value:

Qui est là?—**Personne**! 'Nobody!'
Que faites-vous?—**Rien**. 'Nothing.'
Vous y êtes allé?—**Jamais**. 'Never.'
Plus de questions! 'No more questions!'
Aucune idée! 'No idea!'

However, though *rien* has completely lost its positive value and likewise *personne* (pronoun, as distinguished from *une personne* 'person'), *jamais* and *plus* have not (*Si jamais vous le voyez . . .* 'If ever you see him . . .', *J'ai plus de travail que vous*) and *aucun* retains a positive value in literary usage in the one expression *d'aucuns* = *certains* (*D'aucuns disent que . . .* 'Some people say that . . .').

In modern literary French, the negative particles *pas*, *point* may not be used in conjunction with *personne*, *jamais*, etc. However, this was possible in OFr and even in the 17th century, e.g.

'Je n'ai du moins **pas jamais** lu que . . .' (Molière)
'Je ne veux **point** rendre de mauvais office à **personne**' (Guez de Balzac)
'On ne veut **pas rien** faire' (Racine)
'Vous ne me jugez **pas** digne d'**aucune** réponse' (La Bruyère)
and is still current in popular French, e.g. *J'ai **pas rien** trouvé, je connais **pas aucun** homme.*[7]

[5] In OFr *rien* sometimes meant 'person', e.g. *la rien que je plus amoie* 'the one I loved most'.

[6] In OFr, *jamais* referred only to the future ('nevermore'); with reference to the past, one used *onques*, *onc*, (<Latin *unquam*), e.g. *que je n'en vi onques nul tel* (Chrétien de Troyes) ('for I never saw such a one'); *onc* is occasionally used as late as the 17th century, especially by La Fontaine, e.g. *Je n'appris onc à les manger ainsi.*

[7] Bauche, 121.

256

19.7. *Double negation.* The fact that nearly all other negative constructions involved the use of *ne* led to the introduction of *ne* even when there was a negative word in the phrase, such as *ni* (in OFr, *ne*) < Latin *nec* 'neither, nor' or *nul* < *nullum* 'no' (adjective):

Je **ne** cherche **ni** lui **ni** son frère
Je **n**'ai **nulle** envie de le voir.

This was already the usual construction in OFr.

(Note that *nul*, both as a pronoun = 'nobody' and as an adjective, is now largely restricted to literary usage; in speech, *personne* and *aucun* are preferred.)

Here too, contrary to modern literary usage, it was possible to insert *pas* in 17th-century French, e.g. *On ne peut **pas** mettre **ni** deux participes, **ni** deux gérondifs* (Vaugelas).

ADDITIONAL BIBLIOGRAPHICAL NOTE

D. Gaatone, *Étude descriptive du système de la négation en français contemporain,* Geneva, 1971

20 Word order

20.1. *Introduction.* In this section we are concerned only with affirmative sentences; interrogative sentences are discussed in Chapter 21.

In ModFr, as in modern English, the order in which the various elements of the sentence succeed one another is to some extent predetermined. There is, for example, no possibility of modifying the order of the different elements in a sentence such as:

Le garçon/voit/le chien

On the one hand, the order:

Le chien/voit/le garçon

means something totally different, and on the other hand, such orders as:

*Le garçon/le chien/voit
*Voit/le garçon/le chien

are not acceptable French utterances.

The normal word order in ModFr therefore is Subject-Verb (SV) and the direct object (except the personal pronouns *me*, *le*, *les*, etc.) follows the verb.

In certain circumstances, however, a degree of freedom of choice is left to the speaker. Each member of the following sets, for example, is possible:

(a) Le livre que mon frère a acheté
    Le livre qu'a acheté mon frère
(b) L'autre jour j'ai vu mon ami Pierre
    J'ai vu l'autre jour mon ami Pierre
    J'ai vu mon ami Pierre l'autre jour

the distinction between the various possibilities being one of style or emphasis, not of basic meaning.

20.2. *Latin.* In Latin, the area in which the speaker had a measure of discretion in the way he ordered the elements of his sentences for reasons of style or emphasis was much wider than in ModFr and extended to sentences of the type *Le garçon voit le chien*. Generally speaking, the subject tended to come early in the sentence and the verb at the end, so that the Latin equivalent of the French sentence just quoted would normally be:

Puer canem videt.

However, the form of the nouns indicates that *puer* 'boy' is the subject of the sentence and that *canem* 'dog' is the direct object ('The dog sees the boy' would be *Canis puerum videt*) and consequently no confusion arises if the speaker says for example *Canem videt puer* or *Canem puer videt*.

In Latin, then, the function of an element within a clause is not greatly affected by its position, whereas in ModFr the mere position of the nouns in:

Le garçon voit le chien   Le chien voit le garçon

indicates which is the subject and which the object of the verb. 'The fundamental change in word-order from Latin to Modern French therefore consists in its rise as a syntactic device and its decline as a stylistic device'.[1]

20.3. *Old French.* In OFr, there was appreciably less flexibility than in Latin but the ModFr situation, in which the order Subject-Verb is, except in certain special circumstances, the only possible one, had not yet been reached.

If we use the abbreviation S for Subject, V for Verb and C for Complement (which is here taken to include the direct and indirect objects, adjectives, infinitives, participles, adverbs and adverbial phrases, etc.), we can say that OFr is characterized by the two basic orders SVC and CVS, which we illustrate here from the *Roland*:

SVC: 'Li quens Rollant apelet Oliver'[2]
     'Rollant ferit en une perre bise'[3]
CVS: 'Dis blanches mules fist amener Marsilies'[4]
     'Morz est Rollant'[5]
     'Enz el verger s'en est alez li reis'[6]

[1] Ewert, 275   [2] 'Count Roland calls Oliver'
[3] 'Roland struck at a dark stone'   [4] 'M. sent for ten white mules'
[5] 'Roland is dead'   [6] 'The king went off into the orchard'

Other orders do in fact occur, particularly in verse, e.g.

SCV: 'Li quens Rollant Gualter del Hum apelet'[7]
VS: 'Vendrat li jurz'[8]

but it is a well-established tendency of OFr to put the verb in second position, i.e. to favour the orders SVC and CVS.

As we saw when discussing personal pronouns (**11.5.3** (a)), the subject pronoun was often not expressed where it would follow the verb, e.g. *A Carlemagnes irez* 'You will go to Charlemagne', in which case we have the order CVSǪ (SǪ = 'no subject'). Likewise in *Carles repairet* 'Charles returns' we have the order SVCǪ (CǪ = 'no complement'). For convenience, we shall use the abbreviations SVC and CVS to include SVCǪ and CVSǪ.

20.4. *The functions of the first position.* The first position in a sentence may serve one of two functions:

(a) it may be occupied by an element that serves to link the sentence with what has gone before, an element that may be the subject or a complement of some kind (e.g. *for that reason, next, amongst those present*); or
(b) it may be occupied by something unconnected with what has gone before, in which case the element in question is thrown into relief.

The distinction between the two functions may be simply illustrated:

(a) *When I entered the room, John and Peter were sitting at the table; John was reading the paper*: here, *John* links the sentence to what has gone before, *was reading the paper* is the new information conveyed by the sentence;
(b) *When I entered the room, one of my brothers was reading the paper, and one was writing a letter; John was reading the paper*; here *John* conveys new information (whereas *was reading the paper* links the sentence with the previous one) and so is thrown into relief.

The new element has been variously referred to as the *but de l'énoncé* or the *psychological predicate*: in the sentences just quoted, the psychological predicate in (a) is *was reading the paper* and in (b) *John*.

We have seen that OFr favoured the constructions SVC and

---

[7] 'Count Roland calls Gaulter del Hum'   [8] 'The day will come'

CVS. Gradually, the order CSV came to be used more and more frequently, particularly when C was an adverbial expression serving as a link with what went before, e.g. in Froissart:

'apres disner, le conte de Foeis emmena les chevaliers en ses galeries'
'pour celle doubte, la contesse Florence de Bisquaie se parti de son pays'
'car au lez devers la riviere on ne le peut approchier'

20.5. *Inversion of the Subject in Modern French for grammatical reasons.* Throughout the OFr, MidFr and ModFr periods, the order CSV has made steady progress, i.e. there has been an ever-increasing tendency to put the subject before the verb whether or not there was an initial complement. The characteristic orders of ModFr are therefore SV[C] and CSV[C]. Nevertheless, CVS remains in certain circumstances, including the following:[9]

(a) when the initial position is occupied by an adjective which acts as psychological predicate and is therefore thrown into relief:

'Heureux est l'écrivain qui peut faire un beau petit livre' (Joubert)
'Combien différent du vôtre est l'enseignement que j'écoute dans le livre de la Nature!' (Gide)

(b) after nouns introduced by *quel*, which are likewise psychological predicates and thrown into relief:

'Quel plaisir m'ont fait les boutiques!' (Romains)

(c) after certain adverbs and adverbial expressions such as *aussi, à peine, peut-être, sans doute, tout au plus:*

'Aussi se hâtaient-ils vers le nouvel hôtel' (Giraudoux)
'A peine Françoise était-elle descendue que . . .' (Proust)
'Peut-être certains chefs-d'œuvres ont-iis été composés en bâillant' (Proust)
'Tout au plus peut-on démêler, dans cette singulière attitude, la bouderie d'un enfant très personnel' (Bertrand)
'Sans doute eut-il regret de ses paroles' (Proust)

[9] For a full discussion of word-order in ModFr, see A. Blinkenberg, *L'Ordre des mots en français moderne*, 2 vols., Copenhagen, 1928–1933, and R. Le Bidois, *L'Inversion du sujet dans la prose contemporaine (1900–1950)*, Paris, 1952. Most of our ModFr examples are taken from these works.

It is to be noted:

(i) that in (a) and (b), CVS is possible only if S is a noun (or the equivalent, e.g. a demonstrative pronoun), not if S is a personal pronoun or *on*: a sentence such as **Heureux suis-je!* is not now possible;

(ii) that in (a) and (b) we have 'simple inversion' of the subject, i.e. the order CVS, whereas in (c), if S is a noun, we have 'complex inversion', i.e. CSnVSp: type *Sans doute mon père viendra-t-il*—the construction **Sans doute viendra mon père* is not now possible.

20.6. *Inversion of the subject serving as psychological predicate.* The examples quoted in 20.5 represent an inheritance from OFr in which the use of VS after an introductory C is a grammatical feature that conveys no particular emphatic or other stylistic effect. A quite different category is made up of examples in which the grammatical subject is the psychological predicate, i.e. the subject is the important element and the rest of the clause leads up to it. Far from being a mere relic of OFr usage, this construction seems to be becoming increasingly common:

VS: 'Suivit une âpre discussion en russe, à laquelle je ne pouvais prendre aucune part' (Duhamel)
'Restait à réaliser la deuxième partie de leur programme: louer une maison au Pays' (Maurois)
'Descendent un jour place Vendôme un Anglais et une Espagnole' (L.-P. Fargue)
'Peuvent être envoyées sans autorisation ... les marchandises suivantes ...' (Administrative text)
'A mesure qu'approchait l'époque de l'offensive' (Romains)
'Comme le conseillait M. de la Minière' (Régnier)

It should be noted that in English, the equivalent sentences would in many cases by introduced by a meaningless 'there'—e.g. *There followed a sharp discussion in Russian* ... for the first example quoted above.

CVS: 'Alors commença une journée d'une folle agitation' (Proust)
'A ce moment surgit un petit homme en casquette' (Benoît)
'D'autre part fondait, dans un doigt d'eau, une tablette de chocolat' (Colette)
'Il se doutait bien que dans l'esprit de la jeune fille devaient se mêler des faits de valeur inégale' (Romains)

20.7. *Inversion of the Subject for reasons of stylistic variation.* A further category of examples of VS consists of those in which this order is neither a grammatical requirement nor a means of leading up to the psychological predicate, but a stylistic variant on the order SV: the choice is determined by rhythmic considerations and there is little or no difference of meaning or emphasis. This construction is characteristic particularly of subordinate clauses:

(a) VS in relative clauses, in particular those introduced by *que*; this construction is rare in OFr and MidFr, but is now very frequent:

'Rappelez-vous ce que vous a dit le docteur' (Proust)
'La vie est semée de ces miracles que peuvent toujours espérer les personnes qui aiment' (Proust)
'L'entrelacs de lianes où ne peut les atteindre mon filet' (Gide)
'La sueur dont ruisselait son cheval' (Benoît)

In all of these examples, the order SV (. . . *ce que le docteur vous a dit,* . . . *où mon filet ne peut les atteindre,* etc.) is also possible:[10]
(b) VS in other subordinate clauses:

'Le chien gémissait toujours, quoiqu'eût cessé tout bruit de pas' (Mauriac)
'Avant même que fût séchée l'encre du décret . . .' (Proust)
'Tant qu'avait vécu son époux . . .' (France)
'Il suffit que j'y pense pour que m'en revienne le goût' (Duhamel)

In these examples too the order SV is possible (*quoique tout bruit de pas eût cessé,* etc.).

20.8. *The increasing use of inversion.* If the 'normal' word order in ModFr is SV, nevertheless the use of inversion—i.e. of the order VS—is on the increase, if only as a literary affectation. In his work on the subject, Le Bidois concludes that 'l'inversion du sujet, loin d'être en recul, est de plus en plus fréquent dans la langue écrite et jouit même, auprès de certains auteurs, d'une

---

[10] Many examples of the construction RELATIVE VS fall into the category of those in which the subject is the psychological predicate, e.g. *Cette merveilleuse perspective que forme la Galerie des Glaces* (Bertrand), *la Bosnie, où se parle un dialecte serbe* (Richet). Here, the order SV (* . . . *que la Galerie des Glaces forme,* * . . . *où un dialecte serbe se parle*) is not possible.

263

faveur quelque peu inquiétante'[11] and remarks that H. W. Fowler's comments on 'the lamentable craze for inversion' evidenced by some English writers 'pourraient s'appliquer *mutatis mutandis* à certains écrivains de notre pays'.[12]

20.9. *Substitutes for some vanished functions of word order.* Though the use of VS is on the increase in ModFr, its role is a different one from that which it had in OFr.

ModFr has largely lost the facility of throwing any element into relief merely by putting it in first position. This function is now performed by the expression *C'est . . . que*: *C'est Jean que j'ai vu*; *c'est ici qu'il habite* or by placing the direct object in final position: e.g. OFr *Branches d'olive en voz mains portereiz* (*Roland*), ModFr *Vous porterez en vos mains des branches d'olivier*.

Though the order DIRECT OBJECT—VERB—SUBJECT is no longer generally possible, the direct object can still occupy the first position and serve as a link with what has gone before, provided it is recalled by the appropriate personal pronoun, e.g. OFr *Les dis messages ad fait enz hosteler* (*Roland*), ModFr *Les dix messagers, il* **les** *a fait loger là-dedans*; cf.:

'Ce sonnet, elle le méditait et s'en nourrissait tout le jour' (Maurois).

[11] *Op. cit.*, 410.   [12] *Ibid.*, 425.

ADDITIONAL BIBLIOGRAPHICAL NOTE

Paula M. Clifford, *Inversion of the Subject in French Narrative Prose from 1500 to the Present Day*, Oxford, 1973

21 Interrogation[1]

21.1. *Total interrogation and partial interrogation.* A distinction must be made between:

(a) *total interrogation*: what is being enquired about is the existence or not of a given fact or situation: *Are you ill? Did he arrive this morning? Isn't there any bread?*—i.e. we are dealing with questions expecting the answer 'yes' or 'no';

(b) *partial interrogation*: the enquiry relates to the identity of the subject or direct or indirect object of the verb (*Who? Whom? To whom? What? Which child? Which book?* etc.) or to the circumstances surrounding a given situation—e.g. time (*When? Which day?*), place (*Where? In which room?*), manner (*How? How quickly? What with?*), reason (*Why?*).

21.2. *Latin.* In Latin:

(a) Total interrogation was expressed by means of the interrogative particle *-ne*:[2] *scribit* 'he is writing', *scribitne?* 'is he writing?'

(b) Partial interrogation is expressed, as in English and French, by interrogative words (e.g. *quis* 'who?', *quando* 'when?', *ubi* 'where?', *cur* 'why?', *qualis* 'what kind of?').

21.3. *The* VERB-SUBJECT *construction.* The Romance languages have abandoned the Latin system of total interrogation; in the expression of partial interrogation, the use of interrogative words is supplemented by other devices.

The OFr interrogative system depended primarily on the use of 'inversion', i.e. the word-order VERB-SUBJECT. As in the case of affirmative constructions (**20.3**), this order VS, insofar as it serves a grammatical rather than a merely stylistic function, is not characteristic of the Romance languages generally and is probably to be attributed to the influence on French of Germanic speech-habits when the Franks abandoned their own tongue in favour of the Romance speech of northern Gaul.

---

[1] For a recent treatment of interrogation in French see H. Renchon, *Études de syntaxe descriptive*, II, *La syntaxe de l'interrogation*, Brussels, 1967.
[2] Latin also used the interrogative words *num* and *nonne*, e.g. *num scribit?* 'He's not writing, is he?', *nonne scribit?* 'He's writing, isn't he?'

The order VS is still a normal interrogative construction in French if the subject is a personal pronoun (*Veux-tu? Où est-il?*)[3] and, in certain circumstances (see below), is also possible if the subject is a noun (*Que dit ton père?*). In OFr, the modern restrictions on the use of VSn [Sn = *sujet nominal* 'noun-subject'] did not apply:

'Vialt donc Yvains ocirre monseigneur Gauvain?' (Chrétien de Troyes) *Does Yvain then wish to kill my lord Gauvain?*
'Comment pot soufrir Fortune vostre destruiement...?' (*La Mort le Roi Artu*, 13th cent.) *How could Fortune allow your destruction...?*

21.4. *Limitations on the* VERB-SUBJECT *construction.* The construction VSn is no longer possible in total interrogation, having long since given way to the construction SnVSp (or VSpSn) [Sp = *sujet pronominal* 'personal pronoun subject'], i.e. Sn no longer serves as grammatical subject of the verb but is recalled or anticipated by the appropriate Sp: ***Votre sœur*** *vient-elle nous voir? Sera-t-il là demain* ***votre frère***?

This construction is found as early as the *Roland*: ***L'aveir Carlun*** *est* ***il*** *apareilliez?* '(Is Charles's treasure made ready?). By the 14th century it was already common (e.g. ***la ville de Pau*** *siet* ***elle*** *pres de ci?* (Froissart) 'Is Pau near here?') and by the 16th century it predominates over VSn.

In partial interrogation, both constructions are possible in most circumstances: e.g. *Combien coûte ce livre?/Combien ce livre coûte-t-il? Où travaille votre sœur? /Où votre sœur travaille-t-elle?* However, on the one hand, VSn is still preferred in modern literary usage after *que* 'what?': *Que cherchent les enfants?*[4] and, on the other hand, VSn is no longer used in the following circumstances:[5]

(a) when the direct object is a noun: *Quand votre frère finira-t-il son travail?* (not **Quand finira votre frère son travail?*)
(b) with a noun or adjective as complement of verbs like *être* or

---

[3] With *je* however, VS now rarely occurs elsewhere than in the future and conditional tenses (*Que lui dirai(s)-je?*) and in the present tense of a few common verbs (*ai-je? suis-je? puis-je? que dis-je?* etc.); forms such as *chanté-je? dors-je? vends-je? veux-je?* have gone completely out of use.
[4] VSp even occurs occasionally when the interrogative expression is itself the subject of the verb, e.g. **Quel dieu malin** *oblige-t-il donc ces maîtres à parler comme des épiciers?*—see Renchon, *op. cit.*, 58 and 273.
[5] For a fuller discussion see Renchon, *op. cit.*, 67–75.

devenir: *Comment cet homme serait-il sage? En quelle année M. Pompidou devint-il président de la République?*

(c) after *pourquoi*: *Pourquoi vos enfants ne viennent-ils pas nous voir?*; in the 17th century, however, Bossuet could still write *Et pourquoi commandent les hommes?*

(d) where the use of VSn would separate the verb from some element closely associated with it: *Comment l'Empereur montait-il à cheval?* (Hugo) (not **Comment montait l'Empereur à cheval?* which would split the expression *monter à cheval*); *De quoi celui-là fait-il semblant de s'occuper?* (Anouilh) (to avoid splitting *faire semblant*).

21.5. est-ce que . . ., etc. An alternative interrogative construction, based, however, on the construction VS, involves the expression *est-ce que* (i.e. the interrogative (VS) form of *c'est* + the subordinating conjunction *que*). This seems to have been first used in *qui est-ce que, qu'est-ce que* which occur occasionally in OFr; for a while, each element in the construction probably retained its own value (e.g. *Que est iço que est avenud a Saul?* in the 12th-century translation of the Four Books of Kings has the value 'What is this that has befallen Saul?' rather than merely 'What has befallen Saul?'). Froissart, however, uses them so commonly in reproducing direct speech that it is difficult not to conclude that they already have their present weakened value (e.g. *Qu'est ce que vos me dites? Qu'est ce que ge voi* (= '. . . je vois') ?).

This periphrastic construction gradually comes to be used with other types of partial interrogation—e.g. Froissart *Quant sera ce que nos i serons?*[6] It is not, however, until late MidFr that it is attested with reference to total interrogation. It is possible that, in the 17th century, *est-ce que* retained its full value—G. and R. Le Bidois, for example,[7] give Racine's line *Est-ce que de Baal le zèle vous transporte?* the value 'Serait-ce, par hasard, que votre zèle pour Baal, etc. . . .'. However that may be, *est-ce que* now serves in the structure of French as an interrogative particle, fulfilling the same function as Latin *-ne*, and in popular speech has been reduced in certain contexts to [skə]: *où est-ce que . . .* [uskə], etc.[8]

21.6. *Other constructions: introduction.* The reduction of *est-ce que* to the role of a mere interrogative particle is one way in which

---

[6] This example indicates that the tense of the *est-ce que* construction could still agree with that of the following verb.

[7] G. and R. Le Bidois, I, 363

[8] ModFr has also created various 'hyperperiphrastic' forms, e.g. *Qu'est-ce que c'est donc qu'il y a?* (Molière); see Renchon, *op. cit.*, 168–73.

French has succeeded in expressing interrogation while retaining the word-order SV:

Est-ce que vous écrivez?   Avec quoi est-ce que vous écrivez?
Qu'est-ce que vous écrivez?

The language has also evolved other ways of doing this, two for total interrogation:

(i) Vous écrivez?   (ii) Vous écrivez-ti?

and three for partial interrogation:

(i) Vous écrivez avec quoi?   (ii) Avec quoi vous écrivez?
(iii) Avec quoi que vous écrivez?

21.7. *Types*: **Vous écrivez? Vous écrivez-ti?** It is no exaggeration to say that, in educated conversational Parisian French, total interrogation is most frequently expressed by intonation only, retaining the order SV. Maigret, for example, in a Simenon novel, puts the following successive questions to a witness:[9]

Il vous a remis une ordonnance?
Il en a soigné d'autres que vous?
Il venait ici chaque jour?
Il était toujours seul? Vous ne l'avez jamais vu en compagnie d'une ou de plusieurs personnes?
Il ne vous a pas dit son vrai nom, ni où il avait vécu autrefois?

These differ from the corresponding statements (*Il vous a remis une ordonnance*, etc.) in that, whereas the statement has a final falling intonation, the question has a final rising intonation.

In popular speech, the interrogative function may also be expressed by a particle -*ti*, the rising intonation being retained:

Vous avez-ti reçu ma carte? 'Did you get my card?'
Tu l'aimes-ti?
Je serai-ti rentré demain matin?[10]

The origin of this curious particle, which is first attested in the 18th century and which is variously written -*ti*, -*ty*, -*t'y*, etc., is to

---

[9] Simenon, *Maigret et le clochard*, Paris, 42–3.
[10] For further examples of this construction, see Harmer, 61–2, Renchon, *op. cit.*, 83–6.

be found in questions of the following type, in which the interrogative is distinguished from the affirmative (i) by intonation and (ii) by a final syllable [ti] (the *l* of *il* being silent in familiar speech):

Mon frère vient [vjɛ̃] ~ Mon frère vient-il? [vjɛ̃ti]
Mon frère va [va] à Paris ~ Mon frère va-t-il [vati] à Paris?
Mes frères jouent [ʒu] ~ Mes frères jouent-ils? [ʒuti]

and similarly with *est ~ est-il, a ~ a-t-il,*[11] *dit ~ dit-il, chante ~ chante-t-il, dort ~ dort-il, viennent ~ viennent-ils,* etc. As the result of an historically faulty but descriptively intelligible analysis of forms such as these—an unconscious analysis of course—[ti] came to be regarded as an interrogative morpheme that could be added to any person of the verb, not merely to the 3rd person, and so we have forms such as those quoted above. One such form, *(ne) voilà-t-il pas?* is more or less accepted in familiar speech; the others, though apparently making some headway in familiar speech, are still on the whole characteristic rather of popular speech.

21.8. *The order* SUBJECT-VERB *in partial interrogation.* The normal intonation in partial interrogation (Type: *Quand venez-vous?*) is a falling one, and this is retained in all three constructions based on the order SV:

(a) *Type*: **'Vous venez quand?'** Though regarded by many as inelegant, this construction, in which the interrogative word or expression is placed last, does no violence to the normal pattern of French sentences (Subject—Verb—Complement) and it is very common in familiar speech:

Il y en a combien?   Vous écrivez quoi?
Ta sœur habite où?   Cet enfant a quel âge?[12]

(b) *Type*: **'Quand vous venez?'** This pattern, on the contrary, does break with traditional French word order, which requires the order VS (even if only in the expression *est-ce que?*) after an

[11] The *-t-* of *a-t-il, va-t-il, chante-t-il,* etc. is not a reflex of the final *-t-* of Latin *habet, vadit, cantat,* etc. In OFr and MidFr the corresponding forms were *a il, va il, chante il,* etc.: the *-t-* of the modern forms is based by analogy on those verb forms that had retained a final *-t,* e.g. *est-il, dort-il, vient il, dit-il,* etc.
[12] For other examples, see Harmer, 58–9, Renchon, *op. cit.,* 131–2.

interrogative expression that is not itself the subject of the verb (as in *Qui est là? Quel soldat a tiré?*). Perhaps for this reason, it is less acceptable than the type *Vous venez quand?* but is nevertheless not infrequent in familiar speech.[13] In the first two of the following illustrations, for example, the speaker is an educated person:[14]

Combien nous sommes maintenant? De quoi je vais vivre, moi?
Pourquoi tu la manges pas? Où elle est?
A quelle heure il est parti?

This pattern is fully established in speech in the expression *Comment ça va?* for which no alternative construction is in use.

(c) *Type*: **'Quand que vous venez'?** This type—which is not attested till the 19th century—may or may not represent a reduced form of *Quand [est-ce] que vous venez?* It is a feature specifically of popular spoken French and is avoided as a vulgarism even by many who would use the type *Quand vous venez?*:

Combien qu'on vous doit? Quel âge que vous avez exactement?
D'où qu'il sort? Pourquoi que je l'ai pas remise?
Comment qu'il est? Avec quoi que tu les remplaces?[15]

21.9. *The avoidance of inversion.* In one way and another, therefore, the order VS is tending more and more to be avoided in speech. Dauzat indeed goes so far as to say of it that 'cette tournure, courante encore vers 1900, ne s'entend presque plus'[16] which, with reference to popular speech at least, is not much of an exaggeration.

ADDITIONAL BIBLIOGRAPHICAL NOTE

P. Behnstedt, *Viens-tu? Est-ce que tu viens? Tu viens? Formen und Strukturen des direkten Fragesatzes im Französischen*, Tübingen, 1973

---

[13] The following line from the 15th-century *Farce de Maître Pathelin* suggests that the construction has been in existence in speech for several centuries: *Pour qui c'est que vous me prenez?*
[14] See Harmer, 58; for further examples, see also Renchon, *op. cit.*, 129.
[15] For these and other examples, see Harmer, 57–65, Renchon, *op. cit.*, 162–3.
[16] A. Dauzat, *Tableau* . . . , 197–8.

Index of words

A PRONUNCIATION (CHS. 3–5)

French words only are listed, and in their modern form. All parts of verbs are listed under the infinitive, nouns under the singular form, and adjectives under the masculine singular form.

B MORPHOLOGY AND SYNTAX (VERBS)

Verbs are listed here in their modern form, under the infinitive. Names of parts of verbs are abbreviated as follows:

inf[initive]; pres[ent] ind[icative]; pres[ent] subj[unctive]; imp[erative]; fut[ure]; imp[erfect] ind[icative]; imp[erfect] subj[unctive]; pret[erite]; pres[ent] part[iciple]; past part[iciple]; cond[itional].

(s')abstenir 154
acheter: *stem* 186, 203; *pres. ind.* 186; *fut.* 203
acquérir: *inf.* 218
aider: *inf.* 217; *pres. ind.* 181; *past part.* 221, 222
aimer: *stem* 187, 198, 203, 217; *inf.* 217; *pres. ind.* 187; *fut.* 203; *imp. ind.* 198; *pres. part.* 219; *past part.* 222
aller 168; *pres. ind.* 176, 177, 179, 180, 194, 269; *pres. subj.* 188, 189; *imper.* 216; *fut.* 203; *syntax* 150, 238, 239–240
(s'en)aller 154
(s')apercevoir 153, 154; *pres. ind.* 195n.
(s')approcher 154
atteindre: *pret.* 209n.
(s')attendre 153, 154
(s')avancer 154
avoir: *stem* 206; *pres. ind.* 175, 177, 179, 194, 269; *pres. subj.* 176, 181, 188, 196; *imper.* 188, 216; *fut.* 203; *pret.* 206, 211; *pres. part.* 188, 220; *past part.* 222; *syntax* 225–6

(se)battre 152
boire: *stem* 185, 186, 206; *inf.* 218; *pres. ind.* 173, 186n.; *fut.* 202; *pret.* 206, 211; *past part.* 222

chanter 168; *pres. ind.* 169–71, 177, 179, 191, 269; *pres. subj.* 170–71, 180, 191; *imp.* 216; *fut.* 175, 202, 204; *cond.* 172; *imp. ind.*

172, 177, 197; *imp. subj.* 176, 177, 213, 215; *pret.* 175–6, 177, 178, 205, 206, 207; *past part.* 221
clore: *past part.* 224
commencer: *syntax* 150
concevoir: *pres. ind.* 195n.
conclure: *imp. subj.* 214; *pret.* 173, 210, 212; *past part.* 224
conduire: *pret.* 173, 209, 210; *past part.* 224
connaître: *inf.* 218; *pres. ind.* 171, 172; *pret.* 211, 212; *past part.* 224
conquérir: *inf.* 218
conseiller: *inf.* 217; *past part.* 221, 222
construire: *pret.* 209n.
convaincre: *pres. ind.* 172
coudre: *past part.* 222
courir: *stem* 206; *inf.* 218; *pret.* 206, 210; *past part.* 223, 225
couvrir: *pres. ind.* 170; *past part.* 224
craindre: *pret.* 209n.
croire 248; *stem* 185, 198, 206; *inf.* 218; *pres. ind.* 173, 174, 196; *fut.* 202; *imp. ind.* 198; *pret.* 172, 206, 211; *pres. part.* 219; *past part.* 223
croître: *pres. ind.* 172
cuire: *pret.* 209n.; *past part.* 224

daigner: *inf.* 217; *past part.* 221
défendre: *pres. ind.* 172
déjeuner: *stem* 187–8
descendre: *pres. ind.* 172
détruire: *pret.* 209n.

277

INDEX OF WORDS

naître: *stem* 206; *pres. ind.* 172; *pret.* 206, 207
nier: *stem* 187, 217; *inf.* 217; *pres. ind.* 187; *past part.* 222
noyer: *stem* 187; *pres. ind.* 187
nuire: *inf.* 218; *pret.* 209n.

offrir: *pres. ind.* 170
oser: *syntax* 150
ouvrir 168; *pres. ind.* 170; *imp.* 215

paraître: *imp. subj.* 213; *pret.* 172, 174, 175, 176, 177, 178, 205, 206
parler: *stem* 187; *pres. ind.* 177, 179–80, 187; *imp.* 215; *fut.* 202
partir: *fut.* 202
pécher: *inf.* 217; *pres. ind.* 179, 181; *past part.* 221, 222
peindre: *pret.* 209n.
pendre: *past part.* 224
penser 248
percevoir: *inf.* 218; *pres. ind.* 195n.
perdre: *inf.* 218; *pres. ind.* 172, 179; *past part.* 223
(se) plaindre 153; *stem.* 186; *pret.* 209n.
plaire: *inf.* 218; *pres. subj.* 189
pleurer: *stem* 187, 198, 203, 217; *inf.* 217; *pres. ind.* 191; *pres. subj.* 191; *fut.* 203; *imp. ind.* 198; *pres. part.* 219; *past part.* 222
porter: *inf.* 217; *fut.* 202, 204; *pres. part.* 219; *past part.* 221
pourvoir: *fut.* 202
pouvoir: *stem* 185, 206; *pres. subj.* 188, 189, 195; *fut.* 202; *pret.* 206, 211; *pres. part.* 220; *past part.* 222; *syntax* 150
prendre: *pres. ind.* 173, 184, 196; *imp.* 177; *pret.* 173, 184, 208, 209; *past part.* 224
prévoir: *fut.* 202
prier: *stem* 187, 217; *inf.* 217; *pres. ind.* 187; *fut.* 202; *past part.* 222
prouver: *stem* 187; *pres. ind.* 187
punir: *stem* 182; *inf.* 218; *fut.* 202

quérir: *inf.* 218

(se) raviser 154

recevoir: *stem* 185, 186, 206; *inf.* 218; *pres. ind.* 186, 195n.; *pret.* 206, 211; *past part.* 224, 225
(se) réfugier 152, 154
regretter 246
rendre: *pres. ind.* 171
repartir 193
répartir 193
(se) repentir 154
répondre: *pres. ind.* 172; *imp.* 215; *past part.* 223, 225
(se) reposer 153–4
résoudre: *pret.* 210, 212
ressortir 193
(se) rire 153; *past part.* 224
rompre: *pres. ind.* 171; *pret.* 207; *past part.* 223

savoir: *stem* 206; *pres. ind.* 177, 195; *pres. subj.* 188, 189, 216; *imp.* 188, 216; *imp. subj.* 214; *pret.* 206, 211, 212; *pres. part.* 188, 220; *past part.* 222
sembler 243n., *pres. ind.* 171; *pres. subj.* 171
sentir: *past part.* 222
servir: *inf.* 218; *pres. ind.* 192; *pres. subj.* 193; *fut.* 202
souffrir: *pres. inf.* 170
souhaiter: 246
suffire: *past part.* 224
supposer 242

taire: *inf.* 218
tendre: *past part.* 224
tenir: *stem* 186; *pres. ind.* 195n.; *pres. subj.* 188, 189; *imp.* 216; *fut.* 202; *pret.* 212
tordre: *past part.* 225
traiter: *inf.* 217; *past part.* 221
trouver: *stem* 187; *pres. ind.* 187
tuer: *stem* 186n.

vaincre: *pres. ind.* 172
valoir: *stem* 186, 206; *pres. ind.* 172, 195; *pres. subj.* 188, 189; *fut.* 202; *pret.* 206, 210; *pres. part.* 220
veiller: *inf.* 217; *past part.* 221
vendre: *inf.* 218; *pres. ind.* 172, 173, 177, 193; *pres. subj.* 170, 180, 193; *imp. ind.* 197; *pret.* 177, 207, 208, 210; *past part.* 223

279

C MORPHOLOGY AND SYNTAX (WORDS OTHER THAN VERBS)

Words are listed in their modern form. Nouns are given in the singular only, and adjectives in the masculine singular only, even where the reference is to a plural or feminine form.

The following are omitted:

(i) *articles, demonstratives, possessives and personal pronouns; for these, see the appropriate chapters;*

(ii) *words illustrating general features, such as regularly formed adverbs in -ment (see p. 156) and verb forms illustrating the use of features relevant to all or most verbs (e.g. the endings of the future tense or certain infixes).*

dans 160
davantage 159
de 115, 117–18, 120, 154–5, 160
dedans 160
de façon que 242
dehors 160
déjà 159
depuis 160
depuis que 162
dernier 247
derrière 160
dès 160
de sorte que 162
dès que 162
dessous 160
dessus 160
dette 224
direct 106
dont 132–9
dorénavant 159
drap 104, 105
du moment que 165
dur 100, 107, 108, 109, 156

élite 225
émail 103
empereur 95, 97, 102
en (*preposition*) 115, 160
en (*pronoun*) 154–5, 159
enfant 95
ensuite 159
ensemble 159
entre 160
éperdu, éperdument 158
épouvantail 104
ès 115–16
est-ce que 267–8
espoir 187
et 161
étant donné que 162
éventail 104

faible 109
faute que 162
faux 106, 108, 156
ferme (*adj.*) 106, 109, 156

fête 99
feuille 99
filleul 103
fin 107, 110
fleur 96, 97, 100, 102
fors 160
fort 107, 108, 111, 112, 156
fou 103, 103n., 104, 107, 111, 112
(au) fur et à mesure que 162
furieux 111

gai, gaîment, gaiement 158
garçon 98
gars 98
genou 101, 103, 103n., 104
gentil 106
gindre 114
grain 99
graine 99
grand 106, 108, 110, 112
gros 109, 112
guère 159

hardi, hardiment 158
haut 106, 109, 156
heureux 100, 106
hier 159
homme 95, 97
hôtel 100, 103, 105

ici 122n., 159

jamais 159, 256
joie 99
journal 101, 103
joyeux 110, 112
jusqu'à ce que 162, 163, 247

kaki 106n.

là 121n., 123n., 126–7, 159
là-bas 127
large 109, 111

léger 107, 109
lent, lentement 158n.
lequel 132–40
lèvre 99
loin 159
long 106, 110, 112
longe 110n.
longtemps 159
lors 159, 159n.
lorsque 162, 163
loyal 101

maire 114
mais 158n., 159
mal 103, 156
maladif 111
malveillant 220
mamours 129
maximum 114n.
méchant, méchamment 157
médical 112
meilleur 113, 114
même 145
messe 225
messire 129
mets 225
(ma) mie 129
mieux 158
mineur 113n.
minimum 114n.
moindre 113, 114
moins 113n., 158
mois 96
mors 225
mortel 103, 108, 110, 111
mou 103, 103n., 104, 111, 112
mur 94, 97, 100, 101, 102

naguère 159
naval 100, 104, 106
ne 252, 254
net 156
neuf 'new' 105, 110
ni 161, 257
nom 99
non 159, 252, 254–6
nouveau 103, 104, 111, 112